Woken Leader
(Wake up The Leader in You)

Howard Haughton

Woken Leader

(Wake up The Leader in You)

by Dr Howard Haughton

© Copyright (2020) by Dr Howard Haughton – All rights reserved.
It is not legal to reproduce, duplicate, or transmit any part of this document in either electronic means or printed format. Recording of this publication is strictly prohibited.

Preface

Numerous books have been written on the subject of leadership. Many of the earlier writings articulate the virtues of strong leadership an essential part of which is to ensure everyone knows who is in charge. Proponents claim that this style of leadership (commonly known as 'strong man') leaves little room for ambiguity and produces good results. However, over the last forty years, leadership has evolved and there are now several competing theories many of which are based on a shared model of leadership.

Many authors of leadership books adopt an academic or theoretical approach which, sometimes, make it difficult to see how their ideas can be applied in the workplace. As such they tend to be more suited to students of management or leadership.

This book is written for people who want to learn leadership from a modern day perspective. It is suitable for newcomers, students at undergraduate or postgraduate level and more experienced persons. The book comprises a review of key leadership styles, features and attributes in which I highlight and unpack both the benefits and preconditions for applying various approaches to leadership. My overarching philosophy is that we are all leaders and by thought provoking insights into our lives with reflection and visualisation we can provide a space for ourselves to enhance our skills.

I draw on my personal experiences and that of some key influencers and provide practical scenarios from working environments to illustrate the learning. The book is both a commentary on the worldwide state of leadership and the plight and story of black people as leaders given their under-representation in such roles . I have provided an incisive view of organisational functions and best practices and drilled down into the why, the what and how strategies. This is both an organisational management tool and a directional road map for individual growth, self-actualisation and leadership.

Chapters one through ten provides the introductory and theoretical underpinnings of four emerging leadership styles:

1. Empowering
2. Reflective
3. Well-being
4. Stakeholder

These serve as a basis for understanding how people can develop their skills to become a Woke leader. In this respect, the term Woke is used to refer to a style of leadership which reflects a leaders awareness of social, racial, technological and other issues that can affect relations with staff and other stakeholders.

Subsequent chapters provide a structured approach (termed the ABC of leadership) to aid people to understand the relationship between their abilities, belief and implementing a coherent strategy for successful leadership. The applicability of this approach is then illustrated in scenarios taken from work as well as in a more personal setting such as family and sports. An important learning point, from use of the ABC approach, is understanding that enhancing leadership in your private life can positively impact your leadership at work and vice-versa.

In producing this book, I have benefitted from insights gained from numerous persons around the world in various positions of leadership. This has been augmented with years of research into leadership and management. I could only have got this far with the grace of God and for this I am truly grateful. To all those persons that supported my dream of writing this book, I am encouraged by your leadership.

Table of Contents

Chapter 1	1
Why this book	1
Introduction	2
Further reading	7
Chapter 2	9
Could you spot a leader?	9
What is leadership?	10
Exercise	13
Further reading	14
Chapter 3	15
Varying types of leadership	15
Leadership styles	16
Exercise	21
Further reading	22
Chapter 4	23
The empowering leader	23
The traits	24
Benefits of empowering	25
Empowering preconditions	28
Principles of empowerment	32
Empowering versus Laissez-faire	33
Empowering and democratic	36
LA1-Workplace Example	38
Exercise	41
Further reading	43
Chapter 5	45
Reflective leader	45
Traits	46
Reflective versus Empowering	47
Benefits of reflective	51
Preconditions	53
Principles of reflection	55
Building relations through reflection	58
Building knowledge	65
LA2-Workplace Example	68
Exercise	71
Further reading	73
Chapter 6	75
Well-being leader	75
Traits	76
Well-being versus Empowering	77

Benefits of well-being	80
Preconditions	82
Principles	85
LA3-Workplace Example	87
Multidimensional approach	89
Exercise	91
Further reading	93

Chapter 7 — 95
Stakeholder leader	95
Traits	96
Stakeholder versus Empowering	97
Benefits of stakeholder	100
Preconditions	102
Principles	105
LA4-Workplace example	107
Further reading	111

Chapter 8 — 113
Do you practice Woke leadership?	113
Introduction	114
Needs matter	115
Leaders and staff needs	116
Team needs	117
Organisational needs	120
Leadership behaviour	121
Demonstrating self-awareness	122
Demonstrating strategic thinking	122
Motivate	123
Demonstrate well-being	123
Demonstrate dependability	124
Create a shared vision and strategy	125
Facilitate for creativity	125
Facilitate conflict resolution	125
Facilitate shared approach to teamwork	126
Assess quality of outcomes/outputs and process	127
Inspire	127
Empower	128
Facilitate well-being	128
Facilitate for development	128
Switching styles	128
Leadership attributes	130
Exercise	133
Further reading	134

Chapter 9 — 135
Who are your influencers?	135
Introduction	136
Who is influential?	137

Tarana Burke	140
Persistency	143
Demonstrating your passion	144
Demonstrating empathy	145
Satya Nadella	147
Leading by example	149
Inspiring others	151
Encouraging challenges	151
Kenneth Frazier	152
Strategic leadership	154
Innovation/R&D focussed	155
CSR focussed	156
Issa Rae	158
Humour	160
Creativity	161
Mentoring	162
Jesmyn Ward	164
Communication	165
Ann McKee	166
Tenacity	168
Truth seeking/Integrity	169
Chloe Kim	170
Excellence	171
Further discussions	173
Further reading	176
Chapter 10	**179**
Leadership in digital era	179
Introduction	180
Technology maturity model	181
Elimination of jobs	183
Competition	188
Managing risks	190
Example technology risk management	193
Productivity	195
Being nimble	198
CSR	200
Remote working	204
Talent management	205
Building knowledge assets	207
Connected working	209
Further reading	211
Chapter 11	**213**
ABC of leadership	213
Introduction	214
A-Ability	214

Learning point 1	215
Learning point 2	215
Learning point 3	216
Learning point 4	216
Learning point 5	217
B-Belief	217
Learning point 6	217
Learning point 7	219
Learning point 8	219
C-Coherent strategy	219
Learning point 9	220
Learning point 10	220
Putting things together	221
Further reading	224
Chapter 12	**225**
Enhancing your ABC's	225
Enhancing abilities	226
Using strengths to overcome weaknesses	229
Being aware of the strength of others	232
Create a wider appreciation of your abilities	233
Being disruptive	234
Enhancing beliefs	235
Dealing with fears and self-doubt	239
Enhancing coherency of strategy	245
Visualisation	246
Exercise	249
Further reading	250
Chapter 13	**251**
We are all leaders	251
Introduction	252
Family	255
Sports - key steps	260
A leader at my level?	262
Business owner	263
Further reading	266
Chapter 14	**267**
Good & bad	267
Introduction	268
The bottom line	268
NGO	269
My way or the highway	270
It's a man's world	274
Exercise	276
Further reading	277
Chapter 15	**279**
Your aura	279

Introduction	280
Communication	281
Exercise	285

Chapter 16 — 287
The wellness leader — 287
- Introduction — 288
- Feels familiar? — 288
- Circwell leadership — 292
- Governance in well-being — 294
- Embedding wellness — 295
- Further reading — 297

Chapter 17 — 299
Manager versus Leader — 299
- Introduction — 300
- Changing mindset — 302
- Further reading — 306

Chapter 18 — 307
Firing your boss — 307
- Introduction — 308
- Underutilised — 308
- The monies not right — 309
- Weaknesses — 310
- Limited growth — 311
- Poor well-being — 312
- Toxic environment — 313

Chapter 19 — 315
Dear black people — 315
- The sacrifices of others — 316
- Uncle Tom — 316
- Board positions — 320
- Unconscious racism? — 321
- Further reading — 326

Chapter 20 — 327
Afterword — 327

Index — 329

Chapter 1
Why this book

Introduction
Further reading

Introduction

Perhaps more today than at any other time in the past, our voices count. The use of social media has provided an opportunity for individuals to both express their opinions and learn from others, more rapidly than ever, and this includes the field of leadership.

There are fewer excuses for being ignorant. It is as if technology has increased the democratisation of leadership allowing all to have a say. This, however, has added to the increasing amount of information on the subject and is a possible source of confusion for those wishing a gentle but practical introduction to leadership.

Social media and internet articles are full of quips and inspirational comments about varied aspects of leadership. The authors of these articles (influencers) are followed, almost religiously it would seem, by those that share the same view. However, behind the quip lies a history of knowledge borne out of experience and education obtained over a period much longer than it takes to read the article. So, whereas someone might agree with the sentiments of an influencer's postings they might not always be aware of the driving force for such writings.

Good leadership is increasingly viewed as being less about the person at the top and more of an organisation's capacity to support decision making. It is more about corporate social responsibility (CSR) than just share price, more about employee well-being than showing who is the boss and it is more sensitive to the means by which results are achieved rather than the achievements in themselves.

In this respect good leadership takes on more of a stewardship or servant-leader approach. In this approach the leadership of an organisation endeavours to satisfy the objectives of its wider set of stakeholders rather than just to focus on those providing financing. Staff are encouraged to express their ideas, challenge the status quo, and take leadership of projects in a manner which makes best use of their skills and consistent with supporting staff well-being.

It might come as no surprise to some readers that most of the companies I have come across do not consistently operate on a stewardship or servant-leader approach, notwithstanding their growing appeal. Even with rules and best practices, which require companies to disclose more of its governance and environmental traits, this has not necessarily diminished the obsession with profitability and shareholder focus.

For companies listed on a stock exchange quarterly reporting can lead to irrational decision making to ensure the "numbers look good" so as not to adversely impact the share price. This can lead to a type of thinking known as short-termism which seeks to prioritise activities giving results in the near-term but with potential erosion of long-term value.

The type of leadership I refer to in this book is, somewhat, idealistic but does not imply that you need to be perfect to be a good leader. There are no absolutes and what makes you a good leader in one situation might not make you a good leader in another since the effectiveness of your leadership is context dependent. What is important is that you can recognise your strengths and weaknesses across a range of skills and can determine which ones are needed to address your current situation. However, this requires that you work on improving your skills.

The emerging type of leadership is distinct from approaches adopted by past leaders of companies like General Electric (GE) and Microsoft in two main ways. First, they are more about teamwork and less on internal rivalry and second, it requires leaders to be equipped with much more of what is commonly termed soft skills. It is my contention that most, if not all people are capable of being leaders.

Even in an area which requires a high degree of know-how, a less technical person could flourish in this area, as a leader, if they had a moderate level of technical knowledge but with superior soft skills. They could achieve this by building a team around them that possessed the relevant technical skills and empowered them to be excellent. A good leader would learn from her team and be able to coach and guide staff in other skills.

The challenge I have found is that many people are not aware that they possess leadership skills. Many confuse this with management experience or with having a title. However, given the prevailing view that good leadership qualities largely refer to soft skills there is no reason why everyone would not be in possession of them. The real question is to what extent are these qualities developed?

With many people, several leadership abilities lie dormant as if they were asleep. It is my hope that this book will awaken those abilities and provide the motivation for enhancing their capacity and help to develop better leaders. The title of this book bears testament to the fact that we are all leaders but need to awaken to this reality. In other words, we need to be woken leaders.

It is, alas, a fact that some people, even if they have highly developed skills, are not leaders due to numerous reasons. I have found one reason to be a reluctance to assume leadership as it might impact on relations at work or home. Another reason arises from the selection bias of more senior staff preferring one type of person over another. As it relates to the former, I take the view that leadership is something a person must be willing to undertake but not be forced into.

Assuming a role because you can but not because you like it could be a recipe for disaster especially if you do not want to do it. It is important that a leader demonstrates some amount of passion or desire for the role of leadership as this will reflect in the way they interact with others. Since leadership involves inspiring others a leader that has no interest in their role is likely to inspire others to think the same way.

Unfortunately, I have come across selection bias too many times and have fallen victim to its impact myself. This is not to say that all selection bias is bad but when people are passed over for promotion because of gender, race or any other protected characteristic, bias becomes unlawful. Many times, however, selection bias does not occur in an overtly discriminatory way. You might first become aware of it when you realise that you have not been invited to your boss's barbecue party or drinks/meal after work.

You might have noticed that something was wrong when your boss started to become more critical of your work after you started questioning their decisions. If nothing else, you might have been a little concerned after your boss suggested that you need to be more of a team player despite having contributed more to the team than any other. Under these kinds of circumstances, it is fair to say that your chances of becoming a leader or increasing your levels of leadership might be limited and your desire for growth might have to include looking externally outside of your current organisation.

The characteristics of leadership that I detail in this book are not fixed to any organisation. In fact, it need not be with respect to an organisation at all. For example, the skills that you have developed in acquiring and maintaining relationships outside of the work environment are relevant to those required to maintain relations at work.

In a typical personal relationship, there is compromise and understanding of each other's strength and weaknesses etc. The main difference with working for an organisation is that rules of conduct are normally documented and tend to form part of an employee's terms of contract. However, soft skills required to be successful at work are, generally, not detailed in a contract and many employers do not provide the training necessary to support development of these skills.

This book is aimed at those persons that wish to improve their capacity to be a more effective leader. It is not intended that the book guarantee that you will become a leader on having read it or undertaken the advice given. The book is written in a way which presents examples of good and bad leadership and steps that can be taken to enhance key leadership characteristics. Several chapters also contain exercises. Undertaking these will provide you with a guide as to how you compare to the ideals discussed in the chapter.

Although the steps detailed are meant to provide a guide, the reader should bear in mind that even if their circumstances are like those of persons mentioned in the book, the results might differ. We do not all respond in the same way, even under the same set of conditions, to the same stimuli. The guidance provided reflects the better practice of people from several varied organisations, across time and geographic boundaries.

I have spent the best part of thirty years either working for or providing advisory/consulting services to organisations (private and public) around the world. Having started out in my professional career as a computer scientist I have also worked in financial services for global institutions such as Deutsche Bank and JP Morgan. As a consultant, I have provided advisory services to numerous governments on matters related to finance, debt, trade and governance and leadership as well as having established a financial risk management company.

As an employee I have held leadership roles at various levels from junior to executive and continue to be a director of several private companies.

Through my consultancy I have been involved in advising companies on effective corporate governance for several years.

As a black man, I belong to a group of persons that are vastly under-represented at senior/executive and board level among the largest companies in the world. It is my hope that black people, with aspirations to be leaders, will find the book inspiring and useful as a catalyst for change.

Further reading

1. Greenleaf, R (1977), *Servant Leadership: A Journey Into the Nature of Legitimate Power and Greatness*. New York: Paulist Press.

Chapter 2
Could you spot a leader?

What is leadership?
Exercise
Further reading

What is leadership?

The chances are that if you were to pick 100 people at random, from the high street, and ask them to describe what it means to be a leader you would get a variety of responses. It is likely that depending on where the high street is located e.g. the country, the political regime, the average age of the respondent, the predominant religion/culture, and other factors then these are likely to shape the responses.

The Oxford Dictionary of English states that leadership is: "The action of leading a group of people or an organisation". However, has this always been the interpretation of leadership over the ages?

According to the online etymology dictionary leadership derives from the word's **leader** and **ship** and it was only in the late 19th century that it emerged into the more modern interpretation of "characteristics required to be a leader". Delving further into the past reveals that the word **lead** meant "cause to go along one's way" which is derived from the prehistoric West and North Germanic word laithjan.

The historical use of the word leadership took on a more existential meaning than its more modern usage. In the historical context someone that sought leadership was more focused on their own self-enlightenment and improvement without necessarily seeking to assume a governing/managerial responsibility over others.

In modern times we observe the dominance of literature seeking to delineate leaders from others based on good/bad characteristics. Those that have characteristics a, b, c etc. or types 1, 2, or 3 etc. are classed as good and those without are classed as bad.

In relation to employment, such classifications aim to "optimise" the process of identifying good candidates. However, unscrupulous individuals can tweak desirable characteristics to render the employment process discriminatory. This is not to suggest that they should not be used but like any recruitment/management tool they must be used with care. An axiom I like to use derives from the Rotary Four-Way test "is it fair to all concerned". In other words, are the procedures applied to identify, select, and hire, promote/reward and terminate individuals undertaken in a manner that is legally and morally fair to both the organisation and the individual concerned?

Some readers might be surprised by use of the word **morally** especially when decisions can be justified on a legal basis. History has shown, the world over, that legal obligations and moral convictions are not always in sync. For example, segregation and discrimination on the grounds of race was legal in the United States of America up until 2 July 1964 when President Lyndon B Johnson signed into law the Civil Rights Act.

The Act, amongst other areas, made it illegal to discriminate on the grounds of race in relation to employment. However, even in the years preceding the Act, although discrimination was not illegal, there was a groundswell of opinion that it was immoral, and this truth was becoming uncomfortable for the government at the time. Hence, there was a conflict between the law and moral conviction of many people.

Perhaps there was no greater exponent of this conflict than that exemplified by a Baptist preacher from Memphis Tennessee that had the "gall" to organise and lead a march on Washington in 1963 to demand equality. It is evidently clear that without such interventions of moral fortitude the Act might not have been passed until much later if at all. That Baptist preacher was Dr Martin Luther King Jr whose leadership was so profound that it has a lasting impact on not only African Americans but people all over the world.

So, what does history tell us about leadership? For me, it tells me that leadership is principally about developing one's self and helping others to develop. In fact, religious accounts of leadership, as depicted in the Bible and other books provide good examples of the stewardship/servant leader style of leadership I referred to in the introduction.

Whether in private life or in the workplace it is difficult to be an effective leader without relying on the support of others and being willing to sacrifice your "pet project" in favour of the ideas/contributions of others. In so doing, we not only develop ourselves, but we grow because of the development of others and vice versa. This leads to a circular leadership economy in which investing in your employees leads to an investment in you as a leader which, in turn, results in enhanced growth of all concerned.

> "No man is an island, entire of itself;
> every man is a piece of the continent, a
> part of the main"
>
> John Donne

Since humans took their first steps on planet earth, there have been leaders. In many instances, these leaders emerged by circumstances of survival rather than design. Ancient civilisations gave rise to many thousands of leaders within their communities the names of which are long lost. What we do know though is that through generations of war and industrialisation emerged petty kingdoms, principalities, empires, dynasties etc., and monarchies as we know them today.

Some of the earliest recorded civilisations are believed to have first arisen in Lower Mesopotamia and Egypt along the River Nile (both occurring more than 3,000 B.C.E). There is evidence that these civilisations had created systems of governance including central governments, language and writing styles, religion and culture and other socio-economic structures. None of this could have been created without leadership and cooperation.

Exercise

Use a piece of paper to complete this exercise.

Describe what leadership means to you. If you are already in a leadership position, describe what you think has made you a leader e.g. is it your personality or technical knowledge. If you are not in a leadership position describe what you think you need to do to get into a leadership position.

Which of the following resonates more with you?

1. Leadership is more about:
    a. Developing yourself
    b. Managing others

2. Leaders must demonstrate:
    a. Good moral values
    b. Any values that get results

Further reading

3. Press, C. Soanes and A. Stevenson. (2005), *Oxford Dictionary of English*, Revised Edition, Oxford University Press.
4. Harper, D. (2020), *Online Etymology Dictionary*, etymonline.com, viewed October 7, 2020, available at <https://www.etymonline.com/>
5. Rotary International. (2020), *Guiding Principles*, Rotary International, viewed October 7, 2020, available at <https://my.rotary.org/en/guiding-principles>
6. Encyclopedia Britannica. (1964), *Civil Rights Act United States [1964]*, Encyclopedia Britannica, viewed October 7, 2020, available at <https://www.britannica.com/event/Civil-Rights-Act-United-States-1964>
7. Winston, B. (2003), *Extending Patterson's servant leadership model: Explaining how leaders and follower interact in a circular model.* In Proceedings of the 2003 Servant Leadership Research Roundtable. Virginia Beach, VA: Regent University
8. Shaw, Ian, ed. (2000), *The Oxford History of Ancient Egypt*. Oxford University Press. p. 479. ISBN 0-19-815034-2.

Chapter 3
Varying types of leadership

Leadership styles
Exercise
Further reading

Leadership styles

Leaders are often characterised by their style of leadership. Leadership style is how a leader undertakes their duties and provides direction to others. The term style implies that a leader might only have one approach, but this is not necessarily true. In your daily social interactions with people, most likely, you adapt your approach to individuals depending on several factors and so does a good leader when switching from one style to another.

The following diagram depicts the relationship between different leadership styles based on the behaviour of the leader relating to delegation and support.

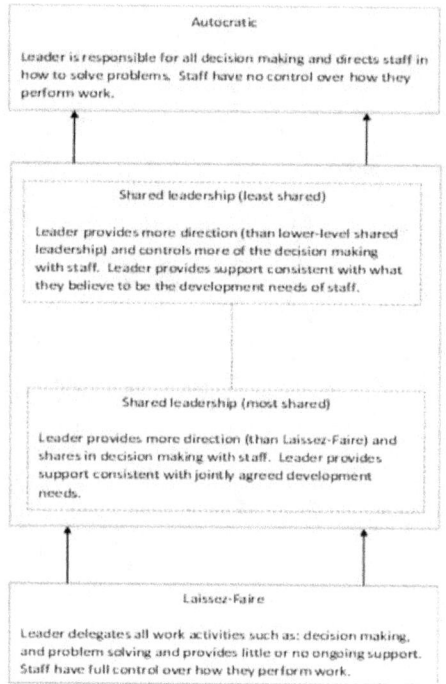

The diagram shows that there are, essentially, three main groupings of leadership styles: laissez-faire, shared leadership and autocratic. The arrows indicate increasing levels of leadership control moving bottom to top. At the same time, as leadership control increases, staff discretion decreases, and leaders facilitate support proportionate to the development needs of staff or what is perceived to be required of them to perform their duties.

When there is less discretion for staff to control how they work, there is more of a requirement for the leader to be prescriptive in terms of what they desire and how this is to be implemented. This reduces the need for staff to act in a creative/innovative manner or to devise strategies for managing risks.

There is also less of a need for staff to be effective communicators since staff are invariably the recipient and not the instigators of communication. Because of all of this, there is much less motivation for leaders to want to support staff development or even identify developmental needs.

When staff and leaders are jointly responsible for decision making and problem solving this results in what is termed shared leadership. The extent to which decisions are shared, autonomy and support over problem solving and the process for arriving at decisions will determine the type of shared leadership.

Who uses which style?

A sector in which an autocratic style of leadership is typically used is the defence (or military) sector. Military leaders give commands and expect their subordinates to follow them in the interests of time and safety. Facebook is an example of a technology company that uses this style at the C-suite level to improve the efficiency of decision making.

Warren Buffett is well known for being a Laissez-Faire leader. His philosophy is to acquire companies that already have self-motivated and highly competent leaders and he sees no point in meddling in decisions best left to those persons.

Companies that make use of shared leadership include the likes of Zappos.

The dashed lines between the boxes in the diagram indicates that there could be several degrees of shared leadership with each higher-level box, somehow, reducing the level of control of staff and hence the extent to which there is shared leadership.

The type of persuasion/influence used by leaders on staff (to get them to do work) differ depending on the level of the box. For example, the closer a leader is to an autocratic style they often make use of threats and instil fear. Sometimes autocratic leaders will use less severe methods such as rewards/penalties as a means of motivating staff compliance.

As leadership becomes more shared, leaders tend to rely less on extrinsic (e.g. monetary rewards or penalties) and focus more on intrinsic motivational methods. Staff which are intrinsically motivated tend to undertake activities because they find some amount of personal value in the work. It appeals to them on a 'higher level' in that it satisfies some philosophical/psychological, cultural aspect or, in general, is aligned to their value system and beliefs.

Examples of intrinsic motivation include recognising efforts of people beyond just that of success, facilitating for learning and development opportunities, enhancing opportunities for teamwork, empowering staff to make decisions and ensuring they buy into and know their role in the department/organisation vision.

As a rule of thumb, more autocratic styles of leadership are better suited to members of staff that prefer detailed instructions and guidance on what to do and how to do it principally because they lack the skills to make decisions and solve work activities without assistance. This style is also suited to those leaders that have strong technical skills since they are responsible for making all technical decisions.

Conversely, more shared as well as laissez-faire leadership styles are better suited to staff that have stronger skills and can make effective decisions. This style is also suited to a wider class of leaders than autocratic since the leader does not have to be as expert as staff in which case they can facilitate for joint decisions or delegated activities to occur to achieve work objectives.

If there is time criticality for decision making, then leadership styles which exhibit higher levels of autocracy tend to be preferred by leaders. Conversely when time constraints are less relevant shared leadership might be preferable since it allows for wider analysis.

When organisational activities are routine and/or staff creativity/innovation is not required by the leader then a more autocratic style of leadership is often preferred by leaders. Conversely, when activities require creative input, and this is valued by the leader then shared and laissez-faire leadership is more preferred.

The style of leadership I see emerging, and is advocated in this book, is one which has the following main attributes, termed LA1, LA2, LA3, and LA4:

1. LA1.
    - The leader(s) do not feel that they are responsible for making all important decisions for their area of responsibility. That is, they are happy to share responsibility and empower others to make decisions and to be led by their staff. The focus of this leader is to empower staff to partake in decision making and problem solving.

2. LA2.
    - The leader(s) accommodates diversity of views and challenges to their recommendations, due to a process of reflective thinking and welcomes feedback on their performance and others to achieve better results. The focus of this leader is on achieving excellence through continuous process improvement.

3. LA3.
    - The leader(s) see it as their responsibility to be knowledgeable of and facilitate for the well-being of themselves and their staff in decisions that are made concerning work activities. The focus of this leader is addressing well-being concerns of staff to improve productivity.

4. LA4.
    - The leader(s) make decisions based on maximising potential positive impacts on stakeholders and taking into consideration their views (beyond just shareholders or those providing financing/funding). The focus of this leader is on better working relationships with all stakeholders.

Each of the above attributes can be viewed as a separate style of leadership but are often combined. As will be discussed a little later, these styles overlap in various respects.

Individuals employing the above style of leadership are not exclusively an LA1, LA2, LA3 or an LA4 leader but they possess characteristics making up each of these different attributes. My experience is that good leaders can exhibit these attributes, to varying degrees, as and when required. This is not to say that individuals do not prefer one style over another. However, better leaders have developed their abilities to be able to accentuate one style more than another based on the circumstances at hand. In other words, an organisation might require a specific type of leadership based on the type of activities they are undertaking, the maturity of the organisation, environmental/regulatory constraints etc.

I describe each of the leadership attributes LA1, LA2, LA3 and LA4 as exhibiting aspects of what I term 'woken leadership'. I use this phrase since an objective of each style is to get leaders to demonstrate that they have an interest in (i.e. are awake to) the feelings/views of others (e.g. staff, clients, and others).

The styles go beyond simply telling people what to do and encourages leaders to better understand the motivations of persons and being conscious of this when making decisions. When this is properly undertaken, leaders will make better and more fair decisions which are not just reflective of their views but incorporate those of others. Going forwards, when I refer to woken leadership it is in the context where a leader is exhibiting a combination of the four styles.

Exercise

Based on the diagram of leadership relationships, which one are you more closely drawn to and why?

Based on the leadership attributes LA1, LA2, LA3 and LA4 which style suits you more and would this be consistent with the role you play in your organisation? Also, do you see any similarities between the attributes and shared leadership?

Further reading

1. Pearce, C. L., & Conger, J. A. (2003), *Shared leadership: Reframing the hows and whys of leadership*. Thousand Oaks, Calif: Sage Publications.
2. Maxwell, J. C. (2018), *Develop the leader within You 2.0*, Harper Collins.
3. Bennis, W. G. (2003), *On becoming a leader*. Cambridge, MA: Perseus Pub
4. Godin, S. (2008), *Tribes: we need you to lead us*, Piatkus Pub

Chapter 4

The empowering leader

The traits
Benefits of empowering
Empowering preconditions
Principles of empowerment
Empowering and democratic
LA1-Workplace Example
Exercise
Further reading

The traits

People demonstrating leadership attribute one (or LA1) are leaders that are aware of the abilities of those around them. They encourage and facilitate others to develop and use their skills in a manner which is of benefit to themselves and others. This leader looks for opportunities to engage and empower individuals to take a leadership role in activities.

The leader is supportive when things go wrong and lets others share in the glory when good things happen. The leader seeks to encourage her staff to contribute to discussions relating to most, if not all, aspects of the operations of their team, department etc., by allowing them to share their views and then making decisions based on incorporating the views of all parties.

Often, empowerment is achieved by group discussions or one-on-one in which persons can express their opinions about what work they are to do and how it is to be undertaken. Ultimately, empowerment results in leaders allowing staff to undertake work in the manner they see fit.

The focus of an empowering leader is the development of staff (or followers).

The good/bad of empowering

An example of good empowering is when a leader has identified persons that are (1) capable and (2) willing to take on a leadership and/or decision-making role and (3) when empowering primarily serves to develop those persons and the wider organisation. Larry Page (from Google) is an example of a CEO that practices this style of leadership. Page was quoted in an interview with Forbes as saying, "My job as a leader is to make sure everybody in the company has great opportunities and feel that they have an impact on what is going around".

An example of bad empowering leadership is when a leader empowers others to bolster their own position (e.g. such as those that delegate to those they like, irrespective of ability) as they know they can count on them for support. Another example is when a leader empowers others and then undermines them by not providing the necessary support to effectively perform their duties.

Benefits of empowering

There are several benefits that can be obtained when empowering leadership is properly executed. These benefits accrue to **leader, organisation, team,** and individual **staff.** I have coined the phrase **LOTS** to characterise these benefits: Leader, Organisation, Team and Staff:

Leader
1. *Improves trust between employee and leader.* Empowering others is an indication that you have belief in them. This belief helps to build trust between employee and leader which is an essential requirement for an effective working relationship. Empowering leaders seek to develop and/or enhance the trust between herself and her employees. They do this by acting consistently and not doing a U-turn (i.e. taking back responsibility) at the first sign of problems. They also act in an open and transparent manner to reduce the likelihood of jeopardising trust.

2. *Improves employee loyalty.* When employees do not feel part of decision-making and implementation processes, they might not be as committed to achieving its objectives, especially if they are not 100 percent in favour of the leader's approach. However, empowering leaders allow others to contribute to decision making which has the effect of making them feel in control of their destiny. When this occurs, employees tend to feel more committed to the leader's objectives and goals since these now become shared or fashioned by employees' input.

3. *Improves effectiveness.* When leaders empower their employees, they free up time so that they can more effectively undertake other activities they are responsible for.

4. *Improves ability of leader to identify areas of strength and weaknesses of employees and facilitate for growth.* When leaders empower staff, they also facilitate for their development and identify ways in which they can be supported to successfully achieve their objectives.

Organisation
5. *Improved productivity.* When staff are empowered to make decisions regarding how they will execute work activities, supported by way of training and development, they often become more proficient and productive.

6. *Improved quality of work and outcomes.* When staff are empowered and adequately supported the quality of their work often improves.

7. *Improved culture.* Subject to staff not being overburdened by empowerment, empowered staff are usually satisfied with their work and the organisation than when there is no empowerment. When staff are satisfied in sufficient numbers, the culture of an organisation becomes more positive.

8. *Improved retention.* When staff are empowered and adequately supported, engagement improves, and they develop a stronger bond with the organisation. Organisations that have good engagement tend to have higher levels of retention.

Team

9. *Improves teamwork.* The collective improvements derived from individual job satisfaction results in overall improved team morale. Further, since teams are empowered to devise strategies for effective cooperative working, this provides an incentive to ensure that staff learn how to better collaborate.

Staff

10. *Enhances employee confidence and self-worth.* Lack of self-esteem and confidence is something that most people have had to grapple with, to varying degrees. Empowering others typically results in a boost to how they see themselves and can lead to improvements in self-esteem. Empowering leaders see it as their responsibility to help their employees maintain high levels of confidence by first enabling empowerment then complimenting them when they achieve and providing support and encouragement otherwise.

11. *Enhances employee leadership skills.* When leaders empower their employees, they give them extra responsibilities. In the execution of these responsibilities the employee is, effectively, assuming a leadership role and developing their skills as a leader. Empowering leaders do not just delegate responsibility and walk away. They ensure that employees are adequately prepared to take on leadership roles prior to assigning such

responsibilities. Moreover, they are on call to provide guidance and assistance as and when required to aid their employees.

12. *Improves employee creativity.* When leaders empower their employees, they facilitate for enhanced creativity from staff since they are now responsible for determining how activities/projects should be implemented and are not, necessarily, tied to specific ways of thinking. However, an empowering leader would not just assume that creativity occurs overnight, they would facilitate for relevant guidance/training to aid staff to think creatively.

13. *Improves employee job satisfaction/morale.* When employees are appropriately empowered and supported (e.g. not overburdened), they get more enjoyment and fulfilment from their job.

14. *Enhances appreciation of wider organisational objectives/goals.* Since employees get to share in more strategic issues (i.e. those delegated by their leader), they also get the opportunity of obtaining a better understanding as to how their efforts feed into and affects wider organisational objectives/goals.

With the above in mind one should note that the empowering leader does not give up on being accountable for her area of responsibility. She is still responsible for ensuring that her staff do what they say they are going to do. In other words, delegation does not imply abrogation. In this respect, the role of the leader becomes a facilitator for their staff to work more effectively. This said, if a leader is not convinced by the suggestions offered, they are still responsible for having a final say over decision making and problem solving.

The benefits, as highlighted above, can be used as a means of assessing the effectiveness of an individual's approach to empowering leadership. Therefore, proper empowering leadership should lead to LOTS of achievement. Persons employing this style of leadership should frequently check to see if they are obtaining the right benefits. This can be undertaken by going through each of the items of LOTS and determining whether improvements have been achieved. To do this a leader should employ the use of relevant indicators to assess improvements in LOTS.

As an example, consider the benefit of improved teamwork. One possible indicator could be the percentage of staff that are happy/satisfied with their role and responsibilities. Another could be the percentage of staff benefiting from knowledge transfer between team members.

Empowering preconditions

To maximise the likelihood of an empowering leadership style having a positive effect, there are some preconditions which should be met:

- *Staff have well-developed communication skills* to enable them to participate in making decisions. If staff are unable to effectively communicate then they are less likely to be able to make valuable contributions to discussions and might find that they are at a disadvantage to others. In this respect it is possible that ineffective communicators end up being assigned work or having to perform activities that they would not have wanted to undertake. This type of situation is likely to result in individuals not feeling valued and reduces the likelihood of obtaining benefits highlighted above.

- *Staff have well-developed technical skills* to enable them to participate in problem solving activities. If staff do not possess the requisite level of technical skills to perform activities assigned to them then they are unlikely to benefit the leader, organisation, team, or themselves.

- *Staff are rationally motivated* to effectively participate in decision making and problem solving irrespective of their skills or other aspects. If staff are not motivated to contribute to effective decision making and problem solving it does not matter whether they are highly skilled or not since they are unlikely to put in their best efforts to achieve outcomes desired by the leader/organisation. Staff are rationally motivated when:

    ◦ *Without additional incentives or fear of repercussions* they are willing to engage in delegated work activities. Although individuals can be motivated by money or other incentives the presence of such rewards are not a true reflection of the value placed on the desired work by staff since, in the absence of such incentives, they might not perform the work.

    ◦ *Self-belief is consistent with demonstrated abilities.* That is, staff are not overconfident, but belief is based on credible evidence of their skills.

- *They believe their work is valued* by the leader and the organisation.

- *They believe they have genuine freedom* to determine how work is undertaken.

- *They believe the intentions of the leader* are non-exploitative. That is, they feel that the leader is not acting for self-benefit or to undermine them in some manner.

- *They believe the leader will facilitate* for the support/development required to undertake tasks.

- *They believe they can take on additional responsibilities* without being overwhelmed or compromising other activities that are still required to be undertaken by the staff member.

- *Leader has well-developed communication skills* to be able to effectively communicate her vision to staff, the results of discussions surrounding the vision and their understanding as to the role/responsibilities of each team member.

- *Leader is capable of inspiring* staff to partake in decision making and other leadership activities. If the leader does not possess the ability to convince her staff to take on delegated responsibilities or contribute to decisions affecting their work this might be an indication of a lack of trust or credibility of the leader. An empowering leader will, therefore, constantly seek to maintain trust with her employees.

- *Leader is welcoming of diversity of opinions* and to be led. If the leader does not welcome challenges or diversity of opinions staff are unlikely to want to actively engage in decisions that might run contrary to that of the leader. This is not to say that they would not take on other activities delegated to them, but it is unlikely that they would try to be as creative as they otherwise would be if they were given more freedom to challenge the leader or the status quo. Moreover, if the gulf between what the leader desires and what staff want is too wide, inflexibility of the leader could lead to break down of relations. An empowering leader is not afraid to show their frailties and to be led by their staff when it becomes clear this presents a better choice for all concerned.

- *Leader has genuine* intentions to delegate. If the leader intends to hold on to the reins of power or control, then true empowerment has not occurred.

- *Leader is aware of their own strengths and weaknesses* and facilitates for the empowerment of staff to support weaknesses as and when required. An empowering leader recognises that they are not capable of making effective decisions all the time, especially for subject matters that they might not be expert. In such circumstance's full delegation and/or partial staff participation could prove the best strategy, but this only works if leaders are aware of and act on their limitations.

- *Leader does not act in an exploitative manner.* The ultimate objective of an empowering leader is to facilitate for the growth of their staff and the organisation. Clearly, if staff perform well then this should also reflect positively for the leader but it should not be the intention of the leader to abuse this relationship to satisfy their own personal goals which compromise staff and/or undermine their motivation.

- *Leader is aware of strengths and weaknesses* of their staff members. If the leader is not aware of the skills and limitations of her team then the likelihood of bad decision-making increases as does the risk of poor execution of operational activities.

- *Leader is willing and capable of facilitating* for the development of her staff either through mentoring or formal training (online or otherwise) and provide necessary resources to support their efforts. If leaders are not able to facilitate for the development of their staff, then this could have a detrimental impact on the leader's effectiveness since this could result in poor execution of operational activities. Moreover, inadequate facilitation could erode the self-belief of staff and deprive them of the necessary support required to be fully empowered.

- *Leader can make timely decisions* when it becomes apparent that agreement and/or consensus cannot be obtained from staff within a reasonable time. Under these circumstances, leaders must be capable of taking charge and lead by example.

- *Organisation-wide acceptance and practice* of empowering leadership. If the practice of empowering leadership is not widely undertaken (and sponsored by those highest in the management chain) in an organisation it is likely that individual efforts might be subject to resistance. For example, if a junior leader empowers their staff but a more senior one does not embrace this style of leadership, this might prove problematic for the junior leader and their staff. Thus, when senior leaders adopt empowering leadership, junior leaders are more likely to be provided with the resources they need to adopt similar strategies.

Principles of empowerment

The above discussions give rise to the following principles of empowering leadership:

> **Principle 1**
>
> Empowering leaders inspire their staff to take on decision making, problem solving and leadership activities. Such inspiration is based on staff having made a conscious decision to trust the leader.

Principle 1 essentially states (ignoring other aspects) that leaders inspire staff if and only if staff have trust in the leader.

> **Principle 2**
>
> Empowering leaders encourage challenges from staff.

Principle 2 recognises that self-determination requires staff to have the choice of being able to challenge existing practices and that this should be encouraged by the leader.

> **Principle 3**
>
> Empowering leaders know the strength/weaknesses of staff and provide adequate development to support them in undertaking their activities.

Principle 3 recognises that staff might need ongoing support to achieve their objectives. Such support playing to the strengths of staff and facilitating for developmental resources for weaknesses.

> **Principle 4**
>
> Empowering leaders can effectively communicate their requirements and expectations of staff.

Principle 4 recognises that although leaders share responsibilities with staff, they still need to provide staff with an understanding of what is required of them and expected levels of quality.

> **Principle 5**
>
> Empowering leaders are willing to be led by their staff.

Principle 5 recognises that leaders are not infallible and that they do not possess all the answers. They acknowledge that true empowerment requires two-way inspiration in which leaders are inspired by staff as well as giving inspiration to staff.

Empowering versus Laissez-faire

Those readers familiar with the laissez-faire style of management should note the contrast with that of an empowering leader. A laissez-faire style of leadership is one in which a leader hands most of the decision making to their staff. Therefore, decisions relating to what work is to be done and how it is to be performed, including levels of quality, are determined by the leader's staff.

The following table highlights the key differences between laissez-faire and an empowering leader:

Laissez-Faire	Empowering
• Decision making delegated exclusively to staff.	• Leader typically transfers decisions to staff but also accommodates joint decision making.
• Staff are expected to work with little or no supervision and devise strategies to solve problems on their own.	• Staff are given, ongoing, guidance according to their level of competency. So, more novice staff are more closely supervised than those showing greater levels of expertise which might not be supervised at all. • Staff can use whatever strategies they see fit if it achieves objectives and is consistent with overall organisational codes of behaviour.
• Responsibility for success/failure is handed over to staff whilst accountability remains with the leader.	• Staff are only fully responsible when the leader completely transfers responsibility and are jointly responsible otherwise. The leader always remains accountable.

Laissez-Faire	Empowering
• Leaders allow staff to exclusively determine the key performance indicators for success. • Staff are responsible for quality assurance of work produced.	• Leaders are responsible for ensuring that any staff key performance indicators (KPIs) can achieve desired outcomes. Leaders are not bound to accept staff KPIs and will replace them with their own if they think they are more appropriate. • Whereas leaders might not be solely responsible for undertaking work activities allocated to staff they play a monitoring role to ensure that the process and outcomes meet (or exceed) their expected standards.
• Leaders delegation of work is not necessarily predicated on skills of staff.	• Leaders empower individuals based on the skills they possess.
• Staff are responsible for devising strategies for how they will work together using whatever methods they see fit.	• Leader and staff are responsible for devising team-working strategies, but the result must be that no member feels that they are not empowered.
• Leader develops vision and strategy without significant input from staff and/or motivation for adopting a shared-vision.	• Leaders motivate a shared vision by ensuring inclusion of staff in decision making as well as execution of activities and ensuring they see how they fit into it. It becomes shared since staff and the leader are jointly responsible for determining what should go in or be excluded and having the final say.

Empowering and democratic

Although similar, there are some subtle differences between an empowering leader and that of a so-called democratic leader. A democratic leader is one that ensures that **all team members** get the opportunity to have an input into decision making relating to what work is undertaken and how problems are solved prior to leaders acting. The final decision, however, is with the leader after taking into consideration the views of staff.

In contrast, an empowering leader is, primarily, driven by knowledge of skill sets when determining who should have a say. This said, an empowering leader is respectful of all opinions and is unlikely to shut someone down because she does not value their skills.

A democratic leader seeks to ensure that work is allocated to all persons if they can undertake such activities and irrespective of their level of competency. In contrast, an empowering leader would judiciously seek to allocate work based on skills not based on equity. If they believed an individual did not possess sufficient skills to undertake an activity this would be assigned to another person, but they would seek to ensure that others of lesser abilities could shadow those more expert (which could include the leader) to develop capacity. So, whereas the focus for a democratic style of leadership is in participation for all, for an empowering leader it is participation for all but with staff development in mind.

Importantly, an empowering leader might decide not to allow wide or any discussion into decision making relating to activities to be undertaken but could allow creative freedom with respect to how individuals execute these activities. The leader would, however, ensure that they would facilitate the support and development necessary to achieve objectives. This would still qualify as empowering since autonomy and self-determination are provided for problem solving. Strictly speaking, this would not qualify as a democratic style of leadership since the requires emphasis to be placed on allowing individuals to have a say for both decision making and problem solving.

More generally, an empowering leader seeks to understand the strengths/weaknesses and aspirations of her staff members and aids in their development to inspire and motivate them to work in the wider interests of the team and organisation.

In conclusion, a democratic style of leadership is empowering but an empowering style of leadership does not have to be democratic. As a result, the democratic leadership style should be viewed as a special case of the more general empowering leadership.

LA1-Workplace Example

Ben works for an investment bank in the city of London and is responsible for ensuring that various transactions undertaken in the day are reconciled with confirmations received from counterparties (e.g. other investment banks). Ben's boss Susan has been working at the bank for sixteen years whereas Ben and other team members have only worked in the bank for a maximum of 4 years.

The reconciliation process, in the bank, has been one of the weaker areas within the firm and Susan has been tasked (by senior management) with the responsibility of implementing revisions which would reduce process times by 30% and increase accuracy by 25%. Susan realises that her department will now be under a microscope and will benefit greatly if she manages to turn things around. She, however, dreads the consequences if things are not improved within the seven months allocated for the process improvement by senior management.

Susan has firm ideas as to how the work should be undertaken and has documented some initial thoughts. Her approach would leverage external expertise in the form of short-term consultants. However, there are those such as Ben that have other ideas. At a team meeting Susan discussed the process improvement assignment with her team. Snippets of the dialogue are as follows:

Susan

As you might have heard I have been given seven months to improve the reconciliation process by senior management.

Ben

Yes. Do you have any thoughts on how we should proceed? I ask because I have been thinking about this matter for several months and a few of us in the team have had some discussions about how we could move forward.

Susan

Yes Ben. I have documented some of my thoughts on the matter and will share them with the team after the meeting. This said, I am keen to know what thoughts you and the team have on the subject. Perhaps we could schedule a subsequent meeting to discuss this?

Team

Various team members state that, considering the importance of the request, more time should be devoted in the current meeting to address the matter.

Susan

OK, I agree. I will present to you my thoughts and then you can present yours.

Susan shared a copy of her documented ideas on the process and then discussed her approach with the team after which Ben discussed the approach he was championing with his other colleagues. Susan questioned every aspect of Ben's proposal and became increasingly assured when he and other team members were able to answer her questions and allay any concerns.

During Ben's presentation it became clear to Susan that the team member's suggestion was superior to her own. She could sense how passionate her team was and how their skills could be used to achieve the required objective. This was important as Ben's approach was that all the work could be undertaken by the team members with, possibly, some help from the Information Technology -IT division. This would not only save on costs but would help to strengthen team morale and empower them to take more control of their own destiny.

Although Susan believed in her approach, having heard the proposal from Ben, she was having serious doubts about her strategy. In her mind she began to weigh the pros and the cons and thought about what could happen if things did not work out. In the case where the work was outsourced, she might be able to get away with blaming the contractors and plead for more time. In the case where the work was undertaken internally, her thoughts was that she would be held more accountable for any failures.

Susan realised that putting off a decision to another time was simply "kicking the can down the road" and she felt that made no sense and that she owed it to her staff to be open and honest. At this point Susan stated:

Susan

During this meeting it has become clear to me that you guys have come up with a suggestion that is much better than mine and I think it will be a winner. Collectively, I know that you have the skills to do a great job and I have confidence in each of you to be able to contribute towards the stated objectives of the process improvement. Please let me know how I can help and what contribution you want from me.

Ben, I think you should take the lead on this project and please let me know if you would like for me to help you in producing the project plan.

Ben

Thank you, Susan, for allowing us the opportunity of sharing our ideas with you and, more importantly, allowing us to take the lead on this important project. We will not let you down.

The above example shows how open Susan was to the support offered by Ben and her willingness to be part of a team being led by more junior staff members. Note that Susan was not passive in accepting the proposal as she wanted to be convinced that her team had thought through the issues carefully and could address her concerns. This is typical of a responsible empowering leader as it makes no sense adopting a strategy that you simply do not have confidence in just because you want to please your team.

A responsible empowering leader is willing to be led but there must be an objectively rationale basis on which this decision is made. However, it would be irresponsible if a leader were to choose their own approach over that of their staff if the staff one was better than theirs. You can read into the word "better" to mean, more cost effective, time saving, wider impact etc. We are all aware, however, that this latter situation often occurs in the workplace. This would be an example of someone not exhibiting the attribute of LA1.

Suppose Susan had decided to go for what she believed to be the option to limit criticisms of her should the project fail. That is, suppose she decided to go for her original approach. Suppose further that the project was successful. Even though the project was successful, Susan would not have demonstrated that she was an LA1 leader. The message here is, **it is not just the result that matters but also the approach you took to get there**.

Exercise

Do you believe that you are an effective empowering leader? (Y/N)

➢ If yes, write down some examples which demonstrate the effectiveness of your leadership.
   1. For each example, write down what **you** specifically did to achieve success.
   2. Write down what you believe **others** contributed to achieving success.

   If you find that you are the centre of what you perceive to be your successes, you might want to ask others whether they think you are an effective empowering leader. It might be that you have not completely relinquished control and enabled others to be as empowered as they could be. In this case, your expectations and those of others you have empowered might not be aligned.

➢ If no, describe examples of where you believe you have fallen short of being effective.
   1. For each example, write down what **you** did or did not do that led to problems.
   2. Write down what **others** did or did not do that led to problems.

   If you find that you are at the centre of your perceived failures, then you should seek guidance or find ways to improve your abilities to mitigate the issues leading to the problems you have identified. If you find that others are the major causes, you might want to ask them about their perception of the reasons why empowerment might not be as effective. It might be that the level of empowerment that you have provided to some might not be suitable to their level of ability and/or personal circumstances. In this case, either some type of tailored support or revision of requirements might help to solve the problem.

I am aware of your abilities.
I encourage you to develop and use your skills for the benefit of all.
I look for opportunities to engage and empower you to lead.
I support you when things go wrong and give you credit when good things happen.

Do I not empower you?

Dr Howard Haughton, 2019

Further reading

1. Fletcher, M. (2017), *Empowering Leadership: How a Leadership Development Culture Builds Better Leaders Faster*, Thomas Nelson, Pub
2. Praszkier, R. (2018), *Empowering Leadership of Tomorrow,* Cambridge University Press, Pub
3. Hao, P., He, W and Long, L. (2018), *Why and When Empowering Leadership Has Different Effects on Employee Work Performance: The Pivotal Roles of Passion for Work and Role Breadth Self-Efficacy*, Journal of Leadership & Organisational Studies Vol. 25(I) 85-100
4. Kim, M., Beehr, T and Prewett, M. (2018), *Employee Responses to Empowering Leadership: A Meta-Analysis,* Journal of Leadership & Organisational Studies 1-20

Chapter 5

Reflective leader

Traits
Reflective versus Empowering
Benefits of reflective
Preconditions
Principles of reflection
Building relations through reflection
Building knowledge
LA2-Workplace Example
Exercise
Further reading

Traits

People demonstrating leadership attribute two (or LA2) are leaders that are constantly seeking ways to improve their own and team performance whilst accommodating the opinion and inputs of others. They actively encourage and act on feedback from others with a view towards understanding what worked and did not work so well and using this to improve future performance for self and team.

The starting point for this type of leader is: *is there anything we could have done differently to improve on the process/result?* In other words, the starting point is a question which seeks to identify whether a better result could have been achieved. This type of leader is striving for excellence and will endeavour to continuously improve until they are not able to obtain a better result. Unlike some types of leaders, the LA2 leader does not answer the question him/herself by using a process of self-reflection alone but relies on the feedback of others.

Since reflective leadership involves an endeavour to continuously improve and relies on collaborative input a major objective of this type of leadership is enhancing learning. This learning comes from individual and shared experiences about some event or aspect of work. Reflective leadership does

To reflect or not to reflect?

I knew someone (in a position of leadership) whose main objective was to be liked by as many people as possible. Under her leadership, the team could not grow technically as she was not able to provide or facilitate for their growth.

She could not understand why her team were not valued as highly as others in the organisation. To compensate for this lack of recognition she increasingly turned to the use of "political" tactics to improve her profile by undermining the contribution of others.

What this person did not appreciate was whereas she thought people liked her, instead they feared and had little respect for her. Her style of leadership was to deflect rather than to accept constructive criticism. Consequently, most of her working relationships were weak and superficial and she provided no positive inspiration for staff members.

This person would have benefitted from understanding that it is better to be respected than to be liked. Her focus should have been to address the reasons for her team's lack of technical growth and the role she and others might have contributed towards this situation.

not work effectively if there is no increase in knowledge coupled with appropriate strategies for improvement.

Reflective leadership is not something that is only meant to be applied at a single point in time, such as when things go wrong. It is a style of leadership which reflects a process of learning and development on an ongoing basis.

Like that of an LA1 leader, LA2 leaders seek collaboration and feedback from their staff members. The motivation for an LA2 leader is not necessarily to obtain consensus or agreement or to fully empower individuals but to derive a better understanding as to how improved solutions to problems can be identified.

Reflective versus Empowering

The following table provides key differences between an LA1 and an LA2 leader.

Empowering	Reflective
• Leader either completely transfers responsibility for making decisions to staff or jointly share in decision making. This is done with a view to increase autonomy and self-determination of staff and enhance team cohesion.	• Leader is responsible for making decisions but seeks opportunities to engage staff prior to acting. This is achieved by soliciting alternative ideas from staff and not just asking staff to comment on the leader's recommendations. This is done with a view to understanding how activities can be continuously improved by reflecting on previous or similar work experiences. • Increased autonomy and self-determination only become relevant if it can be shown to directly contribute to improvements in problem solving (i.e. both the process and the result).

Empowering	Reflective
• Staff are given guidance according to their level of competency. So, more novice staff are more closely supervised than those showing greater levels of expertise which might not be supervised at all • Staff can use whatever strategies they see fit if it achieves objectives and is consistent with overall organisational codes of behaviour.	• Since the focus is on continuous process improvement towards achieving excellence staff engaged in operational activities are those with the greatest level of competency. Consequently, there is less of a need for mentoring and development of staff on a project by project basis. However, outside of a specific project context, a reflective leader will seek opportunities to facilitate for the development of staff based on identified weaknesses. • Staff use strategies that have been shown or are highly likely to result in excellence. Implementation of these strategies might or might not be because of empowerment but could be based on directions from the leader, for example.
• Leader transfers or shares responsibility for decisions and problem solving and remains accountable for them.	• Leader is primarily focused on problem solving and engages in shared decision making only if it helps to improve processes and strive for excellence. The leader remains responsible and accountable for all decisions.
• Operational improvement occurs as a secondary effect of enhanced team cohesion.	• Operational improvement occurs as a direct consequence of processes adopted by team.

Empowering	Reflective
• Leader and staff are responsible for devising team-working strategies, but the result must be that no member feels that they are not empowered.	• Leader and staff responsible for determining the best strategy for team-working based on reflective thinking. This might or might not result in empowerment of all staff in execution of work activities.
• Leaders motivate a shared vision with a view to ensuring inclusion of staff in decision making as well as execution of activities. The focus here is on individual staff members buying into the leader's vision and seeing how they fit into it.	• Leaders motivate a shared vision with a view to understanding how individuals can better work together to achieve team/organisational objectives. The focus here is not just on individual's buying into the leader's vision but for there to be a common understanding as to the most appropriate way to achieve team dynamics and excellence.

Benefits of reflective

The benefits that accrue when reflective leadership is properly executed are:

➢ **Leader**
　1. *Improves trust between employee and leader.* A reflective leader encourages her staff to identify ways in which their own as well as the leader's performance can be improved. This is achieved by reflecting on past and current activities and identifying what worked, what could have worked, what is working and what will work better in the future. This requires transparency and a willingness to engage constructively by all parties. As a corollary, the process also identifies what did not/could not work and the reasons why. This process of reflection and sharing helps to build trust.

　2. *Strengthens commitment to leader's objectives/goals.* When a leader and employees engage in reflective thinking, it enhances the chances that they will end up on the same wavelength. It does not imply that they will be best buddies, but it does lead to mutual understanding if both parties are genuine when sharing. This mutual understanding can help to increase an employee's commitment to their leader's objectives/goals.

　3. *Leader has better understanding of self.* The practice of reflective leadership helps leaders to obtain a better understanding of how they think, work and how others perceive their behaviour. As a leader, improved knowledge of self can help to identify better ways in which a leader can relate to her staff and be more effective.

　4. *Enhances critical thinking skills.* The process of reflective leadership results in leaders engaging in self-examination as well as analysis of the behaviour of others in relation to collaborative work. Reflective thinking requires a person to be rational and open-minded when they analyse and discuss issues and rely on evidence rather than feelings to form conclusions. This process of analysis helps to improve critical thinking.

5. *Improves creativity.* When leaders provide a facilitating environment for reflective leadership, they increase the likelihood of more creative thinking since they are not bound to follow traditional approaches. Reflective thinking constantly strives to find new and improved ways of achieving process and outcome improvement and when properly executed will improve creativity.

- **Organisation**
    6. *Improve organisational effectiveness.* A central theme of reflective leadership is constantly seeking ways to improve how excellence can be achieved. This activity of continuous process improvement helps to improve the effectiveness of the entire organisation.

    7. *Improve organisational sustainability.* Effective reflective leadership will result in better documented procedures and processes for conducting day-to-day operational activities. This facilitates for business continuity when teams change, and new persons come on board as this institutional capacity can be reused.

- **Team**
    8. *Improves shared knowledge & teamwork.* A reflective leader will also encourage her staff to practice reflective thinking amongst themselves. The process of sharing will help to increase the amount of common knowledge within teams and aid individuals in better knowing each other's strengths and weaknesses and how to work better with each other.

- **Staff**
    9. *Employees have a better understanding of themselves.* The practice of reflective thinking helps employees understand how they might appear to others. The process helps individuals to think about their behaviour and how their performance could be improved. When reflective thinking is shared with others, the opportunity arises that individuals can get feedback on their strengths/weaknesses.

    10. *Enhances employee critical thinking skills.* The process of reflective leadership results in staff engaging in self-examination as well as analysis of the behaviour of others in relation to collaborative work. This process of analysis helps to improve critical thinking.

11. *Improves employee creativity.* Since staff are engaged in reflective thinking, just like their leaders, they are free to be creative in how they address problems to achieve continuous improvement.

When the result of reflective leadership is the empowerment of staff to both question decisions and be responsible for how activities are implemented, the benefits of empowerment would also accrue. That is, those benefits for empowering leadership also become those of reflective leadership.

Preconditions

To maximise the likelihood of a reflective leadership style working, there are some preconditions which should be met:

- *Staff have well-developed technical skills* to enable them to analyse past and current work-related activities and make suggestions for improvement.

- *Staff have well-developed communication skills* to be able to effectively articulate their feelings/thoughts regarding working relations and project-related activities.

- *Staff are motivated* to effectively participate in reflective thinking. Staff are motivated when:

    ◦ Without additional incentives or fear of repercussions they are willing to engage in reflective discussions on work-related activities.

    ◦ *They believe either their level of knowledge or those of others* will increase through either self or team reflection.

    ◦ *They believe their opinion is valued* by the leader and team members.
    ◦ *They have confidence in their ability* to effectively contribute to reflective thinking and decision making.

    ◦ *They believe they have genuine freedom* to express their views and opinions in relation to past, current and future work activities.

- *Staff can analyse their strength/weaknesses as well as others* and identify strategies for improvement.

- *Leader has well-developed communication skills* to be able to effectively articulate their feelings/thoughts regarding working relations and project-related activities.

- *Leader has well-developed technical skills* to enable them to analyse past and current work-related activities and make suggestions for improvement.

- *Leader can make timely decisions* when it becomes apparent that time criticality might necessitate curtailing reflective analysis.

- *Leader can facilitate* for the development of her staff including being able to undertake reflective thinking and incorporating this into work activities.

- *Leader can analyse their strength/weaknesses as well as others* and identify strategies for improvement.

- *Leader is welcoming of diversity* of opinions.

- *Leader is willing to relentlessly pursue* reflective analysis irrespective of their or other people's predisposition. They ensure that all opinions are taken into consideration and the process continues until satisfactory outcomes are obtained.

- *Leader is open-minded and willing to accepts the results* of reflective analysis irrespective of whether these reflect negatively on the leader or others. Their utmost priority is pursuit of the truth with a view to improve processes as well as outcomes.

Principles of reflection

> **Principle 1**
>
> Reflective leaders encourage challenges to avoid complacency or apprehension of past experiences influencing present or prospective activities.

Principle 1 recognises that fostering an environment of critical thinking and creativity requires staff to have the choice of being able to challenge existing practices and that this should be encouraged by the leader. It recognises that previous successes are not sufficient for adopting similar strategies and that failures are not an excuse for adopting a no risk approach. The principle applies to the leader and staff alike.

> **Principle 2**
>
> Reflective leaders are tenacious in their pursuit of knowledge to create improved processes and outcomes.

Principle 2 acknowledges that a key objective of reflective leadership is the pursuit of knowledge which they strive for tenaciously by applying reflective thinking in individual and group settings. They are not put off by naysayers or traditional ways of thinking and will seek ways around obstacles to achieve their objectives.

> **Principle 3**
>
> Reflective leaders are excellence seeking.

Principle 3 recognises that reflective leaders do not just strive to do things better. They seek to ensure that learning results in best-in-class and increases the likelihood of continuous process improvement.

> **Principle 4**
>
> Reflective leaders are truth seeking.

Principle 4 recognises that the motivations for undertaking reflective thinking is to uncover the truth. True leaders are not afraid that analysis might embarrass them or others, they simply seek the truth.

> **Principle 5**
>
> Reflective leaders foster ongoing effective communications as they understand that it lies at the heart of reflective thinking and leadership.

Principle 5 recognises that reflective leaders need to be able to ensure that they can effectively guide staff so that the objectives of learning and development through reflective thinking is clear. They do this through communications with staff about the rationale for and objectives of reflective thinking. They also ensure that they and staff document their feelings/thoughts regarding work activities either during or after completion and that these are shared and discussed.

The idea of a boss or a leader providing feedback and appraising staff is well-established in many organisations across the world. Much less common, however, is when staff provide appraisals/feedback on their leader's performance. For this to be effective it requires a leader to recognise that they are not perfect and to expose themselves to criticism from junior staff (or peers). My experience is that this works best for those leaders that are not "politically minded".

Those that are politically minded go to great lengths to project an image of security and competence and often engage in the blame game. They take credit for much but give little effort. They ingratiate with top-level management and typically come across as superficial.

Reflective leadership requires a high degree of transparency and openness. Not all leaders will be comfortable with this. I have come across many people in positions of leadership that take the view that they will only talk to colleagues about work-related events and refuse to interact with those they see as being "too low down in the management hierarchy". Such an attitude is not conducive to maintaining an open and constructive environment in which people feel free to express and share their ideas.

One of the first things a reflective leader should do is ensure that she has a good rapport with her colleagues. However, how often do we really go beyond a superficial understanding of those we work with?

When people maintain relations at a superficial level, they run the risk of incorrectly characterising others. Similarly, when people do not challenge their own assumptions, they become a fan of a club of one. They are likely not to see themselves how others see them, and this could lead to potential lack of team cohesion.

Building relations through reflection

Building a good rapport requires that a reflective leader be driven by obtaining a better understanding of perceptions, about themselves and others.

Perceptions lie at the heart of reflective leadership as detailed in the following list:

1. My perception of me.
2. My perception of what others think of me.
3. My perception of others.
4. My perception of what others think of themselves.
5. Others perception of themselves.
6. Others perception of what I think of them.
7. Others perception of me.
8. Others perception of what I think of myself.

I call the above list, the eight perceptions of leadership. They correspond to views that a leader might have of herself and others and vice-versa. The leader is denoted by the term "My/myself/me and I" and employees by "Others/themselves". So, for example, if I am a leader then I will have a perception about myself which is expressed by the first statement in the above list. What my staff might think of me would be given by the seventh statement in the list.

When there is agreement between what a leader and others think then this provides a basis for mutual co-operation and support in achieving excellence and continuous improvement. However, when there are differences of opinion then this can be a cause for concern as it might indicate inhibitors of improvement.

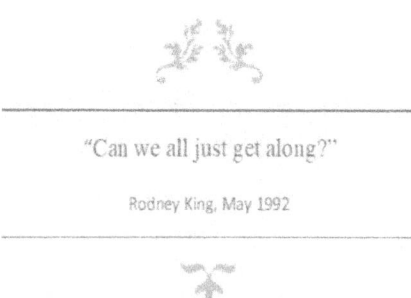

"Can we all just get along?"

Rodney King, May 1992

To understand people's perception of you it requires you to engage in dialogue with them. A practical way to do this is to schedule a face to face meeting. Failing this try an electronic meeting, send an email, or have a telephone call. The general purpose of the dialogue is to set people's minds at ease that nothing they say will be held against them and that you are seeking their candid opinions about you as well as themselves.

As a leader seeking the opinion of others, you would phrase statements 5 to 8 above as a question. For example, what do you think of yourself in relation to XYZ? As to what XYZ is would depend on the circumstances at your organisation. This said, amongst other issues, you might want to consider questions relating to happiness at work, development needs and teamwork.

You would phrase statements 1 to 4 as questions to yourself. The idea is then to analyse the results of what you have produced with those you have received from others. A next step would be to share what you have produced with others. At this point both leader and staff would have the same information.

Unfortunately, in the workplace and elsewhere, you are likely to come across those that do not wish to be transparent and open. They are difficult to pin down and only care about their own opinion. How would you deal with these people, especially if one of them is your boss? Adopting a reflective mindset will help you to better understand yourself and how others compare in relating to those persons that cause you difficulty. You might not be able to get them to share, but you should be in a better position to know how to relate to them.

The table below defines different states of relationships based on whether there are conflicts or agreements between perceptions:

Synchronicity	Conflict	Verify	Resolve
Matching	Unmatched	Matching	Unmatched
1,7 3,5	1,7 3,5	1,2	1,2
1,8 3,6	1,8 3,6	3,4	3,4
2,7 4,5	2,7 4,5	5,6	5,6
2,8 4,6	2,8 4,6	7,8	7,8

Under the column "Synchronicity" if perceptions 1 and 7 (from the above list) match, i.e. my perception of me and others perception of me are the same then a state of synchronicity exists. In this state there is no confusion as to perceptions. That is, there is good understanding between me and others as it relates to perceptions of me.

Note that good does not necessarily mean perfect alignment. It simply means that there is agreement on the fundamental/material aspects. A similar argument holds for the other pair of perceptions listed under the column. The state of "Synchronicity" is the most desirous since it implies that there is less of a gap between the leader and the perception of others.

Perceptions are not necessarily reality even when there is synchronicity. For example, you might think that you are a particularly good strategic thinker and so might your staff, but this does not imply that you are. It might be that your staff are just uncomfortable or afraid of telling you the truth. The onus is on you, as far as possible, to ensure that there is no bias in your assessment of yourself or others of you.

Whereas the state of "Synchronicity" is desirous experience suggests that everyone will not think the same way all the time. This is often likely to be the case in many organisations. Under such circumstances, your focus should not necessarily be to try to get people to think the same as you but to understand why there are differences.

In the state of "Conflict" there are material or fundamental differences between a leader's perception and those of others. A reflective leader would seek to better understand the reasons why these differences arise. Their objective would then be to see if there is anything that they can either clarify or change in their behaviour that would bring about a closer alignment in perceptions.

For this to occur, a leader needs to be willing to accept that they might be wrong or that they need to adjust their style of leadership. It also requires receptibility to change from others. A real possibility is that closer alignment is not achieved but that each party has a better understanding of each other. This is not a failure if both parties can agree to continue to work in the best interests of the organisation.

In the "Verify" state the onus is on the leader or others to verify their perceptions. Since these perceptions relate to their thoughts and not others it becomes important for these to be verified if there are matches.

Verification would consist of simply asking people the relevant question. So, taking the first entry as an example, a leader would ask others what they thought of her and compare that to what she believed others thought of her. If these are the same, then it reaffirms that the leader is in tune with how she thinks others feel about her and their actual feelings. If these are different, it means that there is a state of "Conflict". The leader then follows the same process as discussed earlier.

Healthy conflict

Healthy conflict occurs when persons disagree but maintain high levels of respect for each other and decency.

Persons engaging in healthy conflict hear each other's arguments and the process of discussion can lead to new ways of thinking. This is a benefit to those concerned as well as the organisation.

When persons are disrespectful of each other's perspective, do not listen and treat differences in opinion as an opportunity to make personal characterisations then this is destructive to those persons and the organisation.

"Appearances are often deceptive"

Aesop's fables

In the "Resolve" state the onus is on the leader to understand why they believe there is a difference between what they think and what they believe others think. So, taking the first entry as an example, a leader would ask others what they thought of her and compare that to what she believes others thought of her. If these are the same, then it means that the leader is in tune with how others think however, there is a state of "Conflict" since she believes otherwise.

The fact that a leader believes that there might be differences (even if there are none) could affect the way in which they interact with others. If there are differences between what others think and what the leader believes others think then this might or might not imply that there are conflicts. It depends on how close a leader's perception is of themselves as it relates to others.

Although reflection should be a daily activity, it is impractical to go through the exercise of the dialogue detailed above on such a frequent basis. At a minimum it should be done yearly with the possibility of increased frequency if circumstances change in your organisation. For example, you might have new staff joining at a time at which you would like to conduct the exercise. In this case, it would be more appropriate to exclude this person from the exercise until they had been in the organisation for a period, e.g. at the end of their probation or some longer-time if deemed necessary.

For many, the above might seem a little strange on first reading. After all, we all know what our colleagues think and vice-versa, don't we? The reality is that we do not actually know what others think unless we ask and/or observe them.

The default mode for many people is to assume and act on those assumptions rather than to verify. The risk we run from doing this is that we incorrectly jump to the wrong conclusion. Often when conflict or differences of opinion occur, we do not know the exact reason for such differences, and this is where a structured approach based on reflection proves invaluable.

Building knowledge

In the preceding section, I discussed how a reflective leader could facilitate for an enhanced understanding of her peers and staff. Experience suggests that when people have a good understanding of each other, such as skills/abilities, it makes team work on projects easier to plan and execute. This should be viewed as a necessary first step towards applying reflective leadership to all work-related activities such as projects/events etc.

The diagram below provides an overview of the general process for how reflective learning can take place in an organisation in relation to executing some work activity or situation.

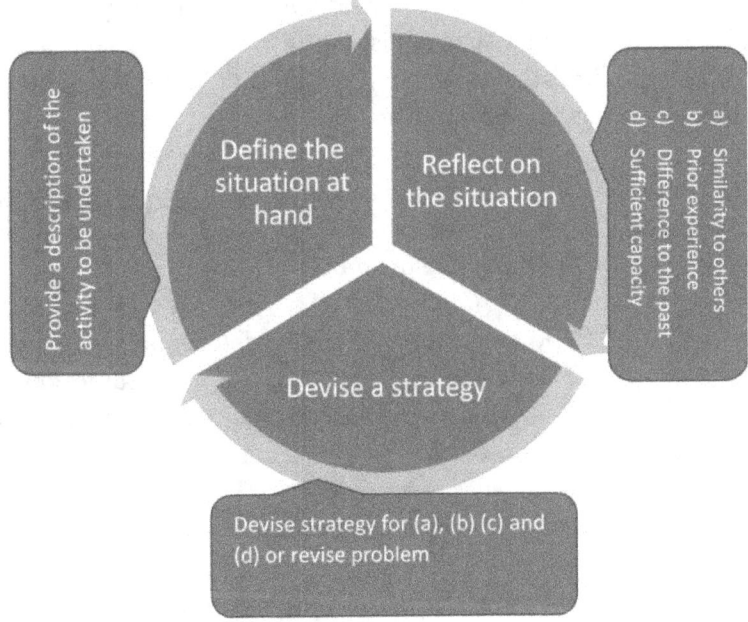

The following provides details relating to the various stages of the process highlighted above:

1. *Define the situation at hand.* This requires a description of the work activity to be undertaken. It does not matter who produces the description, but a reflective leader will want to know that everyone has a common understanding. The reflective leader might want to use their own tools/methods to describe the situation as this could help in their understanding of what is required to be undertaken. They would also encourage others to do the same.

2. *Compare the situation at hand to similar activities you have previously come across.* This involves you reflecting on past experiences and determining what is common and where there are differences. At this point, a reflective leader would want to have a discussion with her team and share her opinion and solicit those of others. Coming out of the discussions there should be answers to questions such as:

    a. *How did we or how have others addressed this type of problem previously?* The result of this should provide a basis for identifying a strategy for addressing the problem.
    b. *What did we learn from our (or others) previous experience that is applicable?* Knowing this will help in determining whether the strategy of (a) can be applied with or without modification. For example, if problems arose in the way similar activities were previously undertaken then what adjustments will people make to avoid these issues reoccurring?
    c. *Are there aspects of what is required to be done different from prior experience?* If there are aspects which are different then this might require a new strategy for these aspects, and this should come out of the collective reflective discussion.
    d. *Do we have the internal capacity to complete the required activities?* Having reflected on (a) through (d) a reflective leader would make a candid assessment on what she believes her team can do and what other resources might be required.

3. *Devise a strategy that reflects a, b, c, and d.* Note that such a strategy might involve changes to the activity description. In other words, reflection might result in a refinement of the activity to be undertaken as issues with its implementation are uncovered and/or further clarity is obtained.

The above type of reflective analysis can be undertaken as often as there are initiatives to be performed in the organisation. By practicing this type of leadership, leaders help to enhance learning and development which can be documented to provide a template for others. This, in turn, helps to improve productivity and quality assurance.

LA2-Workplace Example

Natalie works for a global software technology company and is European head of client relationships. The company produces and supports several products for many clients within the region and their better-known products have won numerous awards over the years. However, customer loyalty has been challenged of late and competitors are beginning to make inroads into their market share.

Natalie believes that she has a great management team beneath her but wonders to what extent things can be improved. She acknowledges that increased competition might be a key factor in explaining a reduction in customer retention rates, but she cannot help but think that her division might be able to do more to help. Natalie decides to have a meeting at which she invites all the European country/regional heads to attend either physically or by video call. Snippets of the dialogue are as follows:

Natalie

Team. I have been thinking about the drop in customer retention over the past fifteen months and wonder how, as a division, we could do things differently to adjust this situation. Is there anything that you think we could be doing differently that could have an impact here?

Franco (head of Southern Europe)

Natalie, we have been implementing our policy of client acquisition and sales for several years. This has worked well for us, but it has its downside. Since this was a policy that you created, I think you know it well, so I will not labour too much on it. Save to say the policy would have us offer services that we have not always been equipped to adequately deliver. In theory we should rely on Product Development for technical assistance, yet we rarely include them in initial client conversations. Further, we should also rely on Product Support for advice on timing for resolving usability issues, but we often contact them as an afterthought.

Some clients complain that they feel misled about product/service functionality and are given the run-around when they raise issues.

Natalie

This is a serious issue, and I can see how this can result in loss of client loyalty. We need to take immediate corrective action. Does anybody else have a view on this?

Jillian (head of Central Europe)

The points made by Franco are valid. At our and your level, I believe we have a good relationship with our peers in Product Development and Product Support, but this is clearly not replicated down at the more junior levels. They should be more integrated into our client acquisition and sales policy and made to feel an integral part of client services.

Bob (UK manager)

I agree that there might be issues with the policy, but Product Support must understand that they are there to support us and not the other way around. When they eventually get around to responding to a client request, they seem to think that they are the ones managing the client relationship. They say things to the client that we have not agreed, and this leads to confusion.

The dialogue continues. What Natalie can glean from the meeting is that there are issues with the existing division policy for client acquisition. Further, there are issues with respect to the type of response and timelines of those responses from Product Support and that relations with other departments could be much better with clearer identification of roles and responsibilities.

The following segment highlights concluding comments from Natalie at the team meeting:

Natalie

I would like to thank you all for being frank and sharing with me your thoughts on this serious matter. I take full responsibility for those aspects of our operating policies/procedures which do not work well and have contributed to the matter. I acknowledge that issues with other divisions are also contributory and I will seek to raise those matters with the respective heads of those divisions.

Franco was correct in pointing out that the policy was created by me, but this meeting has identified weaknesses in that policy, and it needs to change. I think our discussion also highlights that I need to keep better abreast of the issues that arise both within and between our division and others.

I have identified the following list of follow up items to be dealt with as a matter of urgency and welcome your feedback on all:

1. *Initiate the revision of the client acquisition and sales policy. This will be done in conjunction with Product Development and Product Support*
2. *Brief the heads of Product Development and Product Support about our findings and engage them to seek ways to address performance related issues*
3. *Initiate regular feedback sessions where issues can be raised on either one to one or in the group at various levels in the division*
4. *Brief the global head of client services about our meeting and proposed next steps*

From analysis of the above we can see that Natalie adopted an inquiring mind to the issue of falling client retention rates. She was not prepared to just accept that it was due to increased competition. This said, it would not have been unreasonable for Natalie to have just gone along with that explanation and it would have shifted the burden more towards Product Development. However, Natalie exhibited a tell-tale sign of an LA2 leader, she started to ask questions about her own performance and those for whom she is responsible.

Natalie took the opportunity to hold a meeting at which she could learn more about the possible contributors to the retention issue. She was prepared to listen to the views of others and although she might not have expected it, she accepted the criticism of her policy and its impact on the organisation. Further, Natalie has sought to initiate feedback sessions which can be used as the basis for supporting continuous process improvement.

Exercise

Do you believe that you are an effective reflective leader? (Y/N)

> If yes, write down some examples which demonstrate the effectiveness of your leadership.
>   1. For each example, write down what **you** specifically did to achieve success.
>   2. Write down what you believe **others** contributed to achieving success.

   If you find that you are the centre of what you perceive to be your successes, you might just be doing what is required of you. However, it would be extremely useful to ask others whether they think you are an effective reflective leader. It might be that your perception of your achievements does not align with those of others.

> If no, describe examples of where you believe you have fallen short of being effective.
>   1. For each example, write down what **you** did or did not do that led to problems.
>   2. Write down what **others** did or did not do that led to problems.

   If you find that you are at the centre of your perceived failures, then you should identify which aspects of your leadership you need to improve. If you find that others are the major causes, you might want to ask them about their perception of the reasons why reflective leadership has not been effective. This could form the basis for identifying areas of improvement for them as well as yourself.

I rely less on yesterday's victory but use the lessons to learn how I could do even better tomorrow

Am I reflexive?

Dr Howard Haughton, 2019

Further reading

1. Smith, A. and Shaw, P. (2012), *The Reflective Leader: Standing Still to Move Forward*, Canterbury Press, Pub
2. Shepherd, N and Smyth, P. (2012), *Reflective Leaders and High-Performance Organizations: How Effective Leaders Balance Task and Relationship to Build High Performing Organizations*, IUniverse Pub
3. Brown, J. (2006), *A Leader's Guide to Reflective Practice*, Trafford Pub
4. Matsuo, M. (2016), *Reflective Leadership and team learning: an exploratory study,* Journal of Workplace Learning, Vol. 28, No. 5, pp. 307-321

Chapter 6
Well-being leader

Traits
Well-being versus Empowering
Benefits of well-being
Preconditions
Principles
LA3-Workplace Example
Multidimensional approach
Exercise
Further reading

Traits

People demonstrating leadership attribute three (or LA3) are leaders that are consciously motivated to create a harmonious working environment as a means of achieving wider organisational objectives. To be clear, the focus of the leader is to create an environment which is conducive to enhancing the well-being and productivity of staff. They recognise that staff happiness and welfare have an immediate impact on the reputation and profitability of an organisation.

This type of leader utilises knowledge of persons strengths and weaknesses to provide them with growth opportunities which plays to strengths and aids in the management of weaknesses. The leader actively seeks to reduce the likelihood of mental or physical distress at work by recognising the unique needs of each staff member and facilitating ways in which they can better achieve their objectives.

Rather than to look for reasons to criticise, an LA3 leader looks for ways to develop persons skills and nurture a working environment which is welcoming and accommodating of diversity of culture and opinion. They realise that different people communicate in different ways and can easily become frustrated if they think others do not take them seriously. Often, the leader encourages and recognises the

Do the right thing

Tim Cook, the CEO of Apple, is reported in Fortune as saying that he begins sending emails at 4:30 a.m. It is also said, based on a profile in Gawker, that he is the first in the office and the last to leave. This seems to work for Tim and perhaps, those around him but it might not work for many.

I am aware of persons who dread the sound of their mobile devices going off late at night or early morning as it might be from the boss. It reminds me of a line from the Jaws 2 movie "just when you thought it was safe".

For those persons that do not have the desire to regularly work much more than their contractual hours or to answer emails at antisocial times but feeling that they are being pressured into conforming, this might be the start of a stressful situation.

As a leader you are meant to inspire and not to intimidate. A good leader should know when their actions are inspirational and when they are detrimental to the well-being of their employees.

achievements of their staff even when these are for small wins. They realise that support, and recognition is often repaid in terms of loyalty and improved performance.

LA3 leaders ensure that staff members can use their skills and creative freedom to execute their roles/responsibilities but also ensure that staff are exposed to minimal levels of uncertainty in executing tasks. However, this type of uncertainty reduction is the antithesis of the micro-manager that seeks to control the way in which people do their jobs. The leader is more of a macro manager but not to the extent where little guidance is given. An LA3 leader looks for ways to enhance smart rather than hard work to achieve the same outcome and encourages this style of working for their staff.

Well-being versus Empowering

The following table provides key differences between an LA1 and an LA3 leader.

Empowering	Well-being
• Leader either completely transfers responsibility for making decisions to staff or jointly share in decision making. This is done with a view to increase autonomy and self-determination of staff and enhance team cohesion.	• Leader is responsible for making decisions but seeks opportunities to engage staff prior to acting. This is achieved by soliciting alternative ideas from staff and not just asking staff to comment on the leader's recommendations. This is done with a view to understanding the best way in which staff members can undertake work resulting in non-negative impact on their well-being as well as to maintain team cohesion. • Increased autonomy and self-determination only become relevant if it can be shown to directly contribute to improvements in well-being and does not have materially negative impact on team cohesion.
• Staff are given guidance according to their level of competency. So, more novice staff are more closely supervised than those showing greater levels of expertise which might not be supervised at all. • Staff can use whatever strategies they see fit if it achieves objectives and is consistent with overall organisational codes of behaviour.	• Same. • Staff use strategies agreed by the leader unless, for well-being reasons, alternative approaches achieve the same objectives and is consistent with overall organisational codes of behaviour.

Empowering	Well-being
• Leader transfers or shares responsibility for decisions and problem solving and remains accountable for them.	• Leader transfers or shares responsibility where it can be shown that this results in improvements or does not negatively impact staff well-being. The leader remains responsible and accountable for all decisions.
• Operational improvement occurs as a secondary effect of enhanced team cohesion.	• Same.
• Leader and staff are responsible for devising team-working strategies, but the result must be that no member feels that they are not empowered.	• Leader and staff responsible for determining the best strategy for team-working. The result must be that no member feels that their well-being is impaired.
• Leaders motivate a shared vision with a view to ensuring inclusion of staff in decision making as well as execution of activities. The focus here is on individual staff members buying into the leader's vision and seeing how they fit into it.	• Leaders motivate a shared vision with a view to understanding how the individual circumstances of staff can be accommodated to satisfy well-being needs and achieve work objectives.

If increased autonomy through empowerment is identified as a well-being strategy, then the benefits of empowering leadership would also accrue. Similarly, a Well-being leader knows that they might have to use and encourage reflective thinking if that helps in enhancing staff well-being and productivity.

Benefits of well-being

The following are benefits of well-being leadership:

- **Leader**
    1. *Improves trust between employee and leader.* The leader constantly seeks ways to demonstrate that they have trust in and can be trusted by their employees. They realise that lack of trust can lead to erosion of confidence in the organisation and ultimately increases in absenteeism and resignations.

    2. *Improved knowledge of strength/weaknesses of employees.* A critical and ongoing activity of the leader is to ensure they have a good understanding of the skills and development needs of their staff. These leaders look for ways to ensure their staff get support in a timely manner to increase the effectiveness of employee engagement.

    3. *Strengthens commitment to leader's objectives/goals.* The leader ensures that their staff are comfortable with the type of work they are allocated, the environment in which the work is undertaken, the quantity and the time in which they are to complete the work. The leader ensures that staff are fully aware of what is required of them and, to the best of their ability, accommodates different styles of working. All this serves to enhance the commitment of staff to achieving the leader's objectives and goals.

- **Organisation**
    4. *Improved workplace harmony, collaboration, and retention.* Once individuals see that the organisation caters for their welfare needs, this reduces the likelihood of various types of conflicts and leads to better collaboration and retention.

    5. *Improved employee/organisational productivity.* Employees that feel that their welfare is being taken care of tend to be happier and more productive.

    6. *More predictable revenue/profitability.* Less volatility in productivity improves the ability of organisations to forecast likely revenue

streams.

7. *Improved sustainability.* Organisations with a reputation for well-being leadership, tend to have better brand value than those which do not. They have higher retention rates and less earnings volatility and staff which are more highly committed and productive. These characteristics result in improved sustainability over other organisations.

➢ **Team**

8. *Improved team morale.* When staff are at ease with their well-being, team cohesion improves. One major consequence of this is enhanced productivity.

➢ **Staff**

9. *Workload tailored to individual circumstances.* The leader will ensure that the workload of staff will be tailored to meet their individual circumstances. Consequently, staff will rarely if ever be under-worked or overburdened.

10. *Responsibilities match accountabilities.* In a well-run organisation the leader ensures that staff will not have to account for matters for which they are not responsible, as can be the case when a leader simply "dumps" work on staff.

11. *No stress from micro or macro-management.* Staff receive the level of supervision consistent with their skills and requirements.

12. *Higher level of job satisfaction.* Staff feel more in control of their destiny and motivated to go to work.

13. *Better work-life balance.* Staff are better able to commit to and engage in work activities but retain a high degree of satisfaction outside of work.

14. *Enhanced job security.* Staff that are better able to manage their well-being have improved confidence about their work and ongoing employment with the organisation.

Preconditions

To maximise the likelihood of a well-being leadership working, there are some preconditions which should be met:

- *Leaders have a zero-tolerance for cliques, empire builders, rumour mongers and those that aim to exclude and undermine others.* Employment law tribunals around the world are plagued with lawsuits many of which stem from this type of behaviour. The likelihood is that in many organisations, that are subject to these lawsuits, they have well-written policies concerning bullying/harassment etc. however, the issue is more on the enforcement than lack of policies. A well-being leader makes it their job to not just be cognisant of corporate policies, they also ensure that all their decisions do not lead to harm or well-being detriment of others.

- *Leaders are aware of and practice well-being for themselves.* Leaders that practice well-being in their own lives will find it easier to facilitate for the adoption of well-being leadership for others. It becomes a harder sell if leaders adopt a do as I say not as I do approach as staff might feel confused about the sincerity of the leader. It is also likely that if leaders have poor well-being and coping mechanisms this will also result in poor well-being and coping mechanisms for staff. The opposite is also true.

- *Leaders should be available to discuss and identify solutions to address staff concerns.* In many organisations the process of raising and resolving issues involves a lengthy and convoluted process. The worst case is when management are not or do not make themselves available to have constructive dialogue with staff. A well-being leader will go out of their way and utilise a variety of technology to ensure that, even in their absence, they are able to maintain contact and support colleagues, especially as it relates to staff well-being.

- *Leaders are aware of strengths/weaknesses of staff and facilitate for their development.* A well-being leader will be aware as to how they can play to the strengths of staff and know which areas require further development and facilitate for the same.

- *Leaders empower staff to make decisions and solve problems.* A well-being leader will, as the need arises, empower staff to make decisions about their work activities and determine how they will solve problems.

- *Leaders encourage humour and happiness.* It is widely accepted that people are more productive when they are happy with what they are doing. A well-being leader is adept at making people feel relaxed and engaged with their work. Better leaders can see the funny side of things and encourage staff to converse in a collegiate, respectful, and jovial manner. This increases harmony and happiness in teams and the wider organisation.

- *Leaders undertake continuing development.* There can be few things more frustrating than to discuss matters of well-being with your manager and to realise that they do not have a clue how to help you. It is not uncommon for managers to refer issues to human resources (HR) and for the resolution process to be dragged out so long that staff members feel even more stressed and demotivated. A well-being leader, whilst not being an HR expert, will make it their objective to receive ongoing training and development in matters pertinent to well-being and to facilitate same for their staff.

- *Leaders solicit and incorporate the opinion of others in decisions.* Well-being leaders understand most staff members will want to have a say in work related activities which affect them. They accommodate this, amongst other things, by having a good understanding of their member's strengths/weaknesses and aspirations and working with staff to reflect these in their work and development objectives. If staff have constraints which require them to work part or flexitime, then these are incorporated into work plans.

- *Leaders are open and constructive.* Well-being leaders are aware that being open, transparent, and providing constructive feedback enhances trust and confidence of staff members. They understand that without trust and confidence they are unlikely to retain the loyalty of staff, which will likely result in increased attrition and decreased productivity and in reputational loss.

- *Staff willing to undertake continuing development.* Staff should also be prepared to undertake development in relation to matters concerning well-being. This will provide them with the ability to become more self-aware and able to identify emerging issues for themselves and others.

- *Staff are open and constructive.* If staff are open and honest about their own situation then this provides a basis for which others can intervene and provide help. However, staff also need to be constructive in how they deal with others so as not to cause stress for them.

- *Staff are motivated* to effectively participate in well-being leadership. Staff are motivated when:

    ◦ *Without additional incentives or fear of repercussions* they are willing to engage in practices that will enhance personal well-being and the well-being of team members, including that of the leader.
    ◦ *They believe their opinion is valued* by the leader and their team.
    ◦ *They have confidence in their ability* to be able to effectively use well-being techniques to the benefit of self and others.

- *Organisational commitment to well-being.* If the organisation is generally committed to well-being (i.e., Board approved policies are in place) it increases the likelihood that well-being leadership can be successful. In the absence of senior level approval, well-being might become piecemeal in its application and subject to removal at any time.

Principles

The above discussions give rise to the following principles of reflective leadership:

> **Principle 1**
>
> Well-being leaders lead by example in demonstrating well-being practices.

Principle 1 recognises that leaders are more effective in well-being leadership if they adhere to the same practices they espouse for their staff.

> **Principle 2**
>
> Well-being leaders communicate in a manner to reduce uncertainty and anxiety.

Principle 2 recognises that good communication (both verbal and non-verbal) can reduce levels of uncertainty and anxiety regarding work activities for staff. This clarity helps to alleviate stress caused by worry and unnecessary confusion. In essence, the principle acknowledges that good leadership behaviour begets good well-being in staff with the converse also being true.

> **Principle 3**
>
> Well-being leaders use humour to enhance staff productivity.

Principle 3 acknowledges that when staff are happy, they are more productive and well-being leaders will make use of tactics to create an environment where positive humour is welcomed.

> **Principle 4**
>
> Well-being leaders understand the well-being needs of those they lead.

Principle 4 recognises that well-being leaders need to be empathetic to the needs and desires of their staff to facilitate for their well-being.

LA3-Workplace Example

Ingrid works for an international organisation and is contracted to work between the hours of 8:30 a.m. and 5:00 p.m. each day. This said, she often works upwards of ten hours on a typical day and frequently travels abroad for work assignments.

The organisation operates a policy of flexible arrival time in which they allow employees to get to work by 10:30 a.m. and then work their hours. Most often, Ingrid gets to work by 8 a.m. The organisation also operates a flexible working policy which allows persons to work from home for up to three days a week, but this is dependent on approval by the relevant departmental manager. There are no overarching rules governing the circumstances under which such remote working would be allowed.

Ingrid's boss, Marie, comes to work closer to 10:45 a.m. each day and frequently leaves after 9 p.m. This said, Marie often sends emails at 7:00 a.m. requesting status updates on work which are required urgently. Marie does not like staff working from home as she says, "you don't really know what they are getting up to". This is proving to be a problem for Ingrid as she would like to work from home three days a week. She has expressed her desire to have a more balanced work-home life in which she is better able to manage personal commitments. Marie has refused to approve Ingrid's request.

Ingrid has got so frustrated that she has decided to elevate the issue to Marie's boss, Sunil. After several email communications, a meeting was scheduled at which Sunil, Marie and Ingrid would discuss the matter. Snippets of the dialogue are as follows:

Sunil

Thanks for agreeing to attend the meeting Ingrid with me and Marie. As I understand it you would like to work from home for three days a week as this would help you to better manage various personal matters. Is this correct?

Ingrid

Yes. I have a long commute into work and back and this does not always allow me the time to provide care for others that depend on me. I feel that they are suffering as a result and so am I. As you know the nature of my work does not necessitate that I physically be in any place all the time. I do a lot of research which culminates into a report and this forms the basis for assessing my performance.

The organisation has remote working applications that can be used to facilitate for video meetings and calls. I can also access emails and group chats.

Marie

Yes, Ingrid but we often have impromptu discussions which you would not be able to take part in. Also, I would not be able to supervise the work that you are doing and to monitor that you are spending the required number of hours doing work. At best I could only allow you to work the occasional day from home and this would not be every week and only when things get bad for you at home. Otherwise, if I approve your request then what is to stop others making a similar request and before you know it, most of the department would be empty often.

Sunil

Let me jump in here. Whilst I agree that the optics might be important, I think we need to focus on Ingrid's needs and assess whether these can be facilitated given current policies and departmental pressures.

Ingrid is an extremely skilled researcher who has shown that she can work without close supervision. In fact, this is a requirement of the job. As I understand it, from previous email communications, she would still be able to travel abroad to undertake assignments so there would be continuity there.

I also agree that our technology is appropriate to keep Ingrid in contact with colleagues at work. If there are impromptu meetings, then give Ingrid a call before they start and ask her if she can attend. Otherwise fill her in afterwards.

Do you agree with my conclusions Marie? Are there any compelling reasons why you think Ingrid would not be able to effectively undertake her work if approval is given?

Marie

None other than what I have already mentioned.

The outcome of the meeting was that Ingrid's request to work from home for three days a week was approved by Sunil.

Even from the small amount of information we are given, it seems obvious that there are differences in the management style of Marie and Sunil. Marie's approach is based on distrust for the intentions of persons making requests to work from home. She sees an aspect of her job as *monitoring to ensure that people are working their contractual hours*. She also believes that another aspect of her job is to closely supervise the work of others even when there is no requirement or necessity to do this. It is interesting to note that she never sought to address the needs of Ingrid. Instead, Marie made the issue of the request to work from home about her feelings and how others would perceive such an approval.

Delving further into the work practices of Marie we observe that she has no problem with requesting work to be done prior to the contractual start yet she regularly fails to get to work on time. Perhaps the optics only applies to others. This can be a source of stress to employees as they might feel obliged to respond under time pressure.

I summarise Marie's leadership style as being poor management and not a leader. Her style of management is not positively influential and seems to be focused on ensuring the completion of routine tasks.

In contrast, Sunil appeared to be quite knowledgeable about Ingrid's strengths and the relevance of this to supporting her request to work from home. He was able to understand how Ingrid could use technology to maintain connectivity with colleagues and be able to achieve a more balanced work-home life without affecting the quality of her work. Sunil has demonstrated key aspects of being an LA3 leader in stark contrast to Marie who exhibited none.

Multidimensional approach

Not all companies approach wellness in the same manner. There are those (and I suspect many) that are of the view that wellness is little more than encouraging staff members to take all their annual leave within the year and giving them a day off if they feel a little stressed. However, more forward-thinking organisations go way beyond this.

Disclosures in annual reports and other documents suggest that more and more companies are taking wellness more seriously. The more enlightened provide on-site gymnasium (or free access to certain fitness clubs), exercise classes, free choice of food (including vegetarian and other healthy meals) and access to healthcare services etc. With these types of benefits who would want to leave such a company right? Well, if issues such as race, gender and other protected characteristics are not factored into well-being there is a real risk that these benefits might have little impact on employee retention.

Google is an example of a company that is widely cited as having one of the best wellness packages. This said, the retention rate at Google has been a cause of concern for a while, like several technology companies. Drilling down into the company's diversity (2019) report reveals that retention rates for ethnic minorities that identify as black are the worst amongst other racial categories. A similar picture existed the prior year. When you take into consideration the very highly publicised walk outs and lawsuits against the company leads one to conclude that the wellness of black people (and I dare say other groups) at Google could be significantly improved.

So, being a well-being leader might require you to adapt your approach to your staff not just based on their skills and generic considerations but to also be sensitive to their culture, religion, ethnicity, gender etc., as these also form a part of their well-being.

Exercise

What are some of the things you have done to improve your own well-being at work, and have you observed any improvements?

- ➤ If yes, write down some examples which demonstrate how you have improved.
- ➤ If no, write down what you believe to be the main causes.

If you answered yes, have you also been able to use your good results to the benefit of others? If not, you might have an opportunity of making a positive difference to those around you by using your improved well-being to enhance your relations with them.

If you answered no, find a way of working on those outstanding issues so that they do not cause your well-being to deteriorate any further and/or impact others.

Write down some of the things that you have done to improve the well-being of others that you work with. Are your colleagues more likely than not to agree that you are a positive influence on their well-being?

I have confidence in your skills and trust you to do your job in the best way you see fit and I will be there to provide guidance, should you desire.

I recognise your unique needs and requirements and although you are part of a team, I see YOU.

I encourage you to work smart rather than hard as hard does not mean better.

I play to your strengths and aid you in the development of your weaknesses.

Don't I care for your wellbeing?

Dr Howard Haughton, 2019

Further reading

1. Robertson, I and Cooper, C. (2011), *Well-being: Productivity and Happiness at Work*, Palgrave pub
2. MacGregor, S and Simpson, R. (2018), *Chief Well-being Officer: Building better lives for business success,* LID Pub
3. Mitchell, D. (2018), *50 Top Tools for Employee Well-being: A Complete Tool-kit for Developing Happy, Healthy, Productive and Engaged Employees*, Kogan Page Pub

Chapter 7
Stakeholder leader

Traits
Stakeholder versus Empowering
Benefits of stakeholder
Preconditions
Principles
LA4-Workplace Example
Further reading

Traits

People demonstrating leadership attribute four (or LA4) are leaders that actively seek to influence and make decisions that reflect the interests of those in the value chain of an organisation (e.g. suppliers, staff, clients, regulators). They behave in a manner which demonstrates that they understand and seek to incorporate their views into decision making.

This type of leader makes it their responsibility to understand those that are part of their organisations value chain. They understand what adds value to these entities and how they contribute to the sustainability of the organisation.

This type of leader seeks collaboration rather than to make decisions unilaterally. With internal stakeholders they foster teamwork (both inter and intra-departmental) and with external counterparts they identify possibilities for cooperative ways of working as well as achieving some social good. In either case, emphasis is placed on enhancing relationships and building knowledge.

What do you have at stake?

Unless you work for a not for profit organisation, your organisation is in business purely to make money. This has been the prevailing view of capitalism. The consequences of this has been extremely rewarding for shareholders and senior management whose compensation have been linked to company performance. However, as evidenced by several large and numerous smaller corporate failures, it is generally wider society, employees, and others in a company's supply chain that suffer when the pursuit of profits overshadows other considerations.

Increasingly, whether by way of regulations, pressure from large shareholders, consumers/clients, or other forms of activism, organisations are adopting a multi-stakeholder view of a firm's purpose. They are happy to continue to make good profits but not at the expense of erosion of standards in relation to environmental, social and governance.

An LA4 leader realises that they "can't please all of the people all the time" and this is not their intention. They do, however, try to make the best decisions based on taking into consideration a wide variety of stakeholder issues. They realise that what was important to a stakeholder yesterday might not be as important today. They realise that different stakeholders might have conflicting desires and the relative importance of these might change over time. The LA4 leader, therefore, ensures that they can evaluate the potential impact of incorporating different combinations of stakeholder views into decision making.

Stakeholder versus Empowering

The following table provides key differences between an LA1 and an LA4 leader.

Empowering	Stakeholder
• Leader either completely transfers responsibility for making decisions to staff or jointly share in decision making. This is done with a view to increase autonomy and self-determination of staff and enhance team cohesion.	• Leader is responsible for making decisions but seeks opportunities to incorporate the views of staff and other parties (both internal and where possible, external) prior to acting. This is done with the view of reducing the risks of conflict with stakeholders. • Increased autonomy and self-determination only become relevant if it can be shown to directly contribute to better ways of managing potential conflict and enhancing stakeholder relations.

Empowering	Stakeholder
• Staff are given guidance according to their level of competency. So, less experienced staff are more closely supervised than those showing greater levels of expertise which might not be supervised at all. • Staff can use whatever strategies they see fit if it achieves objectives and is consistent with overall organisational codes of behaviour.	• Same. • Staff use strategies agreed by the leader unless alternative approaches achieve the same objectives, are consistent with overall organisational codes of behaviour and are better suited to enhance stakeholder relations.
• Leader transfers or shares responsibility for decisions and problem solving and remains accountable for them.	• Leader transfers or shares responsibility where it can be shown that this results in improvements or does not negatively impact stakeholder relations. The leader remains accountable for all decisions.
• Operational improvement occurs as a secondary effect of enhanced team cohesion.	• Same.

Empowering	Stakeholder
• Leader and staff are responsible for devising team-working strategies, but the result must be that no member feels that they are not empowered.	• Leader and staff responsible for determining the best strategy for team-working. The result must be that stakeholder relationship is not jeopardised. This does not imply that all stakeholders are equally satisfied as a choice might have to be made to prioritise one party over another. For example, the leader might have to make decisions which limit staff discretion and empowerment if it helps to improve the process of satisfying key external stakeholder objectives.
• Leaders motivate a shared vision with a view to ensuring inclusion of staff in decision making as well as execution of activities. The focus here is on individual staff members buying into the leader's vision and seeing how they fit into it.	• Leaders motivate a shared vision with a view to understanding how staff can best reflect the interests of all stakeholder parties whilst satisfying work objectives.

Benefits of stakeholder

The following are benefits of stakeholder leadership:

➤ **Leader**
1. *Improves trust between employee and leader.* Stakeholder leaders recognise the importance of including staff members in key decision making. They do this by facilitating a framework which enables staff to share ideas within and between organisational silos and challenge status quo thinking. These foster increased synergies and creativity by leveraging existing resources. The result is staff feeling more valued and in control of their destiny which engenders trust.

2. *Employees more committed to leader's objectives/goals.* Staff feeling more included, and able to help in shaping objectives/goals as well as how these are obtained, helps to strengthen commitment to leader.

3. *Builds relations with others in organisation.* Stakeholder leaders facilitate for the sharing of ideas and teamwork across organisational silos. This helps to build the brand/image of the leader with others in the organisation.

➤ **O**rganisation
4. *Improved collaboration between business units/silos.* Stakeholder leaders look for ways in which they might be able to leverage the skills of others within their organisation. This helps to improve synergies between units and overall effectiveness for the organisation.

5. *Improved reputation.* Stakeholder leaders seek to understand and incorporate requirements of external party's key to the successful operation of the business of the organisation. By actively seeking to manage external stakeholder relations, leaders reduce the risk of damage to the reputation of the brand of the organisation.

6. *Improved sustainability.* Stakeholder leaders facilitate for improved organisational collaboration which has the effect of

increasing and disseminating knowledge within the organisation. These leaders also foster opportunities for working with external stakeholders to address technical and/or social/environmental issues. They realise that changing times requires changes in approach to issues which, potentially, go beyond those working in the organisation. By addressing these matters, stakeholder leaders increase the likelihood that the organisation remains relevant and sustainable.

- **Team**
    7. *Improves shared knowledge and teamwork.* Stakeholder leadership has the effect of increasing levels of cooperation both intra and inter business units/divisions etc. This results in improved teamwork and knowledge amongst those participating in the teams.

- **Staff**
    8. *Improves employee creativity.* Leaders facilitate for enhanced creativity as they encourage staff to challenge existing ways of working.

    9. *Improves employee engagement.* Leaders actively seek and value the engagement of staff in all key decision and problem-solving activities.

    10. *Enhances employee self-worth and confidence.* Stakeholder leaders enable staff to demonstrate their abilities to contribute to activities beyond their main core duties. This demonstrates trust which in turn improves confidence and self-belief.

If increased autonomy through empowerment is identified as a strategy that can help to enhance stakeholder relations, then the benefits of empowering leadership would also accrue.

Preconditions

To maximise the likelihood of a stakeholder leadership working, there are some preconditions which should be met:

- *Leaders and staff know how to identify their stakeholders.* Stakeholder leaders understand that the projects they undertake could have an impact on a variety of different stakeholders and they make it a key focus to identify these stakeholders and assess the impacts. They understand that these stakeholders comprise both internal and external parties and that the operations of the organisation have societal implications.

- *Leaders and staff understand, value and are competent in relationship management.* Leaders do not work in a vacuum and need to foster and manage relationships with internal and external stakeholders. To do this a stakeholder leader will engage with others to better understand their requirements and aspirations. The decisions they make will be based on a more holistic and balanced perspective rather than primarily driven by personal or team considerations.

- *Leaders and staff are competent in conflict management.* Given the varied and potentially conflicting needs of different stakeholders, a stakeholder leader constantly seeks ways to avoid conflicts and where this is not possible, they focus on damage limitation.

- *Leaders take a strategic view.* Stakeholder leaders appreciate that accommodating the views of a wide and potentially varying set of parties places the organisation in a better position to be able to make necessary changes to operational and strategic plans before major issues occur. To reduce the likelihood of having to make frequent changes to strategic plans they ensure that sufficient consultation takes place during the drafting of such plans and incorporate stakeholder views on an ongoing basis.

- *Leaders and staff have well-developed communication skills.* Stakeholder leaders serve a variety of different constituents and a style of communication that works with one party might not work with another. This type of leader is adept at finding the right style that will enable effective dialogue.

- *Leaders are tenacious in the light of varied stakeholder requests.* Stakeholder leaders realise that accommodating multiple views might result in unexpected changes to operational plans. They also realise that they might not be able to incorporate all opinions and that these might detract from agreed objectives. They realise that they need to remain tenacious under these circumstances unless circumstances warrant an alternative approach.

- *Leaders are aware of strengths/weaknesses of staff and facilitate for their development.* A stakeholder leader will be aware as to the development needs of their staff and will ensure that support is provided to ensure that they can operate effectively. Such support will include, amongst others, development in topics such as risk, relationship, and conflict management.

- *Leaders and staff are competent in risk management.* With focus on a diverse constituency, it is more likely that risks will arise in the day-to-day leadership. Stakeholder leaders are comfortable with thinking from a risk perspective in that decisions are analysed from the perspective of likelihood and consequence/impact. That is, prior to decisions being made leaders have evaluated the likely consequence (e.g. financial and reputation) on the organisation of things going wrong and the likelihood of this occurrence.

- *Leaders facilitate for stakeholder leadership.* If positional leaders do not facilitate for cross-functional/department teamwork, then the corresponding benefits will not be obtained. Similarly, stakeholder leaders should facilitate for opportunities for staff to engage with external parties if the need arises.

- *Staff are rationally motivated to participate in stakeholder working practices.* Staff are rationally motivated when:

    ○ Without additional incentives or fear of repercussions they are willing to engage in stakeholder work practices.

    ○ Self-belief is consistent with demonstrated abilities. That is, staff are not overconfident, but belief is based on credible evidence of skills.

    ○ They believe their work is valued by the leader and the organisation.

- They believe they have genuine freedom to determine how work is undertaken.

- *Organisation is committed to stakeholder leadership.* If senior management of the organisation is committed to stakeholder leadership then more junior leaders will find it easier to apply. However, in the absence of senior level acceptance, it might prove difficult to implement successfully.

Principles

The above discussions give rise to the following principles of reflective leadership:

> **Principle 1**
>
> Stakeholder leaders vary their communication style to fit that of the stakeholder.

Principle 1 recognises that different stakeholders potentially have different requirements and preferred styles of communication which are accommodated by stakeholder leaders.

> **Principle 2**
>
> Stakeholder leaders lead for all those with something at stake.

Principle 2 recognises that stakeholder leadership is more than just accommodating the usual parties such as the providers of financing. It facilitates for the fact that, increasingly, issues arising under environmental, sustainability and governance form a prominent aspect of stakeholder leadership.

> **Principle 3**
>
> The strategy of stakeholder leaders reflects the strategic intent of stakeholders.

Principle 3 recognises that strategic thinking and stakeholder consultation forms an inherent part of effective stakeholder leadership. It implies that the direction of an organisation is not determined solely by insiders but includes the wider set of value-chain parties.

> **Principle 4**
>
> Tenacity curbs enthusiasm for distracting stakeholder leaders.

Principle 4 recognises that stakeholder leaders stay tenacious in pursuit of agreed objectives in the light of conflicting and distracting requirements. They realise the impossibility of pleasing all parties all the time but stay focused on key objectives whilst working with all stakeholders in a consultative manner. By employing risk and conflict management strategies they can evaluate the impact of varied decisions and incorporate these into the priorities assigned to manage stakeholder relations.

LA4-Workplace example

Marcus works for an engineering company where he is head of emerging technology. The research work undertaken by his department will pave the way for the next generation of technology solutions offered by the company. Marcus and some members of his team have been working on a project which could have a significant impact on the aeronautical industry. Marcus has shared some of the results of this project with his colleague Nathan who heads product development. Nathan is quite enthused by the results but is aware of the politics in the organisation. He knows that his director, David and Marcus's director, Bill do not get on.

Nathan's department also has a research element but mainly focuses on ways of improving existing technologies. The apparent overlap in research capacity seems to be one of the main causes of the rivalry between David and Bill. Moreover, if the current research undertaken by Marcus's team proves successful it could result in migrating from existing to adoption of newer technologies. However, to develop this new technology would require the expertise of the product development department.

David has become aware of the work being undertaken in Marcus's department and has reacted negatively. He says this work is premature as the existing technology, which was solely developed by his division, still has many years of shelf life. He argues that to invest time and money into developing the new technology would be a waste of resources. David has made known his concerns to the company's CEO Mark and has requested a meeting. Mark has responded by saying that he wishes to have a meeting, but this must also include Bill, Marcus, and Nathan.

Mark requested both David and Bill, in preparation for the meeting, to assume the other persons position and to document what they thought would be the advantages and disadvantages of continuing with the research project versus maintaining the status quo. In other words, David would imagine that he were the director responsible for emerging technologies and Bill responsible for product development.

Mark realised that it would take several weeks before this meeting could take place, so he suggested that they meet in one months' time. During this time Mark decided to go through a similar exercise he set David and Bill. In addition, being aware of work ongoing at rival organisations, Mark reached out to one such company with a view to assessing their appetite to engage in a possible joint venture. Mark had senior contacts in this organisation and was aware that they were involved in similar work to that proposed by Marcus.

The day of the meeting arrived.

Mark stated that he had read through the documents he asked David and Bill to prepare. He praised them for their efforts and mentioned that he had one key observation. The documents revealed that both directors would benefit by learning more about each other's departments. Bill identified many more advantages for David's area, than David, when considering continuance of the research project. A similar pattern emerged when David assessed the advantages for Bill, assuming maintaining the status quo. Mark then shared with David and Bill that he had undertaken his own assessment of the pros and cons but wanted to hear from Marcus and Nathan prior to deciding.

Marcus and Nathan discussed how expansion of the research project could be achieved by establishing a project team consisting of members from both departments. David asked for how the team would be coordinated, roles and responsibilities assigned and how the results obtained would be reflected in persons appraisal. Mark interjected. He said I know our appraisal system is kind of rigid and largely reflective of achievements related to departmental work but if this project is to be a success it cannot be held back because we don't have an adequate performance management system. So, let us assume that we have one for the time being and we can deal with the details later, if required.

Marcus and Nathan produced a project plan which was discussed in detail to the satisfaction of the CEO. Mark then mentioned that he had approached a competitor and that he believed a joint venture could be undertaken which would reduce time to production and market. He stated that our firm would be the managing partner in the venture should we decide to go ahead. However, I will only make that decision if we are all in agreement in this room. My own assessment suggests that it makes sense to pursue this research and development project.

This project has advantages in terms of bringing teams closer together in a more seamless way and it is hard to place a value on this. The project could also open collaborative opportunities beyond the one discussed resulting in access to new and bigger markets. Moreover, if you consider the potential environmental benefits of the new technology, we could have a great CSR story here. I dare say this would not hurt the share price either.

Some of you reading this would be able to relate to the issues highlighted in the above example. You probably have this type of situation going on in your firm. The way Mark handled the situation is typical of an LA4 leader. Mark was not quick to judge either way. He put himself in the shoes of others and asked others to do the same. His key concern was ensuring that all relevant parties had an opportunity to have their say. He recognised the importance of opportunities for cross departmental working and was prepared to change business processes to facilitate for same. He identified the potential for joint ventures with rival organisations and the positive environmental impact the project could bring.

Accountability might be mine alone, but it is in my gift to share the glory.

Although I am accountable to self and firm, I also hold myself to wider societal values.

By understanding the desires/values of those around me I am better able to reflect these in my decisions.

I seek opportunities for collaboration even when I can do things by myself.

Dr Howard Haughton, 2019

Further reading

1. Mayfield, P. (2013), *Practical People Engagement: Leading Change Through the Power of Relationships*, Elbereth Pub
2. Anastasi, C. (2018), *Strategic Stakeholder Engagement*, Routledge Pub
3. Blowfield, M and Murray, A. (2019). *Corporate Social Responsibility*, OUP Oxford Pub
4. Freeman, R. (2010), *Strategic Management: A Stakeholder Approach*, CUP, Cambridge

Chapter 8

Do you practice Woke leadership?

Introduction
Needs matter
Leadership behaviour
Switching styles
Leadership attributes
Exercise
Further reading

Introduction

The chances are that many organisations, if asked, would say that their leaders exhibit the style of leadership as depicted by the attributes discussed in the previous chapters. The question is, however, to what extent are the attributes consistently demonstrated? For example, some leaders are keen to delegate responsibility for decisions they do not want to take but have no problem in taking the glory when such a decision has a positive impact or playing the blame game when it doesn't. This is an example where the leader might comply with the "syntax of empowerment" but fails to satisfy the spirit in which it is supposed to be demonstrated.

For someone to effectively demonstrate the leadership styles previously discussed, two things are desirable. The first is that the organisation should have a facilitating environment (i.e. part of its culture) or policies which encourage a style of management depicted by the attributes. The second requires that individuals will need to develop and maintain a range of soft skills that enable them to demonstrate these attributes.

Some might argue that organisations should not attempt to mandate how those in leadership positions undertake their jobs. They say that you can only get the best out of senior management if they are allowed the creative freedom to manage in the way they see fit.

My response has been to say, what is good for the goose is good for the gander. That is, why not extend this argument to the middle management that report into senior managers and then to those lower down the hierarchy etc. The result would be that all individuals in an organisation could end up feeling that they should not be bound by codes governing leadership conduct.

Most persons agree that culture plays an important part in determining how an organisation goes about doing what it does. However, in an organisation where people are moving in different directions this type of culture can prove problematic in facilitating change and being able to respond in a timely and consistent manner to issues as and when they arise.

Organisations which uphold good standards of corporate governance, for example such as that advocated by the organisation for economic cooperation and development – OECD are better able to address such matters. They are better placed because such standards, if properly followed, require enhanced disclosure of management practices including as it relates to staff welfare and wider corporate social responsibility.

Many countries have stock exchanges which implement some form of corporate governance reflecting listing rules, legal requirements, and better practices. So, companies listed on these exchanges have a requirement to comply or explain or otherwise act in accordance with the exchange's rules. However, there are many organisations that are not listed, and which do not follow any type of formal governance or better practice code. I have been a strong advocate for these companies to also follow governance codes appropriate to their size and industry.

The corporate disasters of the 90's, the early 2000s and those that crashed during the great recession (reflecting the period 2007-2009) are indicative of a failure in leadership. My experience is that good leaders are early adopters of better leadership practices, they are not laggards. They do not see it as an imposition to conform to practices which aim to preserve the sustainability of their organisation whilst developing leaders which exhibit the attributes cited above.

Needs matter

In an earlier chapter I used the term woken leadership to characterise empowering, reflexive, well-being, and stakeholder leadership. Each of these styles appeals to some psychological need that individuals might have. Previous discussions also detailed preconditions that should hold to maximise the chances of the varying styles being effectively implemented. However, these conditions arise as a result of meeting the needs of the agents (Leaders, Organisation, Team and Staff). In a well-functioning organisation, there should be sufficient commonality between the expectations (or needs) of these key agents. These needs are discussed in the sequel.

The following diagram depicts the typical relationship between the agents:

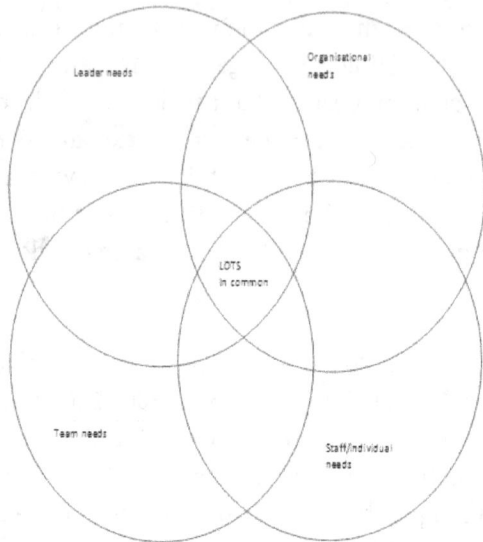

As can be seen, the views/needs of the agents should all intersect. The more the agents have in common, the more the circles are closer together implying increased commonalities between all agents.

It is not likely or desirable to insist on complete alignment between all agents since this could significantly reduce the likelihood of diversity of opinion and stifle creativity. It is, however, possible that a given situation (i.e. set of tasks to be completed and its objective) could result in close alignment across all agents. It is the responsibility of a leader to know when they should push for close or accept wider variations in beliefs across all agents.

Leaders and staff needs

It is human nature to aspire for a better way of life. Some of these needs will cover basic requirements such as food/water, clothing and shelter others might include flexibility of working hours, ergonomics of the workplace and a friendly work environment. Higher level needs might include more and better recognition, further development/training, increased autonomy, and engagement in creative/innovative work.

A leader and her staff will have several needs and requirements some of which are job related and others not. For example, some basic requirements are not job-related such as food, clothing, and shelter.

Generally, when people have adequate resources to provide for their basic requirements their attention, often, turns towards non-physical and then higher-level desires, this type of argument has been popularised by the work of psychologists such as Abraham Maslow.

This said, the possibility also exists that even if an individual can adequately provide for their basic physical needs, they might decide that they want more expensive clothes, food, shelter etc. In this respect, even though a leader might earn more than their staff it is likely that they might still have basic needs requirements, although possibly on a different scale.

There might be situations where staff desire further development/training and where a leader desires to have highly committed individuals. These two desires do not have to coincide and will only become closer if the leader and/or staff are able to compromise and see things from the other persons perspective.

In summary, a leader and each individual staff member will have a set of needs/desires some of which might be similar (or are reconcilable) and others which present potential mutual conflict. It is the role of the leader to figure out how she can get all persons to work together when required.

The result of this might be that some staff members are subject to leadership which is different to others. This argument might run contrary to popular leadership writings, but I am convinced that it works. The point here is not to treat people detrimentally whose views differ from you but to employ methods to get the best form of engagement from them.

Team needs

On a basic level, the team requirements/needs are derived from those of the individuals comprising the team. However, at a higher level, there might already be an "institutional identity" for the team based on the role of the team, how it has performed historically and/or the desires of the leader.

The needs of the team can be expressed as follows:

Why

Every team exists for a reason. This is the why. This why can be expressed as a list of needs:

- The need to contribute to implementation of wider internal organisational objectives.

- The need to contribute to meeting expectations of external stakeholders.

- The need to operate more efficiently and effectively than the sum of the individual (and potentially competing) contributions of people making up the team.

What

Every team should have a vision of what a future state would look like if the "why" were to be successfully implemented. This vision is the "what".

The vision statement should, amongst other things, state what attributes the team will possess when the future successful state has been obtained. It will include statements regarding:

- The contribution the team will be making, at the point of success, to internal organisational objectives.

- The contribution the team will be making, at the point of success, to meet expectations of external stakeholders.

- The value-added of teamwork over that of individual staff contributions.

Each of the items listed above gives rise to a corresponding requirement or need to support the why.

How

Every team should have a mission statement which describes how the vision will be implemented. The statement should cover, amongst other things:

- How the team will collaborate to achieve the contributions to internal organisational objectives and external stakeholders.

- The means by which the team will add value.

Strategy

The strategy should describe a plan for how the mission statement can be implemented. It will address several needs including:

- The need to have a plan describing what work the team will be undertaking and the role of each team member.

- The need to identify how each team member's work contributes to the wider internal organisational and external stakeholders.

- The need to ensure the accountability of each team member for work allocated to them.

- The need to have a list of outcomes and outputs to be achieved/produced, their timing and how the quality of these artefacts are to be assessed.

- The need to have acceptable norms for team-working and communication to achieve the outcomes/outputs.

- The need to have a means by which conflicts will be resolved.

- The need to have a means by which individual team members will be supported for training/development to facilitate team activities.

Organisational needs

The process of identifying the organisational needs is like that of the team. For example, there is a need to have a why, what, how and a strategy but at the highest (aggregate) level of the organisation.

Organisational needs are also documented in firm-wide policies, standards, and guidelines. They provide details enabling individuals to assess whether their basic and high-level needs can be met. The implementation of these policies, standards, and guidelines (as cascaded through an organisational hierarchy) determines the culture of the firm. This culture will, additionally, impose guidelines/constraints on personal behaviour as well as within teams.

Personal behaviours are, typically, driven by the beliefs/values of individuals and are related to individual needs. For example, a staff member might have a passion for fairness and equality and sees this as a fundamental belief. This same staff member might be driven to seek personal recognition for work undertaken in the light of the knowledge that others (subject to the same circumstances) have been promoted and they have not.

Leadership behaviour

The behaviour of any leader will have an influence on how they are perceived and the effectiveness of their position. To maximise the chances of being a successful woke leader there are several behaviours that should be exhibited to address the needs highlighted above.

Leader	
	• Demonstrate self-awareness • Demonstrate strategic thinking • Motivate • Demonstrate well-being
Organisation	
	• Demonstrate dependability
Team	
	• Create a shared vision linked to organisation and external stakeholders • Create a shared strategy for achieving vision • Facilitate creativity • Facilitate conflict resolution • Facilitate shared approach to team-working • Assess quality of outcomes/outputs and process
Staff	
	• Inspire • Empower • Facilitate well-being • Facilitate for development

The items listed on the right-hand side of the above table are the actions that a leader should undertake to address the needs previously discussed. For example, a leader should demonstrate self-motivation and personal well-being. They should show to the organisation that they are dependable; facilitate team creativity and inspire staff.

Demonstrating self-awareness

Demonstrating self-awareness is key to a leader understanding herself as well as how to better interact with those around her. It requires persons to be reflective and conscious of their likes/dislikes, strengths/weaknesses and how others perceive them. A self-aware person consistently asks others for feedback so that they might improve their performance as well as that of others. This feedback can be obtained by 360-degree reviews, self-reflection or from a development coach, to name a few.

Demonstrating strategic thinking

Demonstrating strategic thinking helps a leader to move from a tactical (here and now, or short-term) to a more longer-term view. Such thinking helps to improve the likelihood that decisions are taken in the long-term interests of a team/organisation when considered as a going concern. Strategic thinkers:

➢ Focus on the bigger picture and can assess trends, changes, and potential disruptions within their market. They do this by regularly analysing the market and understanding the factors of change. They are aware of changing regulations and the potential impact on business operations as well as the role of technology in shaping future direction.

➢ Ask "what-if" type questions with a view to identifying a vision and stress-testing their assumptions about the future. They do this through several means including, visioning, model building and simulation, team brainstorming.

➢ Develop a "risk-focus" with a view to being able to identify, measure, evaluate, manage, and monitor potential risks that could affect the ongoing operations of the business area the leader is responsible for.

- Allocate time for reflective thinking. They understand that planning for the future must take into consideration what has happened so far as well as the current situation. They assess what has and what has not worked so well and remain open-minded about possibilities.

Motivate

If leaders want to motivate others, then it helps if they start with self-motivation. Self-motivation does not mean that you do not have negative thoughts, but it does mean that you do not dwell on these without having a means of mitigating or reducing the impact of negative consequences. Leaders who are self-motivated use knowledge of themselves (obtained through self-awareness) to identify their motivational needs. Self-motivated leaders:

- Have a clear focus on what their personal and wider goals/objectives are. They realise that having clear goals make it easier to derive a strategy for achieving their result.

- Seek counsel from positive influencers. They are aware that constructive feedback and guidance are likely to build their confidence.

- Take care of their physical and mental health.

- Show gratitude, even for the small successes. Success comes in different forms and, often, not immediately. Self-motivated leaders will be grateful for small wins and use this as a confidence booster to persist for the bigger prize.

- Understand how their needs can be addressed within the context of team/organisation objectives. Knowing this helps a leader to be able to work towards organisational objectives whilst also satisfying personal needs.

Demonstrate well-being

Demonstrating that you not only know about but adopt good personal well-being practices is a sign that you are in touch with your feelings. Setting a good example is key for many aspects of leadership and most importantly that of well-being. In a later chapter I discuss a framework I have developed for well-being leadership in organisations. However, below I highlight a few things a leader can do to enhance their own well-being:

- Nurture a diverse circle of confidants. Leaders that demonstrate good personal well-being understand the importance of being able to talk to others about their feelings concerning work or otherwise. They do not surround themselves with yes people but with those that are capable and willing to give constructive feedback. They understand that to get truly diverse opinions they need to have a diverse set of confidants.

- Widen your social and community interests. Leaders with good well-being practice understand that broadening their social interaction helps them to get involved in diverse activities that could benefit others outside of their organisation. They understand that demonstrating altruism not only helps to develop needed social skills, but it helps to build their confidence in self.

- Do not worry but strategise. Everyone worries about something at some point. However, when you persist to think negatively and about the things you believe you have no control over you are likely to cause yourself some form of mental illness. Good leaders know what they can control and what they cannot, and they choose not to focus on negative thoughts. They strategise about how they can manage potential risks and, if necessary, cope with undesirable consequences.

- Keep body and mind active. Good leaders understand that by continuing to read and acquire knowledge (relevant to and outside of their work) they enhance their ability to appreciate themselves and others better. They understand that by maintaining good physical health they enhance their chance of maintaining motivation and the ability to continue to undertake work.

Demonstrate dependability

Someone that shows themselves to be dependable is likely to be highly valued in their organisation. Good leaders realise that dependability goes beyond a leader showing favour or "sucking up" to those above them. They realise that standard measures of dependability such as timeliness, good quality work and flexibility are necessary but not sufficient conditions. They understand that people will judge them by how they treat others so being respectful to all persons and being fair are just as important as other attributes. In other words, they understand that dependability is not about playing games and getting people to be on your side, but it is about being there for others/yourself and being honest in your interactions with people.

Create a shared vision and strategy

Good leaders realise that without a shared vision and strategy staff have no common focus. This lack of common focus can lead to persons pursuing their own interests to the detriment of the organisation. Good leaders ensure that staff are aware and can see how they fit into the vision.

Facilitate for creativity

The poet John Donne wrote that "no man is an island". He understood that people are better as a collective rather than as individuals. In the same vein, a leader does not know everything and should aim to encourage their staff to be as creative as they can be in the execution of their work activities. However, not everything needs to be undertaken in a creative manner and it is up to the leader to understand the exigencies of the organisation and know when it is required to be expedient or imaginative.

Facilitate conflict resolution

No two people think exactly alike. There will, undoubtedly, be occasions when team members disagree and are not able to find a compromise. Under these circumstances it is the role of the leader to provide direction and aid in resolving conflicts. A key objective of the leader is to facilitate for all parties (i.e. the leader and the opposing persons) to have a common understanding of the two sides of the argument. The following are key pointers to bear in mind in resolving conflicts:

- ➢ Good leaders do not take sides. They listen to both sides of an argument and make sure they understand the points being made. They repeat back (to both parties) their understanding of what is being communicated and ask for confirmation.

➤ Good leaders facilitate for and expect effective communication from all sides. They insist that persons document their issues in writing as well as verbally during face to face discussions. They realise that when persons are required to document their concerns, they, generally, tend to think about it more thoroughly than when they verbalise. This also provides a non-confrontational way in which both sides can express their views. By also facilitating verbal discussions, the leader provides both sides the opportunity to carefully listen to what the other side has to say without interruption.

➤ Good leaders encourage problem identification and resolution and avoid personalisation. They steer the discussion in a direction which requires both sides to focus on the root of the problem without having to resort to finger pointing. The objective is for all parties to constructively identify how to resolve the problem.

Facilitate shared approach to teamwork

Teamwork lies at the heart of operational efficiency of an organisation. However, we all know that teamwork is more than just having a collection of individuals working near each other. There are a few key things a leader must do to facilitate shared approach to teamwork:

➤ Demonstrate that they trust and respect their employees. Good leaders realise that a team is not a team where there is no trust or respect for each other. This is likely to be exacerbated if the leader has a lack of trust/respect for staff as it could impact how she views them, chooses to work with them, reward them etc. The presumption of a good leader should be that their staff are trustworthy until they prove otherwise.

➤ Treat all staff members fairly. Good leaders know that one way to cause divisions within a team is when they treat some people more preferentially than others with no objective justification. They ensure that they are transparent in their dealings with all staff and do not have favourites.

➤ Be willing to be led by their staff. Good leaders know when to lead and when to be led. They understand that to truly share they must give up complete control and responsibility for some areas of work.

- Understand the strengths/weaknesses of their staff. Good leaders will understand the skills that persons bring to a team and how they can be utilised effectively. They will also know and be able to facilitate for the development of skills to aid staff in the undertaking of their duties.

- Work with staff to define the workflow rules/practice. A leader knows that even the most gifted set of individuals need to have clear procedures defining how they communicate and help to progress work from one state to another. A leader will work with a team to ensure all persons are aware of the rules.

Assess quality of outcomes/outputs and process

A key aspect of leadership is ensuring the quality of the outcomes/outputs an organisation produces. This can be achieved in several ways, but it is important that the leader either aids in the assurance metrics or agrees to those that staff have developed. As important but often ignored is the process used to derive these outcomes/outputs. A leader will want to ensure:

- The process is ethical. They will want to make sure that no laws/regulations or codes of conduct have been breached in delivering the results.

- The process is well understood. They will want to ensure that there is sufficient organisational know-how to be able to repeat or improve on the process. In the eventuality of staff changes this provides a means of enhancing the sustainability of the process.

Inspire

It is a basic requirement that all persons who adopt a shared-leadership style must also inspire their staff. Even when a share-leadership style is employed there is no guarantee that staff members will 'go beyond the call of duty' and make even greater commitments for the wider organisation or team. This, typically, only occurs (outside of intimidation) when staff members feel inspired by the leader and/or when they feel by so doing, they will satisfy some physical or higher-level need. Good leaders, therefore, will inspire individuals by showing how their work is related to their needs. They will also inspire staff by acting genuinely, showing trust, facilitating for their development, being fair and acting ethically.

Empower

For staff to participate in decision making and problem solving they need to be empowered. As previously discussed, empowerment requires that leaders must genuinely want to delegate/share and provide ongoing support but also ensure that persons are motivated to take on shared responsibilities.

Facilitate well-being

A good leader realises that if staff well-being is poor then morale is likely to be low and so will productivity. They understand that the team performs well when members are comfortable with their well-being. They know that well-being should, among other issues, incorporate matters relating to the type of work, how the work is conducted and the environment in which the work is done. They realise that what might be suitable for those that are later in their career might not be as important for those that are near the start of theirs. In a later chapter, I provide a framework for well-being leadership which can be used to provide guidance to leaders on this subject matter.

Facilitate for development

Good leaders understand that they need to ensure the continued development of their staff if they are to maintain their loyalty and they are to remain effective. When staff see that their leaders are happy to invest in them, often, this is repaid several times over in commitment and improved engagement.

Switching styles

There are several reasons why an individual might want to emphasise one leadership style over another on some occasions but not on others. For example, it is unlikely that all persons in a team (or a leader's direct reports) will share the same values, have the same level of experience and desire similar things from work.

It might also be the case that an organisation is subject to relatively frequent change in its business environment leading it to make corresponding changes to its operating practices. As such, leaders need to be flexible and realise that one style might not be appropriate all the time given such variations in staff and market conditions. Switching between the styles of woke leadership is very straightforward when persons are capable of and demonstrate the above behaviours consistently.

Previous chapters have highlighted the preconditions for maximising the likelihood of successful employment of the styles discussed. Successful in this respect means improved engagement of staff. In many instances, better engagement should also result in enhanced productivity. Consequently, a particular style should only be applied when all the conditions are satisfied.

The question arises as to what a leader should do if the preconditions for a leadership style is not satisfied. If the main reason arises from a lack of support from higher up in the organisation, short of trying to convince a change of view, there might be nothing the leader can do about this situation. In attempting to change the views of more senior management (or the Board) the leader should focus on the potential benefits of employing the leadership style when compared to the status quo.

If the reason arises primarily from a failure of the leader to satisfy certain conditions, then these should be addressed prior to acting further. It becomes harder to be an effective leader when there are deficits in your ability to lead so these should, ideally, be resolved prior to employing a particular style.

If the reason arises from a failure of a staff member not satisfying certain conditions, the leader could introduce the style but work to support the staff member in addressing any issues. Whilst development is ongoing, it might be necessary for the leader to combine a directional approach (more autocratic style) with the selected style until the staff member has satisfied the preconditions.

Leadership attributes

Whereas an organisation can create an enabling environment it is up to an individual to make the decision that they wish to develop or employ their abilities not just for their benefit but for the edification of others. Therefore, understanding the type of abilities required to bring about woke leadership is essential and will be further developed in the next chapter but for sake of clarity are listed below:

* Persistency.
* Passion.
* Empathy.
* Leading by example.
* Inspiring others.
* Encouraging challenges.
* Strategic.
* Innovative.
* CSR focused.
* Humorous.
* Creative.
* Mentor.
* Communicator.
* Tenacious.
* Truth seeking.
* Excellence seeking.

The above abilities are possessed by all people to varying degrees. Moreover, all the emerging leadership attributes discussed earlier, i.e., LA1, LA2, LA3 and LA4 all rely on these abilities. The following table provides a guide to understand which abilities have the biggest impact on the respective attributes/ leadership styles.

Leadership attribute	Abilities
Empowering leader - LA1	• Inspiring others • Encourage challenges • Develop/Mentor others • Communicator
Reflective leader - LA2	• Encourage challenges • Tenacious • Excellence seeking • Truth seeking • Communicator
Well-being leader - LA3	• Leading by example • Communicator • Humorous • Empathetic
Stakeholder leader - LA4	• Communicator • ECSR focused • Strategic • Tenacious

So, for example, whereas LA1 leadership relies on all the sixteen listed abilities, it is more influenced by those highlighted in the table. Different organisations and even different times in the same organisation might require leaders to emphasise one style over another. To do this, leaders would need to accentuate those abilities in the table (for the relevant style) and rely less on others.

Take heed, relying less does not mean ignoring these skills. The issue is the extent to which a leader needs to rely on an ability in the first place and their existing proficiency in that ability. It is difficult to imagine an organisation in which leaders are humourless. However, for an organisation that has a strong need for stakeholder leadership it would be a mistake to assume that having humour skills would not be of value to that organisation.

Leaders with a poor sense of humour can come across as being serious and unapproachable. This does not bode well for inspiring others. Hence the reader should appreciate that weaknesses in one ability could have negative consequences for others.

Given the above abilities a next step is understanding which ones are strengths and which pose weaknesses and how abilities can be enhanced. In a subsequent chapter I describe the ABC principles which I have developed as a means of mechanising leadership enhancement.

Some people might wonder why such a framework is necessary since leaders do not ordinarily follow a formal approach, they just lead. Well, my experience has been that when I have asked an expert to explain how they do what they do, i.e. what makes them a leader, many have struggled to articulate the reasoning behind their success. This should come as no surprise to those that have been involved in software development where knowledge elicitation and other cognitive psychology techniques are often used to obtain user requirements.

These leaders have simply forgotten the ABCs of their business and/or assume that everyone already has a certain level of knowledge. Consequently, they tend to provide high-level descriptions of their success, often missing out key components.

The purpose of the ABC principle is to provide a simple framework which encourages individuals to assess their leadership skills by understanding their abilities (A), enhancing their beliefs/confidence (B) and having a coherent strategy (C) for achieving their objectives. The principles can be applied by all types of people whether they are already in positions of leadership or whether they are aspiring. You can apply the principles to your everyday life for both personal and professional growth.

Exercise

For each of the abilities listed above, provide a description of what you think it means to (1) perform it well and (2) perform it badly.

Which abilities do you think you possess and regularly demonstrate? Do you perform them well?

Further reading

1. OECD. (2015), *G20/OECD Principles of Corporate Governance*, OECD, viewed October 7, 2020, <http://www.oecd.org/corporate/principles-corporate-governance/>
2. Ferrara, M and LaMeau, M. (2012), *Corporate Disasters: What Went Wrong and Why*, Gale Research Incorporated Pub
3. Enrich, D. (2018), The Spider Network: *The Wild Story of a Maths Genius and One of the Greatest Scams in Financial History*, WH Allen Pub
4. Maslow, A. (2011), *Hierarchy of Needs: A Theory of Human Motivation*, www.all-about-psychology.com Pub
5. Donne, J. (1636), *No Man is an Island*, Villard Pub
6. Hersey, P. and Blanchard, K. H. (1969), *Management of Organizational Behavior – Utilizing Human Resources*. New Jersey/Prentice Hall
7. Hersey, P. and Blanchard, K. H. (1977), *Management of Organizational Behavior 3rd Edition– Utilizing Human Resources*. New Jersey/Prentice Hall.
8. Covey, S. (1989), *The 7 Habits of Highly Effective People*, Free Press Pub

Chapter 9

Who are your influencers?

Introduction
Who is influential
Tarana Burke
Satya Nadella
Kenneth Frazier
Issa Rae
Jesmyn Ward
Ann McKee
Chloe Kim
Further discussions
Further reading

Introduction

The UK has gone through unprecedented political/constitutional crisis in relation to its exit from the European Union (EU) – Brexit. The fact that the majority of the United Kingdom and Northern Ireland voted to leave the EU and that parliament had frustrated the process for over three years shows that there was a big gulf between the wishes of most of the people and parliament. It is evident that the majority of parliament were Remainers and those that voted in the referendum were Leavers.

So, what is the relationship between Brexit and leadership? The impasse that took place in the House of Commons between the elected officials has shown that they were unable to work collectively to implement the mandate given to them by the people of the UK. Instead they pursued their own self-interests and showed a remarkable lack of leadership.

This has led to growing discontent towards our political leaders and other countries have and are experiencing similar issues. For example, France, Germany, and Italy have seen voters' rejection of the traditional party leaders and party system and made it clear that they want more of a coalition style of government.

Arguably one of the biggest contributors to this dissent of the status quo is due to populism. A significant example of this saw the election of the 45th President of the United States, Donald J Trump. Common amongst all these examples is the lack of trust of established leaders/parties that populist voters cite as a key reason for their voting decisions.

At present, the world is going through turmoil from the impacts of the Covid-19 virus and, yet again, so-called leaders are playing politics with people's lives. After it became patently clear that Covid-19 was highly contagious, several leaders chose not to wear face masks or take timely measures to safeguard lives. Instead they choose to project an image to underplay the potency of the virus and to pander to the wishes of 'big business' in delaying social distancing measures and business closures. Undoubtedly this has contributed to the unnecessary loss of many lives across the world and again, has caused people to question the integrity of our political leaders.

In some countries, the impacts of Covid-19 have been compounded by the horrific events surrounding the death of George Floyd and the shooting of Jacob Blake both of which police were responsible for. These events have reawakened issues which lay dormant concerning the treatment of Black people and ethnic minorities (BMEs) in general.

Even the Covid-19 pandemic has illustrated how decades of discriminatory workplace practices and public policies has resulted in higher death rates amongst BMEs than white people. Yet, despite all of this, there has been little true leadership shown by politicians to redress this issue causing many within BME communities to doubt whether business/political leaders really want change.

Who is influential?

Although I have barely touched the surface of the changing attitude towards political leaders the question needs to be asked as to whom modern society puts their trust in and are influenced by be it politically or otherwise. Along with a variety of other factors, changes and improvements in communications, equality, and human rights and social, cultural, and religious values have had an impact on workplace dynamics and perceptions of leadership. Below I have undertaken an analysis of the Time Magazine 2018 100 most influential list of people to illustrate this point.

Profession	Percentage
Activist	12%
Professionals	8%
CEO	3%
Author	2%
Entertainer	28%
Entrepreneur	7%
Politician	20%
Royalty	3%
Scientist	6%
Sports	6%
Artist	5%

I have grouped individuals based on the category I believe they belong to and determined the overall percentage that the category contributes to the total. Most of the categories should be self-explanatory but I will explain the chief executive officer (CEO) and Professionals classification. The CEO category refers to those persons that are heads (or senior managers) of a commercial, for profit business. The Professionals category refers to those that hold jobs such as Architect, Chef, Designer or Reporter but are not CEO's.

What stands out for you from the list? For me it is that more than 1 in every 4 persons are entertainers. This implies that the category of individuals having the most influence on many people around the world are entertainers. The group having the next biggest impact on many people's lives are politicians and then activists.

Although only a snapshot in time, this result is indicative of an increasing trend where entertainers are having a big influence on the social, moral/ethical, and even political views of everyday people. The United States of America elected Donald Trump, for heaven's sake. In general, the effect of these influencers extends beyond private life into the workplace and all aspects of modern society.

Below, I have selected a cross-section of individuals from the 100 list. I have also provided a one sentence summary of what I believe to be the key factors that has resulted in success for these people. The choice of individuals is influenced by the key factors observed in their behaviour.

The factors also correspond to a set of abilities/characteristics I have observed in good leaders and were highlighted in the previous chapter. I should say that all the persons mentioned possess all the success factors detailed (as we all do) but those in bold are the ones I believe to be dominant:

Name	Key success factors
Tarana Burke (Civil Rights Activist. Founder of Me Too)	Tarana has **persistently** demonstrated a **passionate** and **empathetic** conviction for increasing awareness of social injustice due to acts of sexual abuse.

Name	Key success factors
Satya Nadella (CEO of Microsoft)	Satya has **led by example** and **inspired** a culture of change by building better external relationships, **encouraging challenges** to the status quo, and rewarding innovation and teamwork.
Kenneth C Frazier (Chairman and CEO of Merck & Co.)	Kenneth has **identified that the strategy** for his firm to achieve sustainable growth should focus more on **investments in research and development (R&D)** and life-saving treatments and **improve their corporate social responsibility**.
Issa Rae (Actress, writer, director, and producer)	Issa has used **humour** and **creativity** to heighten awareness of the diversity and talent of people of colour and has used this success to provide a platform for **mentoring others**.
Jesmyn Ward (Novelist and Associate professor of English)	Jesmyn has used literature employing a variety of language styles, as a means of **communicating** emotional/controversial issues, in an uncompromising manner, to a wide audience.
Ann McKee (Neuropathologist and professor of Neurology)	Ann has **tenaciously** strived to use research, even in the face of fierce opposition, to **uncover the truth** about the relationship between sports injuries and degenerative diseases.

Name	Key success factors
Chloe Kim (Olympic snowboarding champion)	Chloe has recognised that **excellence** is not attained by winning gold medals on a few occasions but in the relentless and repeated pursuit of improvements to one's own performance.

In the sections below, I provide some background on each of these individuals and drill down into the success factors.

Tarana Burke

Tarana Burke was born in New York and grew up in a poor area of the Bronx. As a child and a teenager, she became the victim of sexual assault and rape. These experiences ignited her passion to advocate for the support of girls who have been subject to similar abuse.

Tarana's passion for social justice; the arts and culture led to her working for several organisations prior to her co-founding Jendayi Aza. This was an initiative focused on an African-oriented rites of passage program for girls. This later evolved into the "Just Be Inc" organisation which Tarana founded in 2003 whose focus is on the overall well-being of young women of colour.

In 2003, Tarana was having a discussion with a girl who revealed that she had been sexually abused by someone close to her family. It was out of this, and other similar conversations, that led to Tarana coining the phrase: "You're not alone. This happened to me too". Out of this came the "Me Too" slogan.

The trauma of being raped or sexually assaulted can be devastating and result in life-changing impairments. The road to recovery will not be the same for everyone subject to this type of abuse. For some, it might take a relatively short period and for others, they might never fully recover. In the case of Tarana, her determination to help others was a key factor in helping her to constructively move forwards with her life.

Tarana could have let her experiences dictate how she was going to live the rest of her life, as a victim, rather than as a survivor. She could have let the trauma of the events hold her back, prevent her from establishing trust and engaging with wider society. Instead, Tarana developed an interest in community action and social issues and was able to successfully learn and develop skills that would later prove useful in life.

In 2014 Tarana worked as an advisor in the making of the Oscar-nominated film, Selma. She is frequently asked to speak at various events regarding promoting support for survivors of sexual assault and serves as a director to various organisations. The inspiration she has provided to others has resulted in the "Me Too" movement becoming a worldwide cause.

Suppose Tarana had decided that having successfully organised press conferences to highlight and rallies against various types of social injustice she would have achieved her goal and stopped pursuing such initiatives so energetically. She might have become a passive rather than an engaged activist for social justice and might not have formed one of the world's most talked about movements – Me Too.

Tarana was painfully aware that talking about change and implementing change were two different things and the latter required persistence. You can have all the charm in the world, be gifted and have the right qualifications and experience but if you do not have persistence you are unlikely to succeed as a leader.

Have you ever watched a TV interview of a politician and thought this guy's body language suggests that he is not really into what he is saying? Well, it might be because he is an uncharismatic speaker but quite likely it could be because he lacks passion and conviction in what he is saying. This is not something that can be said about someone like Tarana Burke who exudes passion about highlighting and combating social injustice.

I bet, like me, you can recall several departmental or organisational meetings at which your boss or CEO made utterances that were just simply unbelievable as they appeared to be comments made in passing, without conviction.

Without passion, it would have been much harder for Tarana to ignite the interest of so many people to her cause. When she speaks, even on such a painful subject like sexual abuse, you can feel the conviction in her voice and her mannerism is engaging.

The learning point here is that, without passion, your job is made that much harder as you try to influence and guide others as a leader. From my experience, the most believable leaders are the ones who are comfortable in their skin and make you feel comfortable with them.

Have you ever had a discussion with someone and felt that, although they were nodding their head and acting as if they were in tune with your feelings, they were just going through the motions? Sometimes people can be incredibly good at hiding their true feelings but eventually the truth will out.

As the old saying goes "you can't understand someone until you've walked a mile in their shoes". To empathise you must have had experience or be able to put yourself in their shoes. This is a major reason why Tarana Burke has been successful in advocating her cause. This is also true in a work environment.

Empathy is one of the cornerstones of engagement but not everyone practices it. I have come across persons in leadership roles that say they are "hands off" preferring not to get too involved with staff. Those which are of the view that staff should be grateful that they have a job. Those that think people have it easy compared to when they were the same age. There are even those that think it is not their job to "baby sit" staff, they simply do not have the time.

All these views are indicative of persons that do not place engagement as a top priority. Without engagement, leaders are not in an ideal position to understand the dynamics in their area of responsibility. At the very least, a leader should be able to show that they are sympathetic to the needs of their staff and others around them. However, a good leader goes beyond this and tries to be empathetic.

In the next section, I present each of the three characteristics previously discussed and pose them as a challenge for you. In undertaking the challenge, please be realistic. Everyone will not obtain the highest score for all the characteristics. I have previously made the point that you do not need to be strong in all skills but be aware of what needs to be developed and what can be used to support your leadership.

Persistency

In today's working environment and at the level you are at, the chances are that many people working in your sector are likely to have similar levels of skills and qualifications. However, what is likely to set the leaders apart from others is persistency. This is the thing that tells you to keep on going even when everyone around you tells you to stop. It is the thing that says there is a light at the end of the tunnel even when all you can see is darkness.

Everyone is born with the ability to be persistent. However, unless you practice you are unlikely to use it to your advantage. Below are some key steps I have identified and used by good leaders to make persistence work for them:

- **Do not be put off by failure**. Failure is a necessary part of learning. It informs you that you have successfully chosen the wrong path. The important part of failure is understanding why you failed, not the failure itself.

- **Embrace change** and do not be put off by new challenges. Change and challenges are likely to come at you fast and furious and your ability to be flexible and open to these will make you a stronger leader.

- **Do not be impatient**. Most likely, success will not be achieved overnight even in this fast-moving digital era. Time should not be viewed as your enemy but use time to perfect your leadership strategy and approach to implementation.

- **Maintain your strategic focus**. Do not get bogged down with tactical activities to the detriment of your longer-term goals.

Consider asking a colleague/friend (preferably three or more) to give you a rating between 1 and 5 (with 5 being the best) for each of the points noted above. Along with the scores, you could ask each person to provide you with evidence to support their rating. Similarly, rate yourself between the same range and compare the scores. Compare the average of the scores to yours. If the average score is greater than yours then this suggests that people have a higher perception of your ability than you and vice-versa.

So that a sufficient degree of granularity can be obtained in the range of the scores, I would suggest you choose increments of 0.5 between scores. Thus, the lowest score would be 1, the next lowest is 1.5, then 2 and eventually 5.

A strong/weak rating would be any score above/below 3 respectively and a good score is 3. The next step would be to implement a plan to improve your scores. The obvious suggestion would be to focus on your weak areas, but it is important to realise that strengths also need to be maintained.

Over time, it is possible that your score might plateau at a certain value less than 5, suggesting that you might not be able to get a higher score. Do not be too alarmed by this. As time progresses, if your responsibilities remain the same then you should expect to score at least what you have previously achieved. However, if you have taken on additional responsibilities or things have changed then it might be that your score goes down as you adjust to the changes.

Demonstrating your passion

When was the last time you were passionate about your work life? Is your enthusiasm contagious or do you think you are going through the motions and putting on a false smile? It is well known that most people are not working in their ideal role and consider their position as a means of making ends meet. However, there might be more that you can do to make your non-ideal role more bearable. The following are some key steps that I have seen good leaders implement and I recommend for you:

- **Have a clear idea** about what you want and the timescales in which you want to achieve your objectives. Communicate this to your colleagues, loved ones or others. If you do not know exactly what you want and cannot communicate it to others, then it will be harder to satisfy your passion. As a result, you might become more frustrated and stressed.

- **Be ready to offer possibilities/solutions rather than just complaints**. If possible, try and find ways of helping to improve the efficiency/effectiveness of what you or others do so that it would increase its appeal to both of you.

- **Try to engage others** on both work and non-work-related matters. If you only ever talk to folks at work about work, they might get the impression that you are transactional and non-approachable. The objective is not to interrogate people about their private lives or to offer information on yours that you do not want to. The objective is simply to show an interest in others with a view to building closer working relationships.

- **Reaffirm your self-worth.** You should remind yourself (constantly throughout the day, each day) that you have value in the organisation and outside. You are not worthless. Stay positive and project a positive image to others and try not to indulge in idle or fruitless conversations which serve to reinforce negative thoughts.

- **Advertise your achievements and value-added.** Remind people of your achievements and how your skills can be utilised in the organisation. If you have skills which can be used to help other organisational units you should stress this and make an argument to work on cross departmental projects, if possible.

- **Seek guidance from or help to mentor others.** A discussion with your boss or others might identify opportunities for capacity building or other strategies that can be used to help your growth in the organisation. Similarly, you might find that you are able to mentor others and help the organisation in ways you never envisaged. You might find that the effort you put out comes back to you several fold as this demonstrates some soft skills that can lead to promotion internally or set you up for a role externally should you decide to move on.

As with the previous challenge, ask a few people to give you a rating (for each of the above points) on a scale of 1 to 5 and ask for justifications for the scores. Prepare a score for yourself and compare the average scores to your own.

Demonstrating empathy

One of the keys to understanding other people is to show that you can relate to where they are coming from. Empathy is an enabler to building closer relationships with people and enhancing teamwork. However, not everyone consistently demonstrates that they are empathetic. Could this be you?

The following steps have been shown to provide an effective means of helping to improve empathetic behaviour:

- **Improve your listening skills.** Demonstrating that you are listening to people helps when you are required to respond to their concerns. Pausing before you respond and waiting for people to finish talking, before interrupting, shows that you are considerate of their opinions.

- **Improve your body language.** Making eye contact, smiling, nodding, not crossing your arms and not attending to other matters at the same time are all signs of positive engagement.

- **Ensuring that your actions are consistent with your words** reinforces that you are taking people seriously. For example, saying that you will do something and then doing the opposite would not endear you to people.

- **Go out of your way** to give people an adequate amount of time to discuss their issues with you and in private or before/after work if necessary.

- **Respond in a timely manner** to matters raised by others. This demonstrates that you are sensitive to the urgency of their requirements.

- **Ask for feedback** on your understanding of issues raised by others and acknowledge their perspectives. This demonstrates your humility and willingness to understand.

- **Be open-minded and solutions oriented.** This shows that you are not narrow-minded and willing to consider all possibilities.

As with previous challenges, obtain scores and feedback from others as well as scoring yourself.

Take a few minutes to sit down and think of conversations that you have recently had with a colleague, friend/associate, or family member. Were there any that did not go well? Have you noticed a change in the behaviour of these individuals for the worse? Could it be that you were not as empathetic as you could have been? If so, you might want to consider having another conversation with them but this time, making use of the pointers above.

Satya Nadella

Satya Nadella was born in Hyderabad in India. His interest in "building things" resulted in him studying and obtaining an undergraduate degree in electrical engineering from the Manipal Institute of Technology.

Satya discovered that he had a passion for computer science and left India to study for a master's degree, in the subject, at the University of Wisconsin and later he followed this up by undertaking an MBA at the University of Chicago Booth School of Business.

After graduation Satya had a brief spell working at Sun Microsystems before moving to Microsoft, in 1992. He made good progress in moving up the corporate ladder and by 2007 became senior vice president of research and development for its online services division. A little later he became President of Microsoft's server and tools business as well as Executive Vice President for the cloud computing platform. In his time in charge of these businesses he was able to oversee major initiatives such as cloud-based computing, enhancement of office 365 subscription-based services as well as to achieve significant growth in revenues.

On becoming CEO in 2014, Satya achieved quick success in overseeing the takeover of Nokia Corporation's mobile-device business and subsequent streamlining of the company (i.e. reorganising the whole of Microsoft) as well as the acquisition of LinkedIn in 2016.

The reorganisation resulted in the loss of several thousands of jobs. Determined that the culture needed to change he encouraged the breaking down of silos between divisions/departments as well as fostering an environment where staff could challenge management if they believed they had a better approach.

At the time of Satya's appointment, there were not too many analysts that would have picked him for the role of CEO. Less than 15% of fortune 100 companies (at the time) had CEO's that were born outside of the USA. Moreover, Satya was not white and did not go to Harvard or Yale. However, Satya had spent around 22 years at Microsoft so although a foreigner to the USA he was well-established within the world of Microsoft. The organisation was moving in the direction of cloud-based services and, generally, in the areas that Satya had been responsible for and had achieved good results.

You might have heard of the saying "Do as I say and not as I do". This is typically associated with those in a position of authority such as a boss, parent, or other person of influence. Satya Nadella led by example in not just saying the culture of Microsoft needed to change but (on being made CEO) he started the process by changing the format of the CEO talks to staff members.

Satya did this by equalising the level of his physical position to that of staff members so that they could see each other at eye level. Funny thing, he started this practice at an event at which Microsoft released its Office product on the iPad. This sent a powerful message to staff of the importance of building bridges and teamwork in and outside of the organisation.

The benefit to Microsoft of this relationship was that it was able to get its products and services on platforms owned by their competitors but for which Microsoft had a clear competitive advantage. This is a message that leaders in other organisations can learn from, sometimes the best way to compete is to work with and not against your competition.

Without inspiration we are just plodding along. An idea kept to yourself is like running a relay with no one to pass the baton to. Satya Nadella realised that by adopting a "growth mindset" and insisting that different departments work more closely he would increase the chance of inspiring the development of "next generation" products rather than just ideas for the here and now.

The learning point here is that you need to be careful who you take inspiration from and share your ideas with. Ideas are to be shared but with those that can help to shape improvements in your thinking and through teamwork, even with those that might oppose you, the chances of inspired growth in both self and others will increase. For what is an organisation if not just the composite of its resources for which people lie at the heart. If the heart is not inspired the organisation is living on borrowed time.

Have you ever been in a team or other meeting and your boss has said something that you are bursting to challenge but felt concerned about how they would react? If you took your concerns to your boss, in private, and they reacted negatively then you were probably right in not raising the matter.

If your boss: generally, does not tolerate challenges, does not share your ethical values, only cares about the outputs you produce and makes no enquiry about your well-being, has divergent or no plans for your career development, does not make time for you, does not recognise your contribution in public (or at all), constantly tries to find fault with your work then it is probably time for you to leave that organisation.

In pursuing a growth strategy Satya Nadella realised that he had to initiate a change in the culture of the organisation. He encouraged staff to challenge the status quo when they believed there were better ways of achieving objectives. This has helped to break down barriers at the organisation and has led to increased cooperation and productivity.

The learning point here is any organisation that does not care about the opinions of its staff members will become inefficient, complacent and its reputational brand will be tarnished. My experience has been that firms that do not value the opinions of their staff members lose these members (often the best quality) and incur costs to recruit and advertise for lost positions as well as the opportunity costs of covering for the positions whilst recruiting.

Leading by example

The objective of leading by example is to demonstrate how things are to be undertaken to achieve a desirable outcome. In today's world, from a business perspective, this outcome is chosen so that it does not deliberately lead to the undermining of an organisation's stakeholders. This can prove challenging since the interests of varied stakeholders might not be aligned. The focus, however, should be on trying to maximise stakeholder value and it might be that some benefit more than others depending on the circumstances.

The following pointers can be used to improve your ability to lead by example:

- **Be sensitive to your surroundings with what and how to communicate.** In communicating with people your focus should be to inform, be informed and to exchange thoughts in a professional manner. Note that this does not exclude you engaging in general "chit chat" which is a part of building relations. However, this cannot come at the expense of productivity and should not be malicious, undermine or seek to embarrass those present or otherwise. Note also that how you communicate is not always verbal so be careful to be sensitive to your and the body language of others when interacting with people.

- **Being a brand ambassador.** Your position in the organisation is valued, otherwise it would not exist. You should use the opportunity to tell people about the importance of your role in the organisation and the value it brings to its varied stakeholders and how it links to other parts of the business. Note that this is not about you, but it is about the role.

- **Being consistent with words and action.** This helps to build trust and reliance and enhances understanding of each other.

- **Being willing to be led.** Helping others or your team to succeed by supporting their initiatives, even if you are more senior, is an example of good leadership. Further, acknowledging the contribution of others and their feedback helps to build confidence and team spirit.

- **Stakeholder and systems focused.** Seeing things from the perspective of all stakeholders and making decisions based on how it impacts these parties demonstrates that you have enterprise awareness and are not narrowly focused.
- **Humility**. Being able to say when you are wrong and taking the blame for when your team messes up. Finger pointing does nothing positive for moral but showing humility strengthens team loyalty.
- **Engaging and solutions oriented**. Being willing to help and offer suggestions for addressing problems demonstrates your desire to contribute to teamwork. This can help to motivate others.
- **Establish and/or uphold high standards of excellence**. Hold yourself to the same high standards that you expect of others. People will respect you more when you show that you hold yourself to the same rules of conduct/governance as them. This will help to reinforce a positive culture in your organisation.

As with previous challenges, you might want to consider obtaining feedback from others as well as scoring yourself.

Inspiring others

Without inspiration it is impossible to lead effectively. If people do not care about what you say, or do you are less likely to achieve your objectives since people will not be motivated to support your efforts.

Building on the previous discussions, the following pointers can be used to improve your ability to inspire others:

- Be a person that leads by example.
- Be empathetic.
- Be passionate.
- Show humility.

As with previous challenges, you might want to consider obtaining feedback from others as well as scoring yourself on how well you inspire people.

Encouraging challenges

People like to feel that they are valued and that their opinion counts. Do you consistently show appreciation and welcome challenges?

The following pointers can be used to improve your ability to encourage challenges from others:

- Humility. By showing humility and not taking things personally will help to make you more approachable.
- Leading by example.
- Being empathetic.

As with previous challenges, you might want to consider obtaining feedback from others as well as scoring yourself on how well you encourage others to challenge you.

Kenneth Frazier

Kenneth Frazier was born in Philadelphia, USA. He obtained a degree in Political Science from the University of Pennsylvania and a Doctorate in Jurisprudence from Harvard Law School. For the first fourteen years, he honed his legal skills at a leading law firm in Philadelphia and then moved to Merck in 1992 and seven years later he became its General Counsel.

During his time as General Counsel he was responsible for overseeing Merck's defence against a class-action lawsuit involving the painkiller Vioxx. At the time of the suit, estimates suggested potential liability between 20 and 50 billion dollars. Frazier was resolved to fight the cases, and, to date, total payouts have been less than $6 billion.

In 2006 Frazier assumed the additional role of executive vice president and in 2010 became president of Merck & Co. In the following year, he was named CEO, made a board member, and became the first African American to head a major pharmaceutical company.

Proverbs 29:18 (King James Version) states: "Where there is no vision the people perish". The vision referred to here is in relation to Gods revelation as to his plans for us. In many ways the words of the Bible are as applicable to the workplace as it was when the verse was first written.

Organisations need strategic direction to guide its continued sustainability. Kenneth Frazier understood this when he changed the strategic direction of his company to focus on investments in R&D as a basis for ensuring continued long-term growth rather than short-term profits. This strategy has paid off for Merck as evidenced by its improving financials.

An organisation without a coherent strategy is likely to: have no clear way of evidencing how visions are mapped to goals and targets for departments and staff; hire staff with "today" skills who will quickly become surplus to requirements once tactical works complete; have relatively frequent organisational changes; have volatile funding sources; have staff feeling they lack job security etc.

The learning point here is an organisation's strategy should be clearly communicated and each staff member should be able to describe how what they do supports the strategy and how this can be measured.

Companies exist to maximise their shareholders wealth, right? Anyone that still thinks that this is true is unlikely to understand the detrimental financial impact poor reputation can have for an organisation. Do you remember the Volkswagen crisis? This company deliberately aimed to mask the extent to which its vehicles were emitting poisonous gases into the environment. The cost of fines, penalties and other amounts have run into many US $ Billions.

What about BP, remember them? They were responsible for the worst oil spill in US history which occurred in the Gulf of Mexico. Clean-up costs and compensation have amounted to more than US $ 20 Billion.

In recognising Merck's corporate social responsibility, Kenneth Frazier has stated that Merck should have a key focus on making a difference in the lives of people living in the emerging markets. This is a particularly important initiative since many pharmaceutical companies are deriving an increasing proportion of their revenues from these markets.

Kenneth Frazier also made clear his social consciousness when (in 2017) he rebuked President Donald Trump over his response to racially motivated attacks in Charlottesville. Some might have questioned the wisdom of his comments, but Kenneth knew the issue was bigger than him or the President. He understood that the tone is set at the top and the approach of the CEO to environmental and societal issues can influence the perception of the organisation.

Organisations do not operate in a vacuum and the consequences of its business practices and in some instances the personal practices of senior personal will have an impact on the fortunes of the firm.

A good organisation would have a well-written CSR policy which is available and communicated to all stakeholders e.g. staff, shareholders and customers, suppliers of goods/services. Amongst other topics the policy would cover how business activities are integrated into CSR initiatives, how the policy is consistent with relevant laws/regulations, specific areas of focus (e.g. children with autism), third parties the organisation will partner with, aims/objectives and targets along with timescales (including how the policy contributes to sustainable development).

Strategic leadership

Strategy lies at the heart of any type of organisation. However, to run successfully, organisations need strategic thinkers. They need individuals that understand that what you do today will impact what you might be able to do in the future. Are you such a person?

The following pointers can be used to improve your ability to be an effective strategic thinker:

- **Constructively challenge the status quo and get people on board**. By being able to show people an alternative view, in a manner which identifies strengths/weaknesses, in a non-combative and coherent manner, will go a long way to getting support for your ideas. People tend to get defensive if they are approached in an aggressive (or dictatorial) manner and irrespective of the virtue of your message they are likely to have some push back.

- **Understand interrelations between short and longer-term goals**. Understanding the difference and relations between daily periodic operations and longer-term aspirations helps in seeing the woods through the trees. If you are not able to understand the things you need to do today to get to where you want tomorrow then, most likely, your strategy and tactical measures are blurred, and you might be mixing up the former with the latter.

- **Humility**. Having the ability to reflect on your own weaknesses opens the possibility of letting others provide the type of support you might require in achieving your objectives.

- **Empathy**. Being able to see things from several perspectives is vital in devising a coherent strategy in which all persons feel a part of the process.

- **Understand and anticipate trends and changes**. Understanding past and likely trends as well as pending/potential market, social and environmental changes is a crucial part of strategic thinking and planning. Without inclusion of these considerations, a strategy is highly likely to fail.

- **Succession planning**. Depending on the horizon it is possible that those involved in the formation of a strategic plan might not be working for the organisation once the plan is operational. Planning should, thus, involve identifying future leaders and other resource requirements.

- **Growth orientation**. Your thinking should involve you understanding how the value for each stakeholder can be enhanced to improve the sustainability of the organisation.

As with previous challenges, you might want to consider obtaining feedback from others as well as scoring yourself.

Innovation/R&D focussed

An inability or failure to innovate could signal the green light towards a rocky road. If you continue to do the same thing whilst others around you are evolving, you are unlikely to succeed. Organisations do not just evolve. They require individuals to drive the process forward. Are you such an individual?

The following pointers can be used to improve your ability to be more innovative:

- **Continuous self-development**. By continuing to learn about new ideas both within and outside of your main areas of expertise you increase your chance of identifying opportunities for innovation.

- **Persistency**. Most innovative products/services take time to evolve. There is no short-cut to innovation and learning how to deal with failure is part of the challenge of being an innovative leader.

- **Clarity of purpose/vision**. Being innovative means that you have a clear vision or understand the purpose for the product/service you are looking to create. You should be able to use a variety of tools to describe the world in which the product/service exists, its benefits and how people's life would be affected by its use.

- **Passionate**. Innovators often speak about their passion for creating things and finding solutions for problems. Being passionate about generating new ideas or creating new concepts is something that not only helps to motivate you but can be contagious and help to ignite the interest of others in supporting your efforts.

- **Team-oriented**. Few innovations are completely developed by a single individual. Being able to work with others and being facilitative of other viewpoints helps to manage complexity and realise opportunities that might have been missed otherwise.

- **Curious and willing to buck the norm**. Innovation typically comes from people willing to ask questions and challenge the status quo. They are seldom satisfied with mediocrity and constantly seek ways of improving processes.

As with previous challenges, you might want to consider obtaining feedback from others as well as scoring yourself.

CSR focussed

The world is changing. Disasters such as the BP oil spillage and the Volkswagen emissions scandal have thrust corporate social responsibility into the limelight. Further, the United Nations Sustainable Development Goals (SDGs) has propelled climate change as a major issue, government, organisations, and individuals should be focusing on.

Gone are the days when it is all about the shareholders, or is it? For an organisation to effectively satisfy its wider stakeholders it needs to ensure business decisions are taken based on a system's rather than a silos approach. That is, decisions should be based on how it impacts the various stakeholders and the environment, rather than just the bottom line. To do this, an organisation should have individuals capable of understanding the linkages between operational activities and environmental and CSR issues (ECSR). Are you such an individual?

The following pointers can be used to improve your ability to be more sensitive to ECSR issues in decision making:

- **Continuous self-development**. ECSR issues are frequently changing both in terms of form and how they are to be reported. You should ensure that you continue to learn about ECSR issues in general and those which are relevant to your organisation.

- **Risk management**. Incorporate risk analysis into your decision making. For example, when decisions are being made, assess the ECSR impact and modify your strategy if you find that there are adverse impacts.

- **Influence change**. Challenging others to incorporate ECSR into their business decisions/processes. Seeing the opportunities for others to successfully integrate ECSR into their operations is a key step towards influencing change on a wider basis in your organisation.

- **Integrity**. If you are not viewed as being trustworthy it will be harder for you to be taken seriously when it comes to influencing others.

- **Humility.** Being able to put the needs of others before your wants and desires, even if you are the CEO, is indicative of someone that can see the "big picture" and act in the wider interests of an organisation.

- **Charitable/voluntary activities**. Taking part in activities run by charitable/voluntary organisations e.g., Rotary Clubs, provides an opportunity for individuals to be aware of and contribute to environmental and social issues locally, regionally, and internationally.

Issa Rae

Issa Rae was born in Los Angeles, California, USA. Rae graduated from Stanford University, in 2007, where she studied for a major in African and African American studies. However, whilst at Stanford, Rae demonstrated her creative flair by creating music videos and writing and directing plays.

In 2011, Rae's web series "Awkward Black Girl" premiered on YouTube and became a hit to the point of obtaining mainstream media attention. The series, a comedy, follows the life of her fictional character as she interacts with co-workers and lovers and the situations, they put her in.

The series won the Shorty Award for Best Web series in 2012 and another Shorty award in 2013. The success of the series eventually led to other initiatives which would solidify her credentials as someone capable of writing, filming, editing, and producing much of her own work. In 2016, the series "Insecure" was aired on Home Box Office (HBO) and has received praise from many circles.

Can you imagine sitting in an office where people are afraid to talk openly and share their thoughts on either business or personal issues? What about being in an office where humour is not tolerated unless it is at the expense of an employee? If your answer to these questions is yes, then you need to seriously think about leaving that organisation. It is generally accepted that humour has a positive impact on people's well-being which can lead to improvements in motivation and productivity.

Is it right to make fun out of the way a young black woman dresses, does her hair, socialises, and manages her professional development? Of course, especially if the issues raised are dealt with in a sensitive/empathetic and realistic way as portrayed by Issa Rae in the hit TV show Insecure.

Issa Rae has used humour as a means of illustrating the social and cultural habits of a 20-something black woman. Although the show is fictional and deals with everyday issues in the lives of a certain demography it is the way in which humour is used that makes the show relatable to audiences that are not African American. In a similar manner, the "real world" workplace should be an enjoyable environment to work where staff are enthused, happy and keen to be at work.

The learning point here is, given the amount of time people spend at work including the time travelling to and from work (which can be more than 10 hours in total), facilitating for a happy and welcoming environment should be considered a basic requirement of management.

I worked for an organisation that, notwithstanding all the talk and rhetoric of the CEO, simply did not value the creativity I brought to the organisation. This creativity led to notable publications, presentations, and commendations from clients around the world, however, there was no recognition of my initiatives by my immediate manager.

It became clear, the manager was intimidated by me and lacked the capacity to be equally creative. My experience is not unique and a common trait of organisations where this type of activity occurs is "entrenchment" where certain individuals end up running the organisation for their own benefit rather than the wider set of stakeholders. Consistent with entrenchment is adopting a "doing things the way we have always done it attitude". Individuals which resist change will end up like the dinosaurs, extinct.

Isa Rae is a poster child for creativity. Her imagination has resulted in creative material produced for YouTube, television and she is an actress, writer, director, and producer that is in demand and has received international acclamation.

The learning point is without creativity an organisation is starved of the lifeline to support innovation and invention. Without recognition and support the most talented and creative people will leave organisations. Support comes not just in the form of rhetoric and words but taking actions to match the words.

History has shown that less successful people gravitate to those that are more successful. They try to emulate them with a view to obtaining some of the achievements of those they revere. However, sometimes there are those achievers that forget that they were once trying to achieve and fail to support those trying to make it up the corporate/professional ladder. This is not the case for Issa Rae. Issa has not only remembered where she is coming from, but she has made it possible for many others to have the benefit of mentorship through an initiative she established with Columbia Pictures. The initiative will work to promote diversity in creating/writing content.

The learning point is mentorship is not only the preserve of the creative industries but for any profession/organisation. Succession planning becomes that much easier when organisations institute mentorship programmes as it can lead to increased retention, productivity, brand recognition and sustainability (economic and otherwise).

Humour

Having fun at work should be viewed as a natural part of the working environment. Work should not be viewed as a place of suffering or where you go just because you want to cover your bills. However, having fun starts with you and your attitude to being jovial can influence others into making work enjoyable. Unfortunately, the converse can also be true.

Are you a person that can bring joy/fun to others and to yourself?

The following pointers can be used to improve your ability to be more humorous:

- **Humility.** Do not take yourself so seriously. Whenever you realise a fault in your behaviour you could try to laugh out loud (do this in a quiet place though). Embrace it, understand how to change it, and move on. Whenever you receive constructive criticism, smile, and say thank you to the messenger and ask them for more feedback.

- **Take time out.** Before you go to work try taking some time out to think about positive events or something that has made you smile/laugh. Let us call this your happy place. Bring your happy place with you to work and engage with your colleagues in a jovial manner. You might need to take several time outs during the day depending on your situation.

- **Try relating humour to work situations.** Think about events that have taken place at work, whether they have involved you or not, and try and create a joke about the situation. All the usual caveats apply in that the joke should not be abusive, discriminatory, or offensive in any way or likely to breach your terms of employment. Use your sense of discernment to figure out who you can share your joke with.

- **Enrich your vocabulary and play with words**. Liven up your presentations and other communications by using a variety of language styles in a humorous manner. Being able to retain the attention of people using wit, good grasp of verbal and non-verbal communication helps to make people feel more relaxed and amenable to your humorous behaviour.

Creativity

Without creativity there would be no need to think. Creative people/organisations come up with new ideas/concepts. These ideas underpin so many aspects of our lives. Do you think you would have the internet had it not been for someone's creative thoughts?

Are you a creative person or do you facilitate creativity?

The following pointers can be used to improve your ability to be more creative or be facilitative of creativity:

- **Continuous self-development**. Things change and what might have been viewed as creative at one point might no longer be viewed as such given changing circumstances. Continuing to enhance your capacity to think creatively by attending courses/workshops and events as these will help the creative process.

- **Get to your happy place**. Although negative emotions can spur creativity it is more likely that people will be more creative when they are happy at what they are doing.

- **Humility**. If you are not facilitative when it comes to challenges to your points of view, you might find it difficult to learn and accept that you might be wrong on occasions. Being receptive to other people's ideas helps to open you up to possibilities that you might not have thought about which could enhance the creative process.

- **Take time to tune in to your inner thoughts and tune out noise**. Although being creative is a process it might not always be possible to blank out "noise" and concentrate on creative ideas. By noise, I mean anything that distracts you from being creative. You should try and find time and a place where you are able to focus.

- **Be expressive and use a variety of media**. Do not feel compelled to only express your thoughts in a limited number of ways. For example, use natural language, formal expressions (e.g. mathematics or Unified Modelling Language - UML in computer science), pictures, sound, or other notations to convey your thoughts.

- **Brainstorming**. Actively share and encourage others to share ideas, to challenge and to build links between concepts. The main idea is to encourage group thinking with a view to ensuring the creative process is more holistic and robust.

- **Ignore hierarchies and boundaries**. Creativity is increased when organisational leaders allow staff members (at any level and for any department) the freedom to make suggestions and develop ideas which can improve the standing of the organisation. So, for example, a person working in research and development should not be prevented from developing an idea for the marketing division if it can be shown to be an improvement on the status quo.

Mentoring

Many organisations do not have a formal mentoring program in place but somehow think that they are doing a great job at developing their staff. Mentoring can help to build capacity for the next generation of leaders and help maintain the sustainability of an organisation.

Are you someone that seeks to mentor others or desires to be a mentee? The following will aid you to be a better mentor/mentee:

- **Willing to listen/humility**. If you are not willing to listen or take instructions, then you will not make a good mentee. Being guided by those with better experience is an invaluable part of capacity building and can help you to avoid pitfalls. Note that I said, better and not necessarily longer experience. As a mentee it is not so much the length of experience that matters but the quality and diversity and its relevance to your requirements.

- **Empathy**. If you are empathetic then you can be sensitive to the style of mentoring that will be most beneficial to your mentee. Similarly, a mentee must be capable of being empathetic to the nuances of the mentor and determine how best to engage with them.

- **Good communications**. Being a good technical person or an organisational leader does not imply that you are able to effectively communicate to others what is required for them to be just as good. Knowing how to communicate is just as important as to what you communicate. Also knowing how to provide constructive feedback, whether you are the mentor or mentee, is fundamental.

- **Leading by example**. Being a good mentor involves showing mentees how to behave as well as how to undertake technical activities. Hence, being a mentor goes beyond talking as well as simply using the mentee as a lackey.

- **Set realistic targets and measure development**. A good mentor can set realistic targets and measure the performance of their mentee on an objective basis. As a mentee, you need to be aware of what you can achieve well and your areas of weakness. Both mentor and mentee should have a commonly agreed set of objectives for the mentoring and when it will be completed by.

- **Trustworthy**. Trust is an essential element of being a mentor and mentee. A mentee needs to know that what is shared with a mentor is not discussed with those not needing to know. A mentor needs to know that the mentee can maintain confidentiality for matters that are for their ears only.

- **Self-development and relevancy of skills**. Just because you are senior in an organisation does not imply that your skills are relevant to mentoring. Mentors should ensure that their skills are relevant for the guidance they are required to give to mentees. Good mentors will continuously update their skills and experience rather than relying on dated achievements.

Jesmyn Ward

Jesmyn Ward was born in Berkeley, California, USA and grew up in DeLisle, Mississippi. Ward graduated from Stanford where she obtained a BA in English and an MA in media studies and communication. Ward later went on to obtain an MFA in creative writing from the University of Michigan.

The joy of successfully completing both her master's degrees were marred by the tragic death of her brother in 2000 and the occurrence of hurricane Katrina in 2005. Those painful memories have helped to influence Ward's books which although based on fiction, paint a sense of reality for the characters and events depicted in her writings.

Jesmyn Ward has managed to capture the imagination of many people describing real situations based on fictional characters of life in the south of the USA for black people. Her varied use of language styles has made her books attractive and compelling reading for people of all backgrounds and race.

Jesmyn's writing skills has resulted in her being awarded the US National award for fiction not once but an unprecedented twice for a female. Although many of us may never attain the literacy skills of Jesmyn the workplace does require individuals (especially managers/supervisors and senior leaders) to have developed proficiency in communication to be able to effectively communicate with staff.

Have you ever exchanged emails with your boss and wondered whether they had fully understood your point of view? It might have been that you were at fault and so you went back through the chain and now you are convinced that you are not imagining things.

You start to reflect on other email exchanges and notice that this behaviour was there all along. In the emails, you see where your boss responds to your points either glibly or not at all. You talk to others and they relay similar experiences. If this situation has occurred in your organisation then, most likely, your boss has a problem with their written communication and perhaps other issues.

The learning point is that everyone is not the same and language styles must be varied to effectively communicate with people of different backgrounds and needs. Without effective communication it is highly likely that the wrong message will be conveyed which could demoralise staff and erode commitment and productivity.

Communication

Communications in an organisation is like the flow of blood through the human body. Poor communications can lead to all types of problems, but an effective communicator can revive and sustain peoples commitment in working for the best interests of an organisation.

Are you a good communicator? In a later chapter, this subject is discussed in more detail and a list of things you can do to improve your communication skills are detailed, few of which are highlighted here:

- **Listening.** To be a good communicator you need to be able to listen to what people are saying and it is a little difficult to do this if you are someone that likes to speak over others. Responding effectively to people requires you to have heard them in the first place.

- **Variety of styles.** Everyone is not receptive to the same learning style and some might respond better to pictures than words, for example. As an effective communicator you should have a variety of styles that you can use to get your message across including the use of non-verbal communication.

- **Humility.** Being genuine and humble are endearing factors which helps to enhance your authenticity as an effective communicator.

Ann McKee

Ann McKee was born in Appleton, Wisconsin, USA. McKee graduated from the university of Wisconsin and Case Western Reserve University School of Medicine with her bachelor's and medical degree, respectively. McKee is currently the director of neuropathology for a group of hospitals run by the United States Department of Veterans Affairs in Greater Boston and a professor of medicine at Boston University.

McKee's early career saw her switch from internal medicine to neurology and then to neuropathology in which she has a key focus on neurodegenerative diseases. In this latter respect, McKee has spent decades studying the brain of those subject to head trauma or had been actively involved in combat sports. Although McKee had made several important findings, over the years, it was not until more recently that her work has began to receive national and international commercial significance.

Based on research conducted from 2008 McKee found similarities in the formation of a disease known as chronic traumatic encephalopathy (CTE) in several former national football league (NFL) players. A similar pattern was found in the brains of other persons involved in combat sports and those affected by head trauma. The implication being that some combat sports can eventually lead to athletes suffering from CTE. You can imagine the commercial/financial consequences of this if people start to shy away from such sports due to its potential dangers.

Ann McKee can be described as tenacious. Even in the face of fierce opposition to her work (from other scientists and the American National Football League, in particular) McKee has persisted in her research of the links between sports injuries and degenerative brain disease.

McKee could have decided to give up her research and continue as a well-respected academic or move to a different field of research. However, her conviction was not to waver, and this has led to ground-breaking research in pursuit of having an earlier detection system for the disease CTE. For this, Dr McKee has since received recognition worldwide for her work.

The opposite of someone that is tenacious is someone that is fickle or indecisive. Have you ever worked for someone who seems to change their mind so frequently they end up confusing themselves as well as others? I once worked for someone that cared more about aligning herself to whatever was the flavour of the day for the CEO for fear "her department" would be marginalised otherwise. The consequence of this flip flopping was to cause increased uncertainty regarding the job security for staff members, reduced morale, and increased levels of stress. I suspect that the CEO saw this wavering trait as a frailty and not a strength of my ex-boss.

The point is that, sometimes as a leader, you should be prepared to accept criticisms, be exposed to uncertainty, and not liked. However, remain true to yourself and work tenaciously to achieve your objectives.

As mentioned in an earlier chapter the rise of populism is, in part, due to the perception of voters that they are unable to trust traditional political organisations and politicians. However, the private sector is not immune to this "political" way of behaviour. In many private sector organisations, there will be numerous individuals who believe that the only/best way for them to succeed is to be a political animal. Often, this politicking comes at the expense of the loss of integrity in decision making and the vilification of those that seek the truth.

Dr McKee has relentlessly pursued the truth even when taking an alternative route might have been easier for her. You do not have to be a Christian like me to accept that seeking the truth and working in the interests of all is the morally right thing to do. In John chapter 8, verse 32 of the Bible, Jesus says: "the truth will set you free". The implication being that if you act on the truth then you are without blame.

The learning point here is that people who know better should do better and those that do not should seek to know. Knowing what is right and doing something else is likely to result in erosion of the reputation of an organisation by both internal and external stakeholders. This erosion could also quickly spread to the bottom line and hence sustainability of a firm.

Tenacity

Tenacity is the ability to persevere in the light of adversity, uncertainty and to adapt strategy, in the light of changing circumstances, to achieve long-term objectives. Without tenacity individuals and organisations fall into the trap of working hard but not smart.

Are you tenacious? Below are some pointers to aid your ability to be tenacious:

- **Plan**. Being tenacious requires that you have a longer-term objective/goal. To achieve your objectives/goals you will need to have a plan as to how you will move from where you are to a state when you have succeeded. For an organisation, this plan could be a strategic/operation plan. For an individual this could be your ambitions for your personal and/or professional life.

- **Embrace failure**. Being tenacious requires that you be capable of learning from and accepting your mistakes and not being put off by failure.

- **Embrace changes**. Being flexible/adaptable to incorporate changes in your strategy/plan to achieve your longer-term goals.

- **Driven**. Understanding the factors driving your long-term goals is important to knowing whether you are guided by fear or passion. Whatever is your driving force, regularly "checking in" to remind yourself of the reasons why you are striving to achieve your goals is vital. If you are not driven by fear or passion, perhaps you should be striving to achieve other goals.

- **Reality check**. Regularly seek advice from others on the viability of your plans and how you are going about it. As with all things, choose your counsel wisely, do not just ask the opinion of yes people but those that are likely to give a thoughtful and balanced opinion. Being willing to accept advice and incorporate inputs from others will enhance your tenacity.

- **Patience**. You have probably heard the saying "anything worth having is worth waiting for". Even in this technological/digital era, success does not always happen overnight and having the ability to be patient is essential.

Truth seeking/Integrity

It should be the objective of all people, whether in their personal or professional capacity to act in a truthful manner. This extends to the results of your work.

Are you someone that is truth seeking? Below are some tips to help you improve your ability to be truth seeking in your behaviour:

- **Lead by example**. By telling and showing people what you stand for, you are quite likely to get pulled up when you fall short of the mark. This is exactly the kind of feedback that you need to maintain your stance.

- **Humility**. Being open and able to accept your flaws provides the basis for you to be yourself and for others to accept you as you are.

- **Non-political**. By maintaining a professional approach and not giving way to playing politics.

- **Circle of influence**. By maintaining a positive circle of influence with others of integrity you reduce the likelihood of being subject to bad behaviour.

- **Technical abilities**. Quite often, people lie about their achievements and abilities. By continuing to improve your abilities you reduce the tendency to exaggerate your achievements.

- **Communication**. Improving the variety of communication styles and the range of your vocabulary puts you in a position to convey more effectively what you mean to people, reducing your likelihood of unintentional error.

- **Fairness**. People with integrity treat others fairly and are capable of being objective in their behaviour irrespective of whether they are relating to someone at their level (or above) or below.

Chloe Kim

Chloe Kim was born in Long Beach, California, USA. Kim is an athlete that competes as a snowboarder and has been World, Olympic, Youth Olympic and X Games champion in the halfpipe.

Kim started snowboarding at the age of 4 and became a member of the US snowboarding team in 2013. The following year Kim won silver in the superpipe at the X Games and has gone on to become the first person (under the age of 16) to have won two gold medals at an X Games in 2016. In the same year Kim became the first woman to achieve back-to-back 1080 spins in a snowboarding competition. She has become only the second person to have scored a perfect 100 points in a competitive snowboarding game.

Despite the above Kim went on to achieve even more success. In 2016 Kim won gold at the Winter Youth Olympic Games obtaining the highest score at the games and in 2018 became the youngest women to have won a gold medal at the Winter Olympics in the halfpipe.

The word excellent has become an overused word. As parents we use it to shower praise on our children even when we know that another word might be more appropriate. Similarly, we use it in the work context e.g. on the announcement of a better than expected earnings result.

Somehow, I believe that excellence is something that we should all be striving towards irrespective of our achievements to date. This means that excellence is never completely attained but our aim is to do at least as good as last time and better if possible. This is something that Chloe Kim knows quite well.

There are few sports personalities that have achieved as much as Chloe in such a relatively short period. Chloe has won gold medals at every significant level of her sport, including having achieved a perfect 100 points at the 2016 X Games a feat that only one other person had previously achieved. With all these achievements it would be easy for Chloe to become complacent and think of herself as having "reached excellence" and stop working as hard. However, we know this not to be the case as she still strives to be even better than before.

The learning point here is excellence achieved at one point in time does not make you excellent forever and the strive for excellence needs to be ongoing. Since one rarely achieves excellence in isolation it is important to recognise the role that others play in support of an individual's or organisation's growth. In the case of Chloe Kim, it would be her parents, coach and others providing technical, financial, moral, and other forms of guidance. Even if an organisation/individual achieves what may be termed excellence, if this is obtained at the expense/detriment of others then this can tarnish the reputation of the achiever. Where possible, the pursuit of excellence must be undertaken so that it is fair to all concerned.

Excellence

The pursuit of excellence is an ongoing process. Being excellent today does not imply that you will be excellent tomorrow.

Are you striving for excellence? Below are some pointers that can enhance your ability to be excellent:

- **Proficient**. To achieve excellence in a field you should attain a level of proficiency that evidences your ability to perform at a high level. Depending on the field, proficiency might be evidenced by qualifications, experience, achievements, or some other measure.

- **Confidence**. It is generally accepted that confidence in self is a strong motivator to achieving some goal. That goal being excellence, will require an individual to be highly motivated. Improvements in confidence can be achieved by one becoming more proficient and recognising that such an achievement can help to grow towards being excellent. Note that confidence here is predicated on there being improvements in skills or acknowledgement that skills are at an adequate level.

- **Willingness.** If you are not willing to strive for excellence, then it is less likely that you will achieve it. Being ready to go that extra mile to achieve success is a prerequisite to being excellent.

- **Coherent strategy**. Since striving for excellence is a process, a strategy is required for how you will get there. Such a strategy should be frequently simulated, and its strengths/weaknesses assessed. Once a strategy has been found wanting then it should be changed.

- **Perseverance & Tenacity**. Excellence does not happen overnight. Both perseverance and tenacity are required for a possibly long road ahead.

- **Humility**. Being able to acknowledge and act to improve your frailties is essential if you are to improve or maintain high levels of performance.

Further discussions

The factors I have highlighted for each of the influencers mentioned in this chapter exist in all of us. How we develop and use these factors will make the difference between whether we become distinguished and good leaders or just another name in a position of responsibility. Common to all the persons discussed is the fact that they displayed a burning desire to improve. They did not sit back on their laurels.

Good leaders/role models are rarely satisfied with success for the sake of it. As important is how success was achieved. They ask themselves questions such as: could we have improved on the process, have done it for less, have done it quicker etc.

"It's the economy stupid" was a mantra coined by Bill Clinton's election strategist, James Carville, in 1992 to stress the importance of the economy in the run up to the next general election. It was an excellent strategy as it resonated with voters and Clinton beat George H W Bush to the presidency in that same year. The following examples serve to illustrate the importance of adopting a variant of this mantra that I call "It's the process stupid".

It was a sunny day in Mexico City on June 22, 1986. England were playing Argentina in the quarter finals of the football world cup at the Estadio Azteca stadium. The captain of the teams were Peter Shilton and Diego Maradona with a height of 1.83 and 1.65 metres, respectively. Shilton was a goalkeeper and Maradona a forward.

The first goal scored by Maradona will go down as one of the most controversial goals in football history and has come to be known as the "Hand of God". The goal was scored after 51 minutes when Maradona appeared to rise above Shilton to head a badly miscued clearance, from an England player, into the back of the England goal.

The England players immediately complained to the referee as they believed Maradona had not headed the ball but used his hands (in fact the outside of his left hand) to score the goal. Notwithstanding their dissent, the goal was awarded by the referee.

During the game, video footage clearly show that Maradona had used his hands to score the goal. If this was all there was to the story, then you can be forgiven for thinking that this was an error on the part of the referee and recall that video replay was not available to referees at that time.

The real story here is that Maradona knew that he had not scored the goal with his head and his subsequent TV interviews makes this quite clear. He had the opportunity to speak to the referee and tell him that it was not a goal but instead he chose to celebrate. Although Maradona's second goal will go down as one of the best in history, the earlier goal set the tone for how the match will be remembered for an exceedingly long time. Yes, Argentina won the game, however, how they won was not fair to all concerned and to many the end did not justify the means.

"Ba da ba ba ba I'm lovin it" has become a familiar tune to many people around the world and has been the jingle for McDonald's for several years.

It is well known that prior to the Justine Timberlake/Pharrell collaboration, the company was not performing so well. In fact, the share price bottomed at under United States $14 a share in 2003. However, following the global marketing campaign, along with its new jingle, the share price rose to over $125 during the month of April 2016.

The significance of that month was marked by the announcement of the UK labour party that it would not be inviting McDonald's to have an informational stand at the party's conference in September. Rumours abound as to the reason, but it was felt that McDonald's had fallen short in relation to the adequacy of workers' rights.

Was the labour party stance a matter of personal taste or was it based on some more objectively viable grounds? Based on a survey, conducted by job website Glassdoor in 2015, McDonald's came last in the ranking of the top 10 food chains in the UK. Key reasons for the poor rating appeared to be salary, management and issues related to culture and work/life balance. The labour party could have been motivated by these findings coupled with its desire that organisations have good relations with unions. This latter aspect seemed to be an issue with McDonald's globally.

Although the general trend of the share price for McDonald's has been on the rise, it appears that there are issues over business practices which question the integrity of the firm's corporate social responsibility frameworks. From a financial point of view, the firm is doing quite well but do the ends justify the means? Many advocates for sustainable and ethical practices would seriously question whether it does, and this will, inevitably, start to impact its share price sooner than later.

Further reading

1. TIME (2018), *Time 100 List of World's Most Influential People,* TIME Inc.,, Viewed September 3, 2020, <https://time.com/5245849/time-100-2018-editor-letter/>
2. Hogan, M (2016), *The Contentious Tale of the McDonald's "I'm Lovin' It,* Pitchfork, viewed September 3, 2020, <https://pitchfork.com/thepitch/1227-the-contentious-tale-of-the-mcdonalds-im-lovin-it-jingle/>
3. Wikipedia (2020), *Issa Rae,* Wikimedia Foundation, viewed September 3, 2020, <https://en.wikipedia.org/wiki/Issa_Rae>
4. Wikipedia (2020), *Chloe Kim,* Wikimedia Foundation, viewed September 3, 2020 <https://en.wikipedia.org/wiki/Chloe_Kim>
5. Wikipedia (2020), *Ann McKee,* Wikimedia Foundation, viewed September 3, 2020 <https://en.wikipedia.org/wiki/Ann_McKee>
6. Wikipedia (2020), *Jesmyn Ward,* Wikimedia Foundation, viewed September 3, 2020, <https://en.wikipedia.org/wiki/Jesmyn_Ward>
7. Wikipedia (2020), *Kenneth Frazier,* Wikimedia Foundation, viewed September 3, 2020 , <https://en.wikipedia.org/wiki/Kenneth_Frazier>
8. Wikipedia (2020), *Satya Nadella,* Wikimedia Foundation, viewed September 3, 2020 , <https://en.wikipedia.org/wiki/Satya_Nadella>
9. Wikipedia (2020), *Tarana Burke,* Wikimedia Foundation, Accessed September 3, 2020 , <https://en.wikipedia.org/wiki/Tarana_Burke>
10. Adams, R. (2013), *The Art of Persistence - The Simple Secrets to Long-Term Success,* CreateSpace Independent Pub
11. Chodron, P. (2016), *When Things Fall Apart: Heart Advice for Difficult Times,* Shambhala Pub
12. Brown, B. (2018), *Dare to Lead: Brave Work. Tough Conversations. Whole Hearts,* Vermillion Pub
13. Baldoni, J. (2008), *Lead by Example: 50 Ways Great Leaders Inspire Results,* Amacom Pub
14. Thomas, G. (2019), *The Inspirational Leader: Inspire Your Team To Believe In The Impossible,* Independtly Published
15. Schein, E. (2018), *Humble Leadership: The Power of Relationships, Openness, and Trust,* Berrett-Koehler Pub
16. Sloane, P. (2007), *The Innovative Leader: How to Inspire Your Team and Drive Creativity,* Kogan Page Pub
17. Westfall, C. (2018), *Leadership Language: Using Authentic Communication to Drive Results,* Wiley Pub

18. Eich, R. (2015), *Truth, Trust +Tenacity: How Ordinary People Become Extraordinary Leaders,* CreateSpace Independent Pub

Chapter 10

Leadership in digital era

Introduction
Technology maturity model
Elimination of jobs
Competition
Managing risks
Productivity
Being nimble
CSR
Remote working
Talent management
Building knowledge assets
Connected working
Further reading

Introduction

Leadership has traditionally been viewed from the perspective of influencing, motivating, and guiding the work of others and organisations.

In an era where technology is playing an ever-increasing role in influencing people both inside and outside of organisations do we need to modify our view of the term leader? For example, does a leader need to be much more technologically savvy?

With a view to answering the above questions I have produced a list of the key impacts the digital era has and continues to have on organisations. These impacts form the basis for the kind of thinking and analysis required to be undertaken by organisations (specifically its leaders) when considering the use of technology to support business operations:

- Elimination of jobs involving tasks which are easily automated
- Increased competition including the presence of developing economies in the global value chain
- Increased reliance on the management of technology risks
- Significant improvement in productivity levels
- Frequent need to adapt products/services to the changing requirements of client demands and pressure points due to competition, regulators/legal (or social and environmental) environment and obsolescence
- Need to adapt corporate governance policies to address matters related to corporate social responsibility- CSR and Reputational issues
- Facilitate for remote working
- Facilitate for the acquisition of technology experts and create a continuous learning environment for all staff
- Increased the necessity for capturing the knowledge assets within organisations as well as the process and workflows for transforming data into knowledge
- Increased the necessity for more real-time communication, closer inter-departmental working and faster decision making

It seems evident that the above impacts require leadership focus and decision making at various levels of an organisation. Employing traditional management approaches to technology challenges/opportunities is unlikely to result in success for most and in many cases will erode shareholder and wider stakeholder value. What is required is an informed understanding of technology and how its embedding in an organisation can help to improve its sustainable competitive advantage.

In the following I will take each of the above impacts and describe its implications on an organisation and detail leadership characteristics that can aid in maximising its positive potential. As a precursor, I introduce and discuss the application of a technology maturity model.

Technology maturity model

I have given training courses to thousands of people around the world. One thing I can tell you is this, whenever I have sent out a questionnaire asking people if they are proficient in Microsoft Excel, Word or other applications, most people say they are either intermediate or advanced. Some are at these levels but there are many that do not know the level of their capabilities.

In order to assist leaders and organisations determine their technological level of maturity, I have developed a model. The technology leadership capability maturity model (TLCMM) which provides a means of assessing the strength of an individual/organisation's technological capabilities. In this model scores are allocated based on the extent to which there is evidence to support the strength of abilities. Scores can take a value between 1 and 5, where 1 is lowest and 5 is highest indicating weak/strong skills, respectively. The scores are interpreted in the following manner:

Scores	Definition	Interpretation
1	Unaware	Little or no evidence of either knowledge of or demonstration of abilities.
2	Nascent	Some evidence of knowledge/abilities but these are inconsistently applied or just at a superficial level and the impact is localised (i.e. not benefiting a wide class of persons) not resulting in any appreciable improvement in operations.

Scores	Definition	Interpretation
3	Functional	Evidence of knowledge/abilities which are applied at more than a superficial level. However, knowledge/abilities are not frequently updated and benchmarked against recognised standards and/or through formal training. Knowledge/abilities are used to occasionally challenge current modes of operation. However, this does not often translate into changes to business processes and has little impact on achieving efficient collaboration with others or satisfying wider stakeholder objectives.
4	Adaptive	Evidence of knowledge/abilities consistently applied. Skills are frequently updated and/or benchmarked against recognised standards. Evidence that skills are used in conjunction with self-reflection to challenge oneself, the status quo as well as to aid and influence others. Continuous improvement in the application of skills has not yet been obtained but business processes are responsive to changes in technology or practices.
5	Excellent	Consistent demonstration of knowledge/abilities for development of self and others where skills are benchmarked against recognised standards. Continuous improvement in the way in which you/organisation apply skills for your/organisations benefit. Likely early adopter of technology or practices and seamlessly integrating it into business/operating model and resulting in efficient collaborative business processes.

The maturity model can also be used visually as shown below:

Unaware 1 → Nascent 2 → Functional 3 → Adaptive 4 → Excellent 5

It should be the objective of all leaders/organisations to get to level 5 of the maturity model. My experience is that most are at the nascent to functional level and do not have a clear strategy as to how they will effectively transition to a higher level.

There are organisations/individuals at level 5 and similarly those at level 1. I have come across organisations that have slipped from a high level, such as a 4 to 3. A key point to bear in mind is that all skills need maintaining and care should be taken to ensure that complacency does not set in.

The TLCMM can be applied for each of the technology impact areas subsequently discussed in this chapter. The discipline of assessing the maturity of leadership should help to focus leader's attention on the areas required to maintain/upgrade skills/abilities.

Elimination of jobs

There have been various degrees of automation dating from hundreds of years BC to the present day. An example of this is the windmill (dating back to that used by the Persians in AD 500-900) which was traditionally used to mill grain and pump water. Prior to this, these activities were largely undertaken by humans with the use of various implements.

Today, amongst other things, the concept of a windmill makes use of turbines for converting wind power into electricity. One thing remains constant is the concern people raise relating to their fears resulting from the introduction of automation. It is true that automation has resulted in loss of jobs, as did the introduction of the windmill, but they have also created opportunities and it is these opportunities those affected should try and use to their advantage.

In an office context, society has witnessed the introduction of portable computers, local and wide area networks which have facilitated for the "instantaneous" delivery of communications from one location to another that might be in another country. No doubt, this has had an impact on traditional postal services.

Office software such as Microsoft Office and similar products has significantly reduced the need to employ staff purely to undertake clerical activities.

These tasks are generally viewed as being routine or repetitive and quite easily automated. However, Big Data, Artificial Intelligence (AI), Robotics and the Internet of Things (IOT) make it likely that non-routine, complex tasks can also be automated.

There are relatively few areas where technology will not have an impact going forward. It is even happening in football. The video assistant referee system (VAR) is a piece of software that aids a match official (i.e. another referee sitting in a room) to review the decisions of the referee on the playing field. Here the VAR system has not replaced the field referee but is used to aid in the decision making. As far as I am aware, use of the system has not affected the pay of the referee or the hours she/he works.

In making decisions, related to the introduction of automation, there are several factors that should be taken into consideration. I have found the following to be key:

➢ The expected economic benefit of automation. This would include analysis of the financial costs and benefits, internal rate of return (IRR), net present value (NPV), payback periods and other financial measures.

➢ The expected internal impact on staff morale and wider societal implications. Although automation might improve business processes it could also have potentially negative consequences in terms of how staff respond to the change. Such changes could also have wider social impact if job losses disproportionately affect a region.

➢ Expected organisational changes both human and business/operational processes. Almost surely the introduction of automation will involve some modification to how existing processes are undertaken. Such changes might require new/revision to existing roles including documentation of new processes.

➢ Capacity building required of staff members to effectively make use of the technology. It cannot be assumed that staff members will have the requisite skills to be able to effectively make use of the technology. Some estimate of the type of training requirements should be undertaken prior to moving forward.

➢ Changes required at the board level (i.e. its constitution) and/or the nature of the flow of information to the board. Depending on the extent to which an organisation will be dependent on new technology it might be beneficial to make changes at the board level. For example, by providing training to board members or changing board committees (or members) to reflect a more technologically savvy composition.

➤ The means by which the organisation keeps abreast of technological changes and incorporates this into its business model. Technology as well as its use changes rapidly and an organisation should be able to assess the potential impact of obsolescence, upgrades and other changes on its business model when deciding on automation.

➤ The means by which the organisation will maintain inclusivity to ensure an equitable balance regarding gender, disability, or other protected categories of persons. It is possible that technology might have a disproportionate effect on one set of people over another e.g. females versus males, able bodied versus disabled. Analysis should be conducted, prior to deciding on automation, about these potential impacts.

A combination of the above factors could be used to determine the adequacy of employing automation. The weight applied to each factor is a matter of choice and can influence the outcome and what works for one industry might not work for another. However, I would encourage numerical values (or a scaling system) to be established for each factor. For example, you could consider a scale of 1 to 5 with 5 being the highest and 1 the lowest score. Minimum levels (or scores for each factor) could also be adopted beneath which the proposed automation might not be optimal.

As can be appreciated deciding whether to use automation in an organisation can involve several non-trivial and possibly interrelated activities. The impact is not necessarily confined to one part of a firm and can have significant impact on its culture. Such decision making requires leaders that have a firm grasp (or appreciation) of at least the following capabilities:

- Knowledge of the technologies to be employed.
- Ability to assess or appreciate how the operations of the organisation will change due to the introduction of the technology.
- Ability to influence change and empower others in the organisation to take on increased leadership responsibilities.
- Ability to assess the strategic implications of employing technology.

- Ability to assess or appreciate the wider social/environmental and reputational implications of employing technology.
- Ability to be sensitive to and assess the implications of technological change on diversity.

In 2019, the UK's office for national statistics (ONS) published analysis it undertook into the impact automation could have on the workforce in the coming years. They estimated that around 1.5 million workers in the UK were at risk of losing their jobs to automation. Those with the highest risk are women and those working part-time. Education, however, would appear to provide a partial means of hedging against this risk.

The ONS estimates that if your educational attainment was at the general certificate of secondary education (GCSE) or below your risk was 39% and it dropped to 1.2% if your education level was to degree standard. The statistics will be different in other countries, but the general message is likely to be the same.

One thing that should be clear from the above list of technical capabilities (as with others discussed later in this chapter and book) is that the required abilities to make the decision about automation might not be possessed by just one person.

This being the case, decision making should leverage the skills of a variety of different personnel whose skills meet the above capabilities. Even if the decision is to be made by a single person and you do possess the skills to do the required analysis it is always better to engage others to verify your work. This provides a signal to show that you value their expertise and opinion. This is an important step in demonstrating LA1 (empowerment) of the advocated leadership style discussed earlier.

Tesla - AI gone too far?

In 2018 analysts at Alliance Bernstein raised concerns over the amount of automation at Tesla. The concerns were, essentially, that Tesla could not justify its expenditure on attempting to automate much of its final assembly (i.e. putting parts into the shell of a car) in terms of cost benefit analysis.

The main source of Tesla's problem was automating the assembly of the many tens of thousands of parts required to be installed into the Model 3. The analysts claimed that not even the Japanese (arguably the world's best car makers) attempt to automate most aspects of assembly because it is not economically viable and can lead to degradation in quality. There is a feeling that Tesla has overestimated the capabilities of the AI technology being employed at the organisation as well as not having fully understood its implications on operations. In this respect, Tesla seems to have failed to demonstrate that they adequately possess the first two capabilities detailed above.

There is no doubt that Tesla's strategy of employing AI to automate much of the assembly process has cost the organisation considerable amounts of money and has led to many saying that the company is simply burning too much cash. However, this is clearly a strategy which comes from the top of the organisation, i.e. its senior leaders.

Drilling a little deeper into the organisation it appears that turnover at the executive level for people reporting directly to the CEO of Tesla, Elon Musk, is around 44% (within the last year, 2018-2019) according to analysts at Bernstein. Even prior to this period, turnover has been relatively high for Tesla for some time.

Some argue that the high turnover rate is a function of the unique nature of the segment that Tesla is in as well as the high demands placed on leaders by its CEO. My argument is given the clear technology challenges faced by the company, its lack of sustained profitability and high executive staff churn rate suggests that there are several other capabilities (listed above) that are not as effective as they could be. The relatively high level of turnover raises questions about Musk's ability to effectively influence people and build a cohesive team.

Musk has made several comments which had adversely affected the company's share price and dented its reputation. Recall, for example, the disparaging comment he made about one of the Thai cave rescuers. That individual brought an unsuccessful lawsuit against Elon Musk, but the company has likely alienated some potential customers. Also recall the time when Musk smoked marijuana during a live podcast interview. On both occasions, the share price suffered.

Some have described Elon Musk as visionary, a champion for innovation and creativity. However, whilst these characteristics are necessary, they are not enough to guarantee excellent leadership in this technological era.

Competition

The increased use of technology has enabled a much more level playing field for those in developed and developing economies to partake in its application. For example, once an individual can get access to the internet they are able to utilise a myriad of free and/or paid services to learn how to write software code and to develop and deploy technology applications which can be used by individuals located anywhere in the world. Although access to reliable internet service might vary with location, once available, an individual is limited only by their imagination.

For the above reason, developing economies are increasingly becoming part of the global value chain in which individuals/organisations are providing services to support products/services initiated in more developed countries. Beyond this, developing economies are also using technology to rival those produced in more developed economies thus increasing competition within developed markets.

A simple conclusion that can be drawn from these observations is that technology has made geographic boundaries less relevant in determining what might be considered a local or foreign resource or competitor.

Below are some of the factors that you should consider relating to competition from a technology perspective:

➢ Who are your firm's main competitors, where are they located and how do they compete? Knowing who your competitors are, where they are located and compete provides a leader with information that they can use to perform better against their rivals. Not knowing who your main rivals are or making assumptions which cannot be substantiated is a recipe for disaster. If you fail to prepare for the competition, you are competing to fail.

➢ How does the profit margin (or other suitable metric for your industry) of technologically superior organisations compare to yours and the industry average? One way to measure the success of your leadership is to compare the results of standard industry metrics across your main competitors. If you are a leader in an organisation in which what you produce is not a direct good/service offered by you firm (i.e. you provide inputs into other services/goods in your firm) then you should try and find the equivalent metrics. Note however, that this might be a little difficult without inside knowledge about your main competitors' internal operations.

- If possible, determine how the reputation of those organisations technologically superior to yours compare to your institution. This could be achieved by analysing externally available information such as social media and other content to assess what people are saying about them. Other measures could include analysis of share price changes, volatility in the number of members/subscribers or movements in credit rating.

- If possible, compare the organisational structure of those technologically superior firms to your own and assess the implications of the differences. Obtaining a copy of the organisational chart should not be too much of an issue for those entities that practice good corporate governance and, quite often, can be downloaded from their website. Issues arise, however, when the chart is too high-level or is not available.

Some of the key capabilities required to be able to incorporate the above factors into decision making require:

- Ability to understand and apply strategic analysis in assessing the competitive advantage of an organisation.

- Ability to be self-reflecting, analytical, and objective in assessing one's own performance and those of others.

- Ability to assess business practices on reputation of an organisation.

- Ability to assess the implications of organisational structure and its impact on performance.

As an example of the impact of technology on competitiveness, consider the world of climate change advocacy. Climate advocacy has traditionally been dominated by well-known environmental and other larger institutions such as Greenpeace and the United Nations, respectively.

However, use of social media platforms has enabled new institutions and individuals to quickly amass large numbers of followers with considerably less costs than traditional brick and mortar organisations. Unlike traditional organisations that work top-down to deliver advocacy via way of policy guides for governments or publish technical papers, digital competitors being more flexible and radical can get their message out more quickly and engage in collective action having a more immediate impact.

Examples of this new type of advocacy have been around for a little while but recent examples include the UK movement, Extinction Rebellion, and the activist Greta Thunberg. What some non-governmental organisations (NGOs) might not be aware of is that both Rebellion and Thunberg are directly competing with their traditional mode of operation and it seems, they are winning. The fact that small organisations and individuals can have a voice through social media means that advocacy organisations can no longer rely on their traditional models to remain relevant and sustainable. Their competitors are, potentially, everywhere.

As an example of the impact of the digital era on wholesale and retail consumer spending consider the Chinese company Alibaba. Alibaba's AliExpress platform enables Chinese Small and Medium-Sized Enterprises (SMEs) to sell their goods to over 150 countries either to other businesses or directly to consumers. The platform, therefore, facilitates for SMEs from this emerging economy to partake in the value chain of companies around the world.

Managing risks

Just because we live in a technological era does not mean that things cannot go wrong. Sometimes technology fails when you least expect it which is why it is vital to have a risk management process in place to manage failures associated with the use of technology.

There are numerous types of technology risks including cyber-attacks, denial of service, loss of data and hardware and software crashes. Effective management of these risks requires a comprehensive risk policy and procedures framework employed across the whole enterprise. Although it is beyond the scope of this book to provide detailed guidance on the contents of such a policy it is expected that leaders will reflect on the following main factors:

- ➢ Identification of critical systems. These are systems which provide information on which strategic and/or management decisions are based and/or are communicated to external stakeholders. These systems lie at the heart of an organisation and its failure could cause significant delays in business operations and/or material losses. Depending on the type of organisation different type of systems will be classified as being critical. For example, although the performance management application might be viewed as important for an organisation that uses a software tool to control a nuclear power plant it is this control and not the management system that would be classed as critical.

- Frequency and means by which data on critical systems will be backed-up and business continuity in the eventuality of a major failure. A rule of thumb, in relation to the frequency, is how long it would take to recover business following a failure. For example, if recovery of business can be implemented irrespective of whether data is backed up daily or every five minutes then there might be no advantage to doing it every five minutes since this might come at additional cost.

- Means by which legitimate users of technology will be identified and any restrictions on their access. Similarly, how unauthorised users will be prohibited and reported. Many risks to the use of software technology arise from those that have access to the system and having a means of restricting access provides the opportunity to mitigate potential risks.

- Means by which malware, spyware or other malicious activity will be prevented, detected, and cured. Cyber-attacks are increasingly undertaken by individuals outside of the organisation using other software to make the attacks. As such it would be useful to have an automated means of detecting these types of dangers e.g. use of tools like Norton, McAfee etc.

- The organisational structure for the direct management of technology risks and the roles and responsibilities of other individuals in reporting and managing risks. Leaders should recognise that the management of technology risks will be an ongoing activity and an organisational approach will improve the chances of reducing risks. Such a structure would clarify the roles of dedicated Information Technology (IT) teams versus the role of other users.

- The type, level of competency and frequency of training provided to staff on the management of technology risks. Depending on the type of technology risk, the need for training might exist in aiding staff members to better identify, mitigate, and cure risks.

- The means by which remote working will be facilitated. Better organisational leaders are, increasingly, becoming aware of the importance of understanding and facilitating the well-being of its staff members. Remote working has become one means by which this well-being is recognised using technology allowing users access to an entity's email, servers, and other applications. However, using technology to facilitate remote working poses risks and leaders should be aware as to how such risks can be managed.

Some of the key leadership capabilities required to be able to incorporate the above factors into decision making require:

- Technical knowledge of risk management principles and practice in general and how technology risk management can be incorporated into an organisation's wider enterprise risk management framework.

- Technical knowledge of current and emerging technologies that could be employed in the organisation and their potential weaknesses.

- Understanding of the "enterprise value" of data to the organisation across the varied systems employed. By enterprise value I mean the importance of the impact the data has for the firm. Some considerations include how easy it is to recreate the data, whether the data is sent to an external party/stakeholder, if the data is unavailable and/or incorrect whether there are any direct costs (e.g. fines), loss of reputation and the level of confidentiality of the data.

- Understanding as to how to assign roles/responsibilities of users in software systems and how this impacts their work.

- Understanding of the human factors/well-being issues associated with the use of technology.

- Understanding as to how to assess the financial and reputational impact of system failures on effective business continuity.

At some point in your life you are likely to have some relationship with the

Equifax company. Equifax is a consumer credit reporting agency and collects data on over 800 million persons and tens of millions of companies worldwide.

In or around May 2017 through July 2017 the company was subject to unauthorised data access. The breach was detected on July 29 but only reported on September 7 of the same year. The breach affected at least 145 million U.S. consumers. As a result of the breach, Equifax could pay up to US $700 million in fines and penalties.

The severity of the fines imposed on Equifax sends a signal that the integrity of third-party data is of paramount importance to regulatory bodies and those to which the data refers. There was, evidently, a lack of adequate risk management controls in place, poor corporate governance, and corporate social responsibility. In effect, the data breach exposed the poor quality of leadership at Equifax.

Less devastating but as embarrassing is the recent hacking of the Twitter account of Twitter's CEO Jack Dorsey. The relatively simple hack was the second in less than 4 years for the CEO and demonstrates that even highly sophisticated technology companies are not immune to technology threats.

Example technology risk management

Nikolas is head of retail banking at a mid-sized bank. A top agenda, for Nikolas, is to introduce a new digital banking application (app) to keep pace with the ever-changing nature of retail banking. The business requirements for the app have been documented and communicated to the different divisions including IT whose job it is to develop the app. Nikolas is pushing for the app to be launched within 15 months and has developed his business strategy based on this assumption.

The mobile app will contain a host of new features geared at enhancing the customer experience. It is expected that this will contribute towards both retention and acquisition of new customers. The risk management team have concerns about the timing of the launch. They believe it could compromise the bank's ability to properly ensure the integrity of potential security loopholes in the app in that there would not be enough time to develop and thoroughly test these features.

The risk team have been pushing for the integration of various enhanced risk mitigating features, but the IT team (headed up by James) have been pushing back saying that they do not have time to include anything beyond the standard security components and have a hard timeline set by the business. The head of the risk management division, Eric, is not amused and has informed Nikolas that he is not prepared to sign off on the app unless he can be assured that the app can pass various tests related to identity theft as well as others.

Nikolas is adamant that any losses incurred because of security breaches would be covered by the additional revenue obtained from new customers and that the app launch should not be delayed. Moreover, he does not believe the likelihood is high that there will be significant breaches.

If you were the boss of Nikolas and Eric, or a management consultant, how would you advise them to proceed?

The above example relates to experiences I have come across so I will give you the benefit of my approach. The first thing I would do is to get a better understanding of the specific security/cyber-attacks Eric's team would want to test.

I would ask them to describe the means by which such threats could be realised and ask them to assess the likelihood of occurrence for each such threat considering the proposed architecture supporting the app as well as the app features. I would then ask Nikolas to assess the potential loss given the occurrence of each threat. In either case, I would ask for justification (e.g. based on past losses for the bank or industry wide) of these likelihoods and potential loss figures to assess their reasonableness.

I would then ask the head of IT, James, as to which controls, they have implemented that will mitigate against the potential risks identified by Eric. Having assessed these controls, the likelihoods and/or potential losses would be revised to reflect the impact of these controls. Given the revised likelihoods and loss amounts a risk matrix of potential expected losses can be derived and used as a basis for assessing the financial impact of threats.

The approach I have highlighted above is standard in the field of risk management and should form part of the risk assessment process for all types of institutions.

Going back to the banking example, the result of a risk process has revealed that there are several high-likelihood, high-loss scenarios that could occur. Under these circumstances it would make sense to delay the launch if the expected losses exceeded the expected gains. This would be a rational basis for making this decision. However, in the world of retail banking, despite regulations, it appears that many banks produce apps which do not address even the simplest of security breaches. This is an indication of poor governance and, ultimately, leadership.

Productivity

Do you have any doubts that technology can and has significantly improved productivity in all countries and organisations? Although it might seem as if WhatsApp, Email servers and the internet have been around for a lifetime it has only been fifty years since the first computer-to-computer link and thirty years from the "birth" of the World Wide Web.

Imagine the ease with which people can arrange work or social meetings today or instantaneously share documents, pictures, and other forms of communication. These advancements along with automation have significantly transformed our lives to the extent where what previously would have taken hours can now take seconds. This impact on organisations/society force us to adapt to a new way of thinking and behaviour. Those that are nimble enough will gain the full benefits of what technology has to offer but those that are laggards are likely to quickly lose out.

Some of the factors that should be taken into consideration when assessing productivity improvements of employing technology are:

➢ Expected lifetime of technology. As we know, technology changes frequently and decision makers should be cognisant of when likely disruptions might occur and when their technology might become obsolescent. Continued use of obsolescent technology could lead to reduced productivity compared to peer organisations especially if these entities have adapted to the changing environment.

➢ Operational changes. Knowing which aspects of operational activities are to be supported by technology and the impact it will have on workflows.

The introduction of technology, most likely, will have an impact on an organisation's workflow. Almost surely, one impact will be to improve the speed with which a certain activity can be undertaken, and one would expect its accuracy. However, there might be certain activities which are subject to human intervention (which have not been automated for various reasons) and are negatively impacted by the automation. Leaders should be fully aware of these potential impacts.

➤ Technical know-how. If employing the technology results in "new" ways of working that cannot be accommodated in the organisation, then it might not be possible to move forwards. In the Bible, Matthew 26, verse 41 states: "the spirit is willing, but the flesh is weak". Similarly, it might be that an organisation has the will to implement technological change, but its staff might not be capable of making the best of the change due to varying levels of technical deficiency. Hence assessing the technical skills required to both implement and work in the new technology environment should be undertaken as a precursor to implementing change.

➤ Cultural challenges. The culture of a firm can either be an enabler or inhibitor of change. Some of the best laid organisational plans have been thwarted by the prevailing culture of a firm. Hence being mindful of and incorporating the factors affecting current and prospective culture of the firm is a prerequisite to implementing technological change.

➤ Key performance measures. It really does not make much sense "embracing" the digital age if you have no idea as to how to measure the success/failure of your technology investments. It might come as a surprise to some readers however, but increased revenues are not necessarily a sufficient measure of the success of a digital transformation initiative. Irrespective of the measure, what is important is the extent to which any strategy chosen is sustainable. Hence it is possible that an organisation adopts a digital strategy which, in the short to medium term, results in appreciable increases in revenue but this alone might mask inefficiencies elsewhere in the overall strategy whose effect is to erode the longer-term sustainability of the firm.

Some of the key leadership capabilities required to be able to incorporate the above factors into decision making require:

- Up to date and detailed knowledge of technologies to be employed.

- Understanding of business process analysis and workflow design

- Understanding of agile methods of working including iterative process, continuous improvement, collaboration, and empowerment.

- Understanding of the existing skills of staff members, potential staffing requirements and timing, means by which staff can access training and potential review of compensation packages.

- Understanding as to how to assess the interrelationships between the various aspects of organizational culture in framing a strategy for the engagement of staff to improve the likelihood of success of implementing change

- Understanding of how to devise and measure key performance indicators which provide timely and reliable (and preferably predictive) estimates of success of strategy. Of note these measures should be designed in a manner which also maintains the sustainability of the firm.

Although an often-cited benefit of automation is improved productivity, there is growing evidence to suggest that some individuals are not coping with "always being on call". Concerns of having to respond to all emails/messages, to be part of all meetings and to collaborate on shared documents can result in stress, anxiety, and other mental health problems. Good leaders would be sensitive to this and try to ensure that performance measures also incorporate aspects of staff well-being. Examples of this vary but could include limiting staff remote access to work systems whilst they are on holiday, sick or beyond a certain time of day. These types of measures could be documented as part of an organisations policies and procedures.

Individuals also have a responsibility for managing their use of technology. For example, this could involve prioritising the emails/messages that you respond to or even open. You could use status features of emails/messaging systems to indicate that you are busy. Although you might still receive communication, it informs the sender that they might not get a response anytime soon.

Being nimble

Once a firm has successfully implemented technological change there is no need for further change until the technology becomes obsolescent right? Well no, as discussed earlier in this book, technology, and its use changes often and those that do not monitor and accommodate for this are likely to become laggards and potentially lose competitiveness.

Organisations need to be nimble to maintain pace with the changing requirements of their clients and wider society. Technology simply exacerbates the rate at which this nimbleness must be maintained. Prior to social media, consider how long it could take for a piece of negative or positive news to spread across the world. Unless such news made it into the most read newspapers, were broadcast on news programs as part of the widest network or numerous telephone calls were made it might take several days to weeks. Nowadays, within minutes such news can reach most parts of the world through social media.

One poor customer review can erode many years of goodwill in a matter of hours. Being able to quickly innovate and/or adapt to changing circumstances brought about using technology is fundamental to the success of any organisation and their leaders.

Some of the factors that should be taken into consideration when assessing nimbleness are:

- ➢ Culture. The type of culture the leaders of the firm are trying to create and whether this represents a marginal, moderate, or more significant change from the status quo. As discussed earlier, culture can play a big part in either enabling or impeding an organisation's ability to successfully implement change. Since a nimble organisation potentially requires frequent changes (note that these are not necessarily speaking about organisational structure changes) its culture must be conducive to such change, e.g. being responsive and flexible.

- ➢ Strategy. Whilst dealing with various short-term activities, leaders should also keep an eye on the longer-term goals i.e. strategy and assess whether this needs modification in the light of these activities. If an organisation is finding, on an ongoing basis, that it frequently needs to adapt its products/services and/or respond to client/regulatory pressures to such an extent where there is a significant divergence from strategy then it might be necessary to update the strategy to fall in line with business trends.

➢ Performance measures. Being nimble requires an organisation to be cognisant of events taking place both internally and external to a firm. Reliable key performance measures will provide a more real-time indicator as to the occurrence and nature of events occurring as well as providing an objective means of establishing personal performance goals.

Some of the key leadership capabilities required to be able to incorporate the above factors into decision making require:

- Ability to be able to understand the factors contributing to the culture of an organisation and devise strategies to engage staff in implementing change in a manner which is both rapid and potentially disruptive to the firm.

- Ability to assess the strategic impact of rapidly changing environments on the longer-term goals and objectives of the organisation.

- Ability to devise metrics that can be independently verified, measured, and monitored and used as a means of assessing firm/individual performance.

Can you imagine life without your digital camera? Well, in the 1970s the management at the greatest camera company in the world, Kodak, thought the idea of a digital camera to be "cute" but not economically viable. The funny thing is the first digital camera was invented by an engineer at Kodak and management's response to this technology clearly showed they did not understand its potential to disrupt the market and so, killed the idea. However, as we all know ideas do not just die, they simply get transformed into opportunities for an entrepreneurial person/organisation and this is what happened with digital camera technology. The rest as they say is history, Kodak remained entrenched into what it thought was its competitive advantage whilst the world was quickly moving on and this ultimately led to its demise.

At the time of writing this book and depending on which report or survey you read Nokia is ranked the 9th or 10th largest smart-phone maker globally having around 1% of the total market share. However, in the late 90's and early

2000s the company was the world leader. So, what happened?

Nokia was the first to market with a mobile network but was slow to realise and adapt to the potential of data rather than voice as the future of mobile communications. Their focus was on hardware rather than software and instead of being nimble, embracing the disruptive technology they choose to retrench to what they thought was their competitive advantage. Sounds familiar? Yes, just like Kodak, the market was moving away from them and they became a laggard.

Do you remember the company Toys R Us? This company was the go-to store for toys. Other companies such as Walmart were cheaper as was Amazon and the latter was making it easier for consumers to shop at their convenience via web and mobile apps. The problem was the management at Toys R Us were not enthusiastic about the use of online shopping. Their thinking was that they believed customers preferred the experience of shopping in a store and were reluctant to transition to use of digital technology.

They failed to make proper use of market data on the take up of digital technology and were not nimble enough to modify their business model prior to irreversible financial problems. Consequently, the company filed for Chapter 11 bankruptcy protection on September 18, 2017 in the US and subsequently other stores around the world have been affected.

I could talk about how poor the leadership was at Toys R Us, but I think this is self-evident. The leadership committed a cardinal sin in that they were not prepared to abandon a strategy that had made them money and positioned them as a leading player in the toy retailing sector. The problem was that the market was changing around them, and their retrenched strategy was no longer a competitive advantage. Good leadership would have identified this change in the marketplace and positioned the company accordingly so that its business model was more sustainable.

CSR

Corporate social responsibility has been associated with organisations for many years but has gained increasing prominence over the last twenty years largely due to high-profile corporate failures and scandals. CSR initiatives have moved from sponsoring the local football club and including a page or two in the annual report to full-blown policies integrated into strategy and business plans.

I gave an example of a CSR failure earlier in this book when I highlighted the BP scandal due to the oil spillage off the coast of Mexico. However, there have been many others such as Enron, Parmalat, Polly Peck and Lehman Brothers to name a few. Organisations are becoming aware that good CSR initiatives not only help to improve relations with a wider set of stakeholders but can lead to enhanced client loyalty, reduced revenue volatility and better overall financial performance.

Some of the factors that should be taken into consideration when assessing CSR implications of digital transformation are:

- Paper trail reduction. Consider the amount of paper that you or your organisation prints every day. Have you ever wondered how much of this could have been avoided by making enhanced use of electronic media? The use of hand-held devices and cloud technology facilitates for individuals to access documents anywhere and at any time. However, and perhaps most importantly, use of digital technology should require less trees being cut down. This in turn, helps in the fight against climate change and supports sustainability which benefits wider society.

- Improved well-being. The average working person in the UK is likely to be at work for at least eight hours and might travel at least an hour to work and back home each day. This is a significant amount of time either spent at work or doing work related activities and it might be that even when you get home you do not immediately switch off from work. Having the ability to work remotely will save lost time due to travel as well as saving energy costs at work and serves to support reductions in CO_2. Having the ability to work remotely is particularly important for those that either have temporary personal care needs or have a need to care for others. This serves to support improvements in the well-being of staff members.

- Energy smart. Do you work for an organisation that puts up signs saying, "please turn off the lights when not in use"? This is a signal that the organisation is taking their carbon footprint and energy utilisation seriously. However, a better approach would be to make use of smart technology (e.g. sensors) which automatically lower or switch off lights when no motion is detected and/or adjusts the heating/air conditioning in a similar manner.

- Stakeholder consultation. Do you get the impression that your organisation is blind (wilfully or otherwise) to the concerns raised by external and/or internal stakeholders? Well, it might be that your organisation is not making optimal use of social media and/or website blogs/emails to both solicit and respond to issues raised. Delays in responding to issues might be perceived as stonewalling or not taking the matter seriously. This, in turn, could lead to escalation and erosion of reputation. Hence making use of technology to effectively communicate with wider group of stakeholders will serve to support the reputation of your organisation.

- Strategy and business plans. In my experience, CSR initiatives tend to work better when they are not considered an adjunct to core activities but are integrated into the strategic and operational plans of an organisation. In everyday life when people see that what you say and what you do (even when you think people are not looking) are consistent then they tend to have more respect for you. It is the same when it comes to doing business. The organisational story becomes more believable when all aspects of saying and doing are integrated.

Some of the key leadership capabilities required to be able to incorporate the above factors into decision making require:

- Ability to understand and facilitate for automation of business workflows and activities.

- Understanding of well-being and how the organisation can make use of technology to support remote working and improve productivity.

- Understanding of how to best make use of ergonomics and technology to improve energy efficiency.

- Willingness and ability to facilitate for wider stakeholder engagement and receptiveness to implement change in the light of criticisms.

- Ability to assess environmental, social and governance related consequences of strategic and operational business choices.

I do not know about you, but when I travel on an airplane my expectation is that I am going to relax. Other than a smooth take-off and landing, I just want to rest. My expectation is that the staff will treat me with respect (you know give good customer service) and be welcoming of my feedback, or at least that is what they say.

Imagine that you are sitting on an airplane and eagerly awaiting its imminent departure. You then hear an airline official announce that several people must give up their seats to accommodate airline crew. Your name is announced, and you are asked to take your bags and leave the plane. What do you do? This was the situation facing Dr David Dao Duy Anh on April 9, 2017 whilst sitting on a United Airlines flight. He refused to get off the plane.

Much of the details of what happened next has been extensively documented in the media. Dr Dao suffered both mental and physical harm after being dragged off the plane. Had it not been for the video tapes of the incident, which were quickly uploaded on social media, it is debatable whether the airline would have admitted guilt.

The first response of the CEO was to praise his staff for doing such a good job and upholding the firm's policy/procedures as well as branding Dr Dao as "disruptive" and "belligerent". In subsequent interviews, following the responses on social media, the CEO changed his tune and became more conciliatory, admitting that the airline was wrong, and that Dr Dao did nothing wrong.

In attempting to put the interests of his company ahead of those of their customers, the CEO and ground staff lost sight of the primary reason why the company is in business. It is not in business to fly staff members from place A to place B but to serve the needs of its fee-paying customers. Given this lack of focus, their subsequent actions served to erode the reputation of the firm.

The negative press the airline received on social media could so easily have been better managed by having a more conciliatory and respectful tone. The timing of their responses could also have been better. All in all, the debacle showed clear evidence of a lack of an adequate crisis management process utilising social media technology.

Remote working

Some discussion regarding remote working has already taken place in this book. However, some key factors that should be taken into consideration when assessing remote working include:

> Organisational needs. Often, there will be a need for staff members to be physically present at work. However, there may be times when such staff could work from home without any loss to the firm. Organisations should identify opportunities for remote working for its staff members. Access to such opportunities should be clearly set forth in a policy/procedures document and should be seen to be fair to all concerned.

> Needs of employees. As previously discussed, there might be some members of staff that are either in need of care e.g. they are temporarily physically/mentally unwell and would benefit from working remotely. Similarly, those staff that have child or other family members to look after might also prefer more flexible working conditions. This said, others might also prefer remote working if that aids in their productivity and this should be accommodated by employers as far as possible.

> Available technology. If staff are unable to effectively communicate with colleagues or access work documents, whilst working remotely, then some of the perceived benefits are lost and such working might result in reduced rather than enhanced productivity.

> Organisational culture. Even if an organisation perceives that there is a benefit to remote working it might be that the culture of the firm makes it difficult to operationalise its use. For example, if remote working is at the discretion of supervisors/managers then it might be the case that some do not allow it since they want to be able to see staff working. This suggests a lack of trust of staff and/or appropriate outcome/output measures to monitor staff performance have not been developed.

Some of the key leadership capabilities required to be able to incorporate the above factors into decision making require:

- Ability to understand the well-being needs of employees and devise suitable solutions to accommodate those needs whilst also satisfying the legitimate business interests of the organisation.

- Knowledge of the capabilities of technology both inside and out of the organisation and how these might be utilised to facilitate remote working.

- Ability to understand and devise policies/procedures to influence change in organisational culture to bring about desired appetite to support remote working.

- Ability to trust and empower others to work to mutually agreed measures of outcome/output without micromanagement.

Surveys conducted by the office for national statistics and UK consulting companies show that an increasing number of people are working remotely in the UK and that within a few years this could amount to around 50% of the working population.

A key reason for this is that people are being more judicious when it comes to seeking job opportunities and are actively trying to maintain a more balanced work/life ratio. This is particularly the case for Millennials and Generation Z. Organisations which choose to ignore this trend do this at their peril. No doubt, the insights of remote working due to Covid-19 is likely to positively skew organisations towards more flexible forms of working.

Talent management

In this technological era is it business as usual in your organisation? If the answer to this question is yes you might belong to one of those organisations that have long embraced technological change and it now forms part of the DNA of your firm. However, one of the most common mistakes organisations make is to assume that they can undertake technology transformation in a manner without any real consideration given to technical know-how of staff members. Under such circumstances, although change might have occurred it might not be optimal.

With the increased use of AI and other technologies being incorporated into communication and business applications, it is becoming more important to ensure organisations have the right set of skills to maximise potential use of these technologies. Some of these skills will occur in the form of new talent to the organisation and additional capacity will be acquired by the upskilling of existing staff members.

Some of the key factors that should be taken into consideration when assessing human resource/talent management implications of digital transformation are:

➢ Adequacy of existing technical skill set. Imagine being given a brand-new Mercedes formula 1 car and asked to drive it around Silverstone. I dare say many people would love the opportunity of this challenge. However, suppose you were informed that your job and the success of your organisation depended on your ability to get the car around the track in 1 minute, 24.303 seconds. Are you still keen to take on the challenge? You would be well advised to hire the talent necessary to give you a fighting chance of success, wouldn't you? Organisations should assess the existing skills of staff members. This could be done, for example, by compiling a database of skills and determine where there are potential gaps and hence skills requirement which could be filled by new talent or upskilling of existing staff members.

➢ Adequacy of existing recruitment and retention. Technology has facilitated for radical changes in the way in which some industries recruit. For example, LinkedIn has provided a direct channel through which both employers and employees can directly interact with people/organisations matching their preferences. Organisations which have not embraced this type of approach to recruitment would be well advised to do so.

Having recruited talent, the next step is to use digitisation as a means of monitoring staff performance, engagement (e.g. occasional email and other correspondence) and record keeping. Finally, digitisation should be at the forefront of capacity building solutions to maintain/upgrade key skills and organisational competitiveness. Retention is key to most roles but particularly when it comes to hard to fill positions requiring deep technological knowledge. These individuals are likely to be in demand so ensuring that they can maintain their skills is important.

➢ Adequacy of existing line management skill set. Simply because your organisation has technical staff with the capabilities of understanding and leveraging the value of technology does not imply that management are able to maximise this potential. If management are not able to effect changes to organisational structures and rely more on data to drive decisions, then potential gains might be lost due to bureaucratic processes including self-preservation tactics. An example of this type of preservation tactic is refusal to share information and to work in a collaborative fashion and to reduce silos and hierarchies.

The key leadership capabilities required to be able to incorporate the above factors into decision making require:

- Ability to be self-reflective and strategic to be able to understand the weaknesses and strengths of yourself and organisation.

- Ability to devise organisational structures and performance measures that recognise the value of critical roles and high-performing individuals in a technologically driven organisation.

Building knowledge assets

If after having implemented technological transformation you still find yourself responding to requests to provide essentially the same data to different systems/people in your organisation, then something might have gone wrong.

Successful integrated technological change would have resulted in the capture of knowledge assets, i.e. commonly used data forming part of reports or analysis conducted on a periodic basis and relied on by several different parties either internal or external to the organisation. The key here is that those internal staff members needing access to such data should be able to see the same information that you can see and be able to use this in their reports/analysis.

The building of knowledge assets should identify and automate the capture of data/information that would otherwise be undertaken manually and/or used across several different applications. In this way business processes can be simplified, and staff time allocated to undertake higher-level/value work.

Some of the key factors that should be taken into consideration when assessing knowledge asset implications of digital transformation are:

- Criticality of data. There are no universally accepted definitions of data criticality, but my use of the term refers to data which if not produced or lost could cause material financial or reputational loss to the organisation. In general, data should be included in a knowledge asset database (or knowledge base) when it is determined that such data helps in the automation of business processes. This said, try to avoid building databases for information which is infrequently used as part of business processes and whose value is not determined to be critical.

- Users and use of data. Attention should be paid to who will be the users of the data captured and whether such data will require transformation or incorporated with other data, analysed, and then presented to users. In the case where data is required to be further processed it might be necessary to have software code and/or database procedures written which undertakes such processing prior to users accessing data.

- Elimination of activities. A key focus of technology transformation is to improve business processes by automating activities which would otherwise be undertaken manually. Hence, identifying those activities that can be automated needs to be identified. Knowledge assets cannot be identified without knowing which parts of the existing business process is required to be automated.

- Workflow design. Without designing how knowledge assets are to be incorporated into revised business processes the utility of such assets might be compromised. In other words, the introduction of knowledge assets should result in a change in the way an organisation undertakes its activities. For example, the speed, accuracy, and security of activities involving data will be different and require people to work in different ways and new workflows/business processes will be required to accommodate these changes.

The key leadership capabilities required to be able to incorporate the above factors into decision making require:

- Ability to understand and apply business process modelling to identify data, its transmission and how it can be manipulated.

- Ability to understand technical details of specific technologies to be employed in the organisation.

- Ability to understand strategic and operational implications of employing technology and using this to adapt business processes so that they are integrated with the technology.

Connected working

An organisation that has successfully transformed to the digital era will have enhanced communication and workflow facilities over those that have not been so successful. In practice this should result in faster decision making, increased empowerment of individual workers, more seamless interworking between colleagues in different departments/locations (or regions) and less bureaucracy and management hierarchies.

Some of the key factors that should be taken into consideration when assessing connectivity implications of digital transformation are:

- Team area – non-designated desks. Organisations are increasingly adopting the practice of having designated team areas where teams sit in a vicinity but do not necessarily have fixed desks. This encourages individuals to move around the area and develop wider relationships. When coupled with technology enabling mobile/remote working it also enhances business continuity.

- Technology enabled meeting rooms. Organisations with embedded or mobile technology to facilitate Skype or another video conferencing type (including shared working on documents) can maintain connectivity between teams in different geographic locations. In designing the ergonomics of office layouts (specifically meeting rooms), therefore, an organisation should pay attention to incorporating technology to support connectivity of both temporary and more permanent remote workers.

- Staff consultation. Organisations that consult staff as to their preferences and take into consideration their well-being and training needs are likely to achieve a higher rate of success in the acceptability and use of technology.

- Security. Organisations must assess the extent to which intra-office and remote connections are safe and secure. Ultimately this will come down to a combination of automated controls for ensuring authenticity of users, data integrity etc. as well as documented procedures for users to follow when using technology.

The key leadership capabilities required to be able to incorporate the above factors into decision making require:

- Ability to understand how intra and inter-team dynamics can influence the ergonomics of office layout.

- Understanding of available technologies that can be used to facilitate remote sharing of documents and video conferencing.

- Understanding of the relationship between well-being and staff performance.

- Understanding of the appropriate levels of security required and offered by technologies to facilitate enhanced connectivity.

What should be clear from the above discussion is that there are numerous capabilities required to be a successful leader in this technological era. It should also be clear that no one person will possess all these requisite leadership capabilities and will require support from a team of individuals that collectively possess these skills. Leadership in the digital era should focus more on ways in which individuals can collaborate via the use of technology, empowerment of staff and support of their well-being with less emphasis on silos and hierarchies. Do you work for such an organisation? If not, you might want to consider making a change.

Further reading

1. Sekhar, C. (2018), *CAPITAL BUDGETING Decision methods: Payback period, Discounted payback period, Average rate of return, Net present value, Profitability index, IRR and Modified IRR*, Independently published
2. Schwartz, M. (2019), *War and Peace and It: Business Leadership, Technology ans Success in the Digital Age*, It Revolution Press Pub
3. Lopez, L. (2018), *The robots are killing Tesla*, Business Insider, viewed: October 6, 2019, <https://www.businessinsider.com/tesla-robots-are-killing-it-2018-3?r=UK&IR=T>
4. Assis, C. (2019), *Is Tesla's executive turnover really high? This analyst sets out to find the answer*, viewed on October 19, 2020, < https://www.marketwatch.com/story/is-teslas-executive-turnover-really-high-this-analyst-sets-out-to-find-the-answer-2019-08-14>
5. Brewster, T. (2019), *Equifax Just Got Fined Up To $700 Million For That Massive 2017 Hack, Forbes*, viewed October 6, 2020, < https://www.forbes.com/sites/thomasbrewster/2019/07/22/equifax-just-got-fined-up-to-700-million-for-that-massive-2017-hack/#3158cb133e96>
6. Mui, C. (2012), *How Kodak Failed*, Forbes, viewed October 6, 2020, < https://www.forbes.com/sites/chunkamui/2012/01/18/how-kodak-failed/#149529c66f27>
7. Knowledge@Wharton. (2018), *What Went Wrong: The Demise of Toys R Us*, Knowledge@Wharton, viewed October 6, 2020, < https://knowledge.wharton.upenn.edu/article/the-demise-of-toys-r-us/>
8. Baxter, H. (2017), *It doesn't matter what happened in David Dao's life – that can't justify what happened to him on United Airlines*, Independent, viewed October 6, 2020, < https://www.independent.co.uk/voices/united-airlines-doctor-david-dao-drugs-gay-sex-court-documents-oscar-munoz-a7680221.html>

Chapter 11
ABC of leadership

Introduction
A-Ability
B-Belief
Coherent strategy
Putting things together
Further reading

Introduction

The purpose of this chapter is to provide a simple approach to enhance your leadership style. I have developed this approach not because I think leadership is simple. In fact, I believe the factors influencing how people behave and interact with others to be multi-layered and quite complicated. However, I am of the view that the key principles are easy to understand and can be distilled through a relatively straightforward approach that I call the ABC of leadership.

As a way of motivating my approach I want to take you back, way back into time to 1974. On October 30, 1974, a man by the name of Muhammad Ali fought George Foreman for the title of undisputed heavy weight boxing champion of the world. Ali was 32 and Foreman 25 at the time they fought each other in Zaire. Both men were roughly the same height, but Foreman was a little heavier weighing 100 kg compared to Ali's 98 kg.

Ali had a record of 42 wins and 2 losses and Foreman had won all 40 of his fights. Foreman also had a larger number of wins by knock-out with 37 compared to Ali's 31.

Based on current form, there was no way that Foreman should have lost the fight to Ali. In particular, the two losses sustained by Ali were to men that Foreman had previously beat. So how did it happen? I am, like most people, not a sport's psychologist but I put Ali's win down to a simple A, B, C which I have observed in many other successful persons.

A-Ability

Muhammad Ali was a boxing phenomenon. He had won the gold medal at the Rome Olympics in 1960 (at the age of eighteen) and had become one of the best and most talked about fighters in living memory. His technical abilities were not in question.

By the time of the fight in Zaire, Ali had fought some of the most revered fighters such as Sonny Liston, Floyd Patterson, Ken Norton, and Joe Frazier.

What was particularly interesting about Ali was that he constantly reminded people of his boxing prowess. You might say what is interesting about that surely all boxers do that? The way Ali did it was different. He would not just remind people that he was a good boxer he told them that he was the greatest! He used psychology to play mind games with his opponent and to manipulate the press to his advantage. It was not that Ali was overconfident or arrogant, but he was very cognisant of his limitations/strengths and, importantly, those of his opponents.

Learning point 1

> **Be aware of who you are and what has contributed to your achievements so far.** Ali was aware of his technical abilities, i.e. his boxing skills. He was also aware that he possessed several soft skills e.g. communications and strategic thinking. He made the world aware that he was a Muslim and was unwavering in his integrity and pursuit of civil rights. Ali's strong sense of identity and self-awareness were contributory to the significant respect he earned from people around the world.

As surprising as it might seem, many people are not truly aware of who they are, what skills they have and what they stand for. Having a strong sense of identity and self-awareness helps to clarify who you are. Experience suggests that even if people don't agree with your philosophies, they tend to have more respect for you when they have a clear sense of what you stand for and that what you say is what you do.

Ali used his strengths to compensate for his weaknesses (relative to his opponent) but to also put doubt in the mind of his opponents about their ability to beat him. This is a trait of successful sports persons and is increasingly been adopted by the business world e.g. by way of marketing campaigns. An example of this can be seen in some of the Pepsi versus Coca-Cola advertisement wars which has resulted in PepsiCo eroding the early market share dominance of Coca-Cola.

Learning point 2

> **Be aware of your strengths and how they can compensate for your limitations/weaknesses.** Ali was aware of his boxing skills but was also

cognisant that he was several years older than his opponent who was on the rise compared to him. He was aware of Foreman's awesome power and dogged persistence to quickly knock-out his opponents. Ali was aware that it would take something special for him to win the fight. That special thing proved to be his communication skills and his ability to execute psychological warfare.

Simply put, Ali put fear in the mind of his opponents that they could beat him. He beat them mentally in and out of the ring and this would be George Foreman's fate.

Learning point 3

> **Be aware of your opponent's strengths and weaknesses and how these are manifested.** Ali was known to be very studious and prepared well for his fights including studying tapes of his opponent's fights. This helped him to determine the specific skills he needed to work on to either combat his opponent's strengths or expose their weaknesses.

In many instances, Ali would even predict the round in which he would win. He used his ability as an effective communicator to paint a picture of what his fights would look like. He was, essentially, marketing his boxing prowess not unlike how a corporate entity might market their capabilities. It worked, notwithstanding what some pundits might have thought about his chances, the people were on his side. By people, I mean the millions that wished they could have been there but could not attend. Even at the fight tens of thousands chanted "Ali boma ye, Ali boma ye" (meaning Ali Kill him, Ali Kill him).

Learning point 4

> **Create a wider appreciation of your abilities.** Ali was a shrewd businessman. He understood that boxing was how he was earning a living and that a fight well promoted could mean more earnings for him down the road. Ali not only got into the head of Foreman but was quickly adopted as the people's champion in what, at the time, would be the worlds most watched boxing fight. Ali used radio, TV, and other media to create a wider awareness of his appeal during the preparation for his fight. Along the way, no doubt he would have received many boxing tips, apart from those

of his trainer. He took from this what he could to improve his abilities.

Perhaps if you counted the amount of time Ali spent "trash talking" his opponents you might be surprised to know that it would be longer than his fights. This skill, however, proved to be an effective tool in his armoury as he was able to use it to complement his boxing skills.

You see, the talking did not stop when Ali got into the ring, he used it as his "third hand". As well as his boxing skills Ali used his communication skills to confuse his opponent in the ring telling them that they did not hurt him and saying things like "is that all you got George?". This proved to be demoralising to many of his opponents and, undoubtedly, affected their ability to fight how they would have wanted.

Learning point 5

- **Be disruptive**. Whether in sport or business, doing things in a conventional way will not differentiate you from the herd. The use of a seemingly irrelevant skill, in support of other skills helped Ali and applies to other sports and competitive organisational scenarios. The point is good leaders have an armoury of skills and know when they can apply these in an unconventional and potentially disruptive manner. If Ali had "stayed in his lane" and chose to use only his boxing skills, he might not have won the fight.

B-Belief

Underlying Ali's approach to boxing was his positive state of mind. Ali came across as being arrogant to some people but to the discerning what they saw in Ali was someone that was at ease with himself. He was someone that chose to adopt a positive mindset and never thought of himself as a loser. The way Ali talked about his personal aspirations made it clear that he was constantly driven to improve as a man, father, husband, and boxer.

Learning point 6

- **Adopt a positive mindset**. Ali chose to be positive and realistic about the prospects of winning his fights. Most importantly, there was a strong relationship between how Ali lived his personal life and his persona in and around the ring. Walking the walk and talking the talk becomes more meaningful when they coincide. People respected Ali because he did what he said, and his positive mindset endeared people to him. I have no doubt that his mindset helped to improve his confidence in his abilities and helped to sharpen his skills.

Muhammad Ali was a master of disguising his fear of opponents. For example, Ali has gone on record as saying that he feared Sonny Liston. However, Ali was able to turn his fear into awareness of his opponent's capabilities which in turn, led him to study how to beat his opponents and gain confidence and enhance belief in his own abilities.

Without the fear of losing, most likely Ali would not have prepared as much for the fights against Liston and Foreman and he would not have convinced himself that his belief in his abilities were well-founded. In contrast, neither Liston nor Foreman (at the time) believed that they would lose to Ali and this set the tone for the level of training they undertook both physically and mentally.

You see Ali had considered all possibilities and prepared accordingly whilst many of his opponents only considered their abilities without respecting the ability of their opponent. Hence their self-belief was over-confidence which affected their preparation and ability to effectively execute a strategy to win.

The moral here is not to underestimate your opponent/competition. Study what makes them successful and identify their limitations. Embrace fear and understand what is driving any concerns you might have and put steps in place to make fear work for you. Having a sense of fear and nerves is not, necessarily, a bad thing if you understand why you have it and have mechanisms to cope. The rush of adrenaline causes oxygen to flow to the brain, muscles and respiratory system and can make you more alert. Not a bad thing, right? However, too much of one thing is good for nothing, as they say. Too much adrenaline can lead to increased risks of strokes, heart attacks, anxiety, weight gain, headaches, and insomnia to name a few.

Identifying your shortfalls and improving your abilities will help to reduce your fears and will enhance your confidence in self. This is something that Ali did well as do all great winners.

Learning point 7

> **Embrace fear**. Being positive is necessary but it is not sufficient to combat fear. Ali was aware that he had to address the issue of his limitations (i.e. face fear) to diminish its effect. This he did by improving his technical weaknesses (in relation to his opponent) and refining his strengths and using his soft skills to disruptive effect. In the business world it is no different. Leaders need to learn to embrace fear and devise strategies for its management.

Learning point 8

> **Reflect on what has worked and avoid what does not**. Ali was a reflective person. He opined and took confidence in the things which led to his success and learnt from his mistakes. This might seem an obvious thing to do but many people are not reflective. They do not always understand how they or others have contributed to their failure or successes and so do not have a sound basis for moving forwards. Reflection helps to build a better awareness of what might or might not work which serves to narrow uncertainty and helps to build confidence.

C-Coherent strategy

Muhammad Ali's strategy for winning his fights was not that he was simply going to knock the other guy out, although he often joked that this is what he would do. It was not that he would outpoint his opponent, which is what he did on several occasions. So, what was his strategy?

Ali's approach was that he would win the fight in his head prior to going into the ring. Ali would often entice his opponents to enter a war of words with him. He would make fun of their looks and ability and characterise them by way of poems. For many of Ali's opponents this had psychological implications. Simply put he got into their heads and caused them to be confused.

Once his opponents started to react to his antics (e.g. by trying to trash talk him), Ali realised that they were not focusing on his boxing abilities and that he was in control. The war of words had resulted in a psychological victory for Ali and all he had to do was to put his strategy for the fight into action which he did better than most.

Learning point 9

- **Devise a plan to win**. Ali did not just devise a plan like other boxers e.g. do gym and bag work plus running. Ali spent much time in sparring allowing himself to be hit by his partner, whilst he was against the ropes. This technique, coined by Ali as the "rope-a-dope", had the effect of the ropes helping to absorb an opponent's blows whilst giving the impression that they were beating Ali. Once they became tired or missed, Ali would seize the opportunity to throw a combination and steal some points. This was an unorthodox technique but used successfully by Ali. He did not train to fight he trained to win. Similarly, in the business world, leaders should devise plans not just to compete but plans to win. Go beyond what others do, be innovative, nimble, and disruptive.

What Ali did was to demonstrate that many fights are won in the mind before they occur in the ring! Ali was able to conceptualise a coherent strategy for beating his opponent well before he got into the ring. However, unlike many boxers, this strategy was not just in Ali's head but because of his exceptional communication skills it was also in the minds of his opponents.

By giving pundits an insight into his strategy, Ali also gave them the opportunity to critique his approach and provide feedback. For some pundits they probably revelled in the opportunity of ridiculing Ali's strategy, probably saying things like his left hand is too good, his chin is too strong etc. No doubt Ali would have taken all this on-board and combined them with inputs from his trainers and others to refine his approach.

Learning point 10

- **Visualise success and treat it as if you have already achieved it**. Ali gave as much attention to training his mind as he did to training his body. His pronouncements that he would knock out his opponents in a certain round or win on points were not just bravado. He Visualised success and then developed a strategy for how he was going to realise his vision. He lived his vision and everything he did was in support of the vision.

In business, many persons create strategic plans and describe in detail what their aspirations are. Many, if not most of these will fail. Beyond the organisational exercise, people often do not live their life as if their strategy will be realised. When this happens to a critical number of persons in an organisation then that firm will, likely, not achieve its vision.

From an organisational leadership perspective, there is much to be gained by following an approach such as that used by Ali in visualising his fights. One of the key skills of a leader is their ability to think strategically and use techniques such as visualisation or mind setting in order to imagine success. A strategy is based on being able to describe what a future state might look like for an organisation. Without the ability to describe in detail what this state would look, feel like, or taste it is difficult to know if you will ever end up in that state. Moreover, even if you can describe this future state, you need to act consistently towards achieving this state otherwise you run the risk of unintentionally drifting from your intended goals.

Putting things together

Without ability it is difficult to be a true leader unless that position is given for other reasons. There might be some of you reading this saying they know of several people that are in leadership positions but lack the ability to be a leader. You are probably correct. Note, however, that being in a leadership position does not make you a good leader. You can have bad leaders and it is these that I simply refer to as being in a position of leadership. Those that are good leaders, I simply call leaders.

So, being a good leader (or simply a leader) requires you to have the ability to lead and this will be based on a combination of those skills I have detailed in previous chapters. However, as also discussed, there is no single ability which will make you a leader. For example, there is no single characteristic that makes a good teacher a good teacher. Clearly, they need the skills to be able to teach a specific subject but what might differentiate them from others might have more to do with approach than technical skills.

In a later chapter, I discuss what makes up the aura of a leader (non-technical skills). It is this aura that people will, typically, associate with a person's approach to leadership. Readers will recognise that these skills are a subset of those discussed in earlier chapters.

The ability to undertake job A is not necessarily the same as the ability required to undertake job B and to suggest that a fixed list of abilities can be applied across all types of roles/positions is simply fantasy and wrong. Hence when I talk about ability, I refer to abilities relevant to the specifics of the position/activity at hand (technical) as well as non-technical (or soft) skills.

Even with ability, it is unlikely that someone can be an effective leader without belief. However, by this I do not just mean belief in one's own abilities but that others have confidence in your abilities. This said, supposing you have proven your abilities at work, but your boss does not recognise these or give you the credit you deserve. Ignoring narrow mindedness, if someone genuinely has abilities and they are not recognised by their boss, it is likely that this person is feared or there is some type of personal dislike.

Having belief in oneself is a necessary but not a sufficient condition for being an effective leader. Belief without a basis is just overconfidence. However, if you need to rely on the support of positional leaders to demonstrate and be rewarded for your leadership and they do not then your ability to shine will be hampered. You cannot be an effective leader in an organisation where your abilities are not valued. Being an effective leader, therefore, requires one to be able to convince others of your abilities.

Having ability and belief alone might not make you an effective leader without having a coherent strategy for how you will lead. Being able to run the 100 metres in less than 9.6 seconds and having confidence in your ability will not, necessarily, be enough to beat another runner that just happens to be running better than they have in years. There have been many races lost due to poor execution of strategy rather than ability or lack of confidence. Most good runners will tell you that they have already run their race several times over (in their mind) prior to the time at which the actual race is run.

So, belief depends on ability and a coherent strategy depends on your belief and having all three will help you to be a more effective leader.

The ABC principle can be summarised as follows:

1. **Ability**
    a. Be aware of who you are and what has contributed to your achievements so far.
    b. Be aware of your strengths and how they can compensate for your limitations/weaknesses.
    c. Be aware of your opponent's (or those against whom you compete such as colleagues) strengths and weaknesses and how these are manifested.
    d. Create a wider appreciation of your abilities.
    e. Be disruptive.
2. **Belief**
    a. Adopt a positive mindset.
    b. Embrace fear.
    c. Reflect on what has worked and avoid what does not.
3. **Coherent strategy**
    a. Devise a plan to win.
    b. Visualise success and treat it as if you have already achieved it.

Further reading

1. BBC (2014), *The Rumble in the Jungle 40 years on, by those who witnessed it.* Based on interviews by: Ade Adedoyin and Edited by: Ben Dirs
2. Treen, D. (2012), *Overcome "Why Strategic Plans Fail", For a Breakout Strategy*, Trafford Pub
3. Jinks, P. (2018), *Strategic Fail: Why Nonprofit Strategic Planning Fails, and How to Fix it*, TJP Pub
4. Bidwell, J. (2017), *Disrupt!: 100 Lessons in Business Innovation*, Nicholas Brealey Pub

Chapter 12
Enhancing your ABC's

Enhancing abilities
Enhancing beliefs
Enhancing coherency of strategy
Exercise
Further reading

Enhancing abilities

Without abilities it is impossible to be an effective leader. This said, there is no such thing as a perfect leader since no human is perfect. Moreover, no person is born a leader. The skills of leadership must be learnt, and some people will perform better at some skills than others. Experience shows that what might be viewed as essential in one situation might not be as relevant in another. The key to being a good leader is knowing which skill to employ at the appropriate time and to know which need further development.

The steps to enhancing abilities are as follows:

1. Try and obtain feedback from a variety of sources as to how they perceive your leadership qualities. Where possible, such sources should include the views of those within and outside of the workplace. In some organisations, as part of the annual performance review, a 360 review is conducted whereby an employee will receive and give feedback from/to other co-workers. My suggestion would be that you approach either the same set of workers or others and ask for feedback (with examples of behaviour). You should also solicit similar types of feedback from friends/colleagues outside of work. You should ask them to give you a score between one and five (with five being the highest number and scores awarded in increments of 0.5, e.g. 1, 1.5, through to 5) and covering the following:

    a. The effectiveness or otherwise of your communications (both verbal and non-verbal).

    b. The extent to which you are viewed as being inclusive, approachable, and accepting of other opinions etc.

    c. Their perception of your trustworthiness.

    d. Their perception as to whether you facilitate for and are a team-player as per the rules of the organisation.

    e. Their perception as to whether you encourage fair play and are a good decision maker.

f. Their perception as to whether you are a strategic thinker and capable of getting things done.

g. Their perception as to whether you show enough humility.

h. Their perception as to whether you show enough empathy.

i. Their perception as to whether you demonstrate enough perseverance.

j. Their perception as to whether you demonstrate enough tenacity.

k. Their perception as to whether you come across as being confident and/or instil confidence in others.

l. Their perception of how you perform with respect to other soft skills.

m. Their perception as to the strengths of your technical skills. Here you would list the skills that you wish to obtain feedback on.

2. Give yourself a rating. That is, conduct a self-assessment and compare your score to the average of those based on feedback. This analysis provides an opportunity for you to compare your beliefs of yourself to the perception of others. The things to bear in mind when undertaking this analysis are:

   a. The activities that you have performed consistently well at in the past, whether at work or otherwise. It is highly likely that if you have consistently performed well in some activity the skills which contribute towards performing that activity will reflect some of your strengths.

   b. Things that others have consistently said about you over the years and for which you can verify. People can say anything about you but if you verify what they are saying then it might be valid and reflect either a strength or weakness.

   c. The activities you like/dislike. Generally, people tend to perform better at the things they like and not as well otherwise. So, if you like something and you do it often it is likely that you might be good at it.

   d. The activities you find easy. Many people confuse the ease of doing an activity with liking that activity. There are some people that find their job easy to do but they do not like it. So, whether you like it or not, if you find something easy to do then chances are you are good at it.

3. For each of the skills, a score of less than or equal to 3 should warrant more immediate corrective action. This said, you should always strive to improve your skills and not become complacent even if you have scored highly. Use the scores from the feedback as a basis for determining the areas of improvement. What should also drive the priority of the skills enhancement is the extent to which they are required in the near-term (i.e. current or soon to be workplace situations). So, skills required near-term should have a higher priority than those that can wait providing that the latter does not affect any near-term skills.

4. If your organisation can facilitate for your professional development, then that would be the best place to start to address the needs identified in (3). Alternatively, you should seek external course providers where developmental needs cannot be met internally. If your organisation can facilitate but refuses to give you the support for your development, then you should seriously consider your strategy for leaving your organisation.

The above process requires time for persons to provide adequate feedback. My suggestion is that you allow at least two weeks for people to get back to you. Remember, you are asking for a favour and perhaps, some of the people you ask might ask the same of you so please be polite when you make your requests.

If properly undertaken, the process will identify both strengths and weaknesses. A subsequent step would be to identify to what extent your strengths are affected by your weaknesses or supported by other strengths. For example, you might have scored relatively high on some technical skill but lower on being inclusive and accepting the opinion of others. However, it might be that (in your organisation or specific situation) improving your ability to accept the views of others could result in further enhancements to this technical skill. If this is the case, then it makes sense to devise a plan which aims to incorporate both in your skills development.

One thing to bear in mind is that you are not likely to excel across all skills. It might be that you never get a score higher than a certain value. Do not worry but try and find out what is causing this situation and if you are not able to address the matter there are one of two things you can do. The first thing is to see if any of your strengths can compensate for your weaknesses. A more dramatic step, if possible, would be to change direction and engage in activities which do not place such a high emphasis on the skills which are weak.

Having gone through the process of 360 reviews or feedback such as the one I suggest, I know that it's not always easy to get people to commit the time to provide you with the valuable information you need for your development. In this case, your self-assessment becomes all that more important. Make sure you spend time trying to understand why your weaknesses are what you say they are.

Do not get pre-occupied with trying to improve your weaknesses by yourself if you are unable. Instead, seek advice/coaching (or mentoring) or try and "benchmark" yourself against someone (an influencer) that you know has strong skills in the area where you are weak. A word of warning in relation to benchmarking. Make sure you go beyond the superficial and try to understand what drives the influencer to be so strong in a specific skill. Without this it is possible that you could end up trying to mimic the behaviours of someone and not knowing what really makes them great.

Using strengths to overcome weaknesses

As a child (around the age of twelve) I had a fascination with speed. I guess this was quite typical for boys of my age at the time. I liked fast cars, airplanes, you name it. I also loved sports, martial arts such as Karate/Kung Fu and athletic events involving sprint races. This said, I had never been on a plane, driven in a fast car, studied martial arts, or could be considered a particularly good runner. However, this did not stop my imagination from taking me to new highs, being a martial artist or a competent sprinter. I imagined this in the day and dreamt about this at night.

I loved watching sprint races on television and would try and emulate the great 100, 200 and 400 metre runners of the day such as Don Quarrie, Steve

Williams, and Alberto Juantorena. This said, it seemed no matter how hard I tried I was not winning the races I wanted and was not the best in my year at school. I would go to newsagents and read copies of martial arts magazines and occasionally sneak into cinemas to watch a Bruce Lee movie. I studied the moves of Bruce Lee (both sound and action) and, in my mind, was a Kung Fu master although I was far from it.

Little did I know it, at the time, but my relentless passion for martial arts and sprinting helped me to enhance two key skills, perseverance, and tenacity. Even though I was not a member of a martial arts club or track and field I practiced every day in my back yard and wherever I could find the opportunity.

At the age of thirteen my persistence paid off and I was running in a schoolboy 400 metre event at the Wolverhampton & Bilston athletic club. Not only did I win the race, but I broke the stadium record for a schoolboy in the event. From that day on I rarely lost any sprint races held at my school. Without perseverance and tenacity, I probably would not have made that athletics team and certainly would not have achieved the 400-metre record.

When I was around fourteen, I joined a martial arts club (to learn a style of Karate known as Wado-Ryu) close to where I lived. Of course, I knew it all so this was just a formality. However, unlike sprinting where I had the opportunity of racing against friends to test my abilities, I had no similar test for my martial arts abilities. It was mostly based on my reading of books and practicing by myself. Yes, I understood much of the theory but as they say, practice makes perfect, especially for activities like combat sports.

I remember my first fight at the club, I had perfected the Bruce Lee sound and his moves and would now have the opportunity of putting these into action. Within the first few seconds I was winded by a kick to my side by an opponent, one of the three Sensei's (instructors) at the club. It took me several minutes to recover. Subsequent fights had a similar outcome with me losing quite easily to people that I believed I should be able to defeat.

I could not understand what was happening. My poor performance continued for many months when I was approached by one of my instructors who told me that I needed to stop with all the Bruce Lee stuff and just be myself. He told me that I had the capability of being a good fighter but should go back to basics, understand what the sport was about and fight using my natural style. This caused me to rethink the reasons why I joined the club.

The discussion with my instructor, although I did not know at the time, was about my attitude, specifically my lack of humility. It was at that point that I started to reflect on the reasons why I wanted to be a martial artist. You remember me saying that I liked fast things, well I wanted to be as fast as Bruce Lee. However, what was evidently clear was that although I was fast and knew many techniques, my mind was only focused on me and I paid no attention to the abilities of my opponents.

I wanted to win and look good at it and forgot to pay attention to details. My soul searching continued for a few more months and I realised that whilst speed was important in martial arts, patience was as effective. I watched again various martial arts movies, read more books, and paid closer attention to my instructors and opponents. What I learnt was that by waiting for my opponent to strike and anticipating their next move, patiently, I could take them off-guard and deliver a point winning kick or punch. I saw various competitors use this technique to great effect. Would it work for me?

With my heightened awareness of humility and trying my best to be patient I put what I had learnt into effect in my next fights. It worked. I became a better fighter; I was comfortable just being me and I was transformed from someone that not only had a theoretical but a practical understanding of martial arts.

By the time I got to seventeen, I was a competent karate competitor, and my earlier technical weaknesses were compensated by my enhanced skills in patience and humility. I competed in the national club championships for the association that my club was a member of. The event was being held at my club. The walk to the club from my home would ordinarily take around 25 minutes. However, on the day, it seemed to take much longer, minutes seemed like hours and the day was overcast. I was determined not to make nerves or fear overcome me and every step I took I imagined myself executing a particular karate move against an opponent.

By the time I arrived at the club, my fears had subsided. However, I was not impatient to fight but I was keen to observe others, have fun and look out for those opponents that might cause problems for me. This paid off, as I made it to the final of the individual event for my weight category and my club team had made it to the final of the team competition. I went on to win the individual event and was the last fighter for the team event which I also won to hand my team the title.

To summarise, getting your strengths to compensate for your weaknesses involves the following steps:

1. Identify your weaknesses. The best thing is to get others to do this for you.

2. Accept your weaknesses, understand them, why they occur, how they make you react, do not be defined by them and stay positive.

3. Identify your strengths. The best thing is to get others to do this for you, but you must be able to understand that your strengths are what they are.

4. Determine how your strengths interact with your weaknesses. What you are looking for here is a strength which when used diminishes the effect of your weakness.

5. Work to enhance your strengths whilst ensuring your weaknesses do not dominate your strengths.

Being aware of the strength of others

It is quite easy to think that only sports persons need to know the strength and weaknesses of others, namely their opponents. Although in business teamwork is an essential element of working it is important to note that your colleagues are also competitors. They compete for financial and other resources, the attention of the boss and other things. Even in the best run teams, competition exists even if it is unintentional.

Knowing how others compete will prove useful to understanding how you might be able to improve your own skills. Rather than to make you a solo player knowing your competition helps to improve your team skills since your knowledge of self can now be combined with that of the knowledge of the strengths/weaknesses of others.

Unlike sports where you might play to your opponent's weaknesses, in a teamwork setting your focus should be on how to support your colleague's weaknesses and enhance their strengths. If your organisation fosters teamwork and you buy into this, then you are likely to get noticed for your value-added contribution.

If you make a habit of supporting others it might not be long before your dependability is recognised as leadership. This said, it is impossible to discount the case where others see your dependability as a threat and try to thwart your potential growth in your organisation. This kind of politics is, unfortunately, very commonplace. How much of this you tolerate is a function of your personal circumstances and core values. However, if you are not being appreciated at your organisation then you need to make the decision to employ your skills where they are more valued.

When assessing the strengths and weaknesses of others, adopting a reflective perspective will help. You could then produce scores against the list of characteristics as detailed earlier in this chapter. The more you incorporate reflective thinking into your day-to-day activities the better you will be at understanding those you work with.

Create a wider appreciation of your abilities

An often-understated aspect of developing leadership abilities is letting other people know what you can do. By sharing knowledge of your skills with others you get the opportunity to get feedback and potentially valuable inputs into refining your skills. Some considerations to bear in mind when advertising your skills include:

- Knowing the target audience of the persons you wish to influence internally and externally.

- Attracting the attention of senior individuals in your organisation and making them aware of your initiatives.

- Writing and publishing papers in journals/magazines relevant to your industry.

- Use social media such as LinkedIn and others to communicate with people in and outside of your industry.

- Talk about your successful completion of academic/professional qualifications.

- Offer to participate in more work-related activities.

- Talk about your achievements in undertaking vocational activities such as that through a Rotary club or similar type of organisation.

Being disruptive

Society and businesses have, for many years, rewarded conformity and frowned on those adopting unconventional approaches. That is, until those breaking the mould prove successful. In this digital era, we see everyday examples of this in the likes of Amazon, Apple, and Alibaba. These companies would not have been as successful without the brave steps taken by their founders which had the effect of disrupting existing markets/industries.

Some key steps in being disruptive are:

- Being open minded. Do not exclude possibilities because you are not familiar or dislike them. As a leader encourage your staff to do the same.

- Take calculated risks. Try developing an understanding of risk management principles and analyse situations from a variety of perspectives in which data is a key determinant in decision making. Whereas there are many aspects of leadership which are driven by personal preferences of a leader, as far as possible decisions should be based on data and evidence.

- Develop innovative and creative thinking. It is hard to think of a single truly disruptive development in modern times that was not influenced by innovative or creative thinking.

- Develop your reflective thinking skills. Continuing to do the same thing in the same way will likely lead to the same result. By being more reflective you increase the possibility to identify new ways of improving on your previous initiatives.

- Understand your market. Most organisations are in business to meet some market demand. As such knowing your client/customer and what will make them happy today, tomorrow and in the future needs to be a key objective. Since no one has a crystal ball and client needs change frequently it becomes important for individuals to be flexible and organisations to be agile.

Enhancing beliefs

Before I delve into the specifics about how you can enhance beliefs, I want to dispel one myth about failure. Failure only destroys one's belief in oneself if (1) you do not learn from it and (2) you do not have a plan for managing this risk when you try again. In some circumstances, failure will be inevitable irrespective of your approach simply because it is not possible to get a win.

Do you remember the song by R Kelly, I believe I can fly? Nobody really believes that this song was about being able to fly like a bird, or do they? However, supposing I was to say to you that it is my objective to train as hard as I can to build up my strength and muscles so that I might be able to fly. Do you think that this is realistic, and should I be upset if I never achieve my objective? I would say no, it is not realistic, and I should not be upset about failing since it is not possible to achieve a win here without assistance from the use of artificial wings.

So, what is the message? Make sure that the things you put your trust and belief in are realistically achievable. Your challenge is to figure out how to achieve realism, the resources required and how those resources will be utilised towards that end.

The following are some steps you can take to improve belief/confidence in yourself:

1. Achieve success in some personal or business venture. The achievement of success, generally, results in building confidence and creates or reinforces awareness of your abilities for you and others

2. Identify someone that you believe exudes confidence and try and find out what makes them confident. It is tempting to say, only choose positive role models but we know that even "bad guys" have redeeming characteristics. What is important is that you can understand how they maintain confidence and use it to their advantage. Whilst being true to yourself, try and emulate the characteristics of this person. Being true to yourself simply means taking your learning points and implementing them in a way that is natural to you. If you find that there is a gap between your skills and theirs then this gives you an indication as to what you need to work on.

3. Do not give up and constantly remind yourself that you are here for a reason. It is easy to see why some people just give up and take the view that they are worthless. You here it all the time. You know that soft but nagging voice in your inner ear saying: give up, it is not for you, you are not worth it, you are not good enough. Whenever you feel this way quickly respond by affirming that: you are here for a reason and that you are worthy. Stay positive. Take time to reflect on what you have achieved or those people or feelings that make you happy. It is difficult to be prescriptive but there is much evidence to suggest the more often you think of positive things your mind is likely to make you more productive and motivated.

4. Have a supportive network of friends/colleagues on speed dial. It is important that you surround yourself with people who can make a positive difference in your life. I do not mean yes men, people that will say whatever it takes to make you happy but those that are not afraid to say no or you are wrong. These people are there to make you strong and you are there to make them strong. You might also have to make some difficult decisions to separate yourself from negative people, you know those that never have anything positive or constructive to say. This is not so easy and in some instances some of these people might be family members. From experience, my advice is, irrespective of the nature of the relation-

ship, if it is destructive to your health and self-esteem you need to make some changes to correct this situation which could include anything from ignoring negative behaviour/comments to extricating yourself from any circumstances where these people can negatively impact your life.

6. Do not be afraid of failure or to take risks. I have come across many people that are so afraid of failure or to take risks that they always go for the "soft option" and are surprised that they have not achieved more out of life. My advice to all these people is this: without risk you cannot expect to get a positive return. Humans learn by exposure to new things and leaders grow by adapting to new situations. So, to grow you need to take risks and be exposed to new situations and step out of your comfort zone.

7. Accept your weaknesses and devise a strategy for improving your control of them. Your weaknesses just like your strengths contribute to what you are. Playing to your strengths alone is a dangerous thing to do since it ignores the threat posed by your weaknesses. By working to mitigate your weaknesses your focus should be on how their improvements can be used in conjunction with your established strengths.

The following are some steps you can take to improve belief/confidence of others in you:

1. Demonstrate that you have confidence in others. We know that humans are prone to mimic the behaviour of others and as a leader you should start the contagion. My experience has been that if you show confidence and help to build the capacity of other's they are more likely to have confidence in you. Your support of others helps to build trust which leads to confidence.

2. Demonstrate that you have achieved successes in your business/professional ventures or that you have the capabilities. Whereas previous achievements are no guarantee of future performance, it tends to form the basis for which we make decisions about people's abilities and hence the confidence we place in them. Equally important however, even if there is no history of success, is the capability of people to develop into future leaders. Leaders should, thus, be looking to "hire their boss" when making certain hiring decisions. That is, do not be afraid to hire people that can be moulded into leaders that can take your position.

3. Humility and acceptance of weaknesses. You might be surprised but acknowledging and accepting your weaknesses makes it clear to people that you are trustworthy and open to guidance and being led by others. Once genuine people see that you are open to them, they are more likely to be open to you and be supportive of your ideas.

4. Clear and direct communications. If you are not able to give directions in a direct and clear manner, then it might be difficult for people to understand you and what you require/stand for. Being clear, polite, empathetic, and thoughtful in your communications with others will help to increase their trust of you and we know that trust builds confidence.

Evidence shows that once your confidence is enhanced, it provides motivation to improve your abilities. So, becoming good at what you do enhances your confidence and an enhanced confidence gives you drive to continue to improve your abilities.

Dealing with fears and self-doubt

It is well-known that fear and self-doubt are significant contributors to a lack of self-confidence. Negative interactions and events that occur in your life can have a detrimental impact on one's confidence. Things that your parents might have said, the way you were treated by your partner, the lack of support given to you by teachers or authority figures.

Often when negative things happen it causes one to be a little apprehensive about entering situations that might lead to similar results. Sometimes this apprehension turns to fear and leads to self-doubt. By managing fear and self-doubt you put yourself into a good position to enhance your confidence.

The most important thing to bear in mind is that you are here for a reason and stop blaming yourself for your doubt and fears.

Suppose you had learning difficulties which made it harder for you to comprehend lessons at school. Your parents did not have the time to help you with your homework as they were too busy doing other things or resting from work. Your teachers could not devote time to you as the class sizes were so big. That is what it was like for me during most of my early school years.

Whenever the teachers would ask the class questions, I used to pray that they did not ask me because I did not have a clue how to answer the questions. Ask me about football, athletics, martial arts, or some other sport but do not ask me about anything I was supposed to have learnt in class.

At the age of eleven, when I entered high-school, I was placed in the second to last grade of class based on academic ability. There were six different categories for each year, and I was in category 5 out of six. Superficially, I was outgoing and played sports and hung around with other people like me. However, inside I was shy and really wanted to be smarter and perhaps, one day, be someone that we commonly call a white-collar worker.

As a three-year-old I remember saying to my parents that I wanted to be a medical doctor when I grew up.

It was not until the second year of high school that the school realised that I had a learning difficulty. The result of this was that I was to spend 4 days in my regular school and 1 day at an institution which could help me with my learning difficulties. The shame and embarrassment were almost too much to bear for me as others would be made aware of my situation. At that point in time, I was not aware that my "condition" was not my fault, but I acted as if it were. I looked down on myself on the one hand and played the fool on the other to remain popular.

My learning difficulties had set me back in more ways than one. By the time I turned sixteen instead of sitting O Levels (at the time, the highest level of qualification for someone of that age) like some of my friends I was preparing to sit the lower level certificate of secondary education (CSEs). In one of those subjects (mathematics), I was only allowed to sit a special exam whose highest mark would give me the opportunity to take the higher-level CSE the following year. I was that bad at mathematics!

My father was extremely disappointed with my poor academic performance. One Saturday morning he told me that he would be willing to have a conversation with one of his friends who was the owner of a small garage at which he repaired and maintained cars. He thought, perhaps, his friend could train me to be a mechanic.

Ordinarily I would not have questioned my father but on this day, it became clear to me, for the first time, that he really did not think much of my prospects for a successful career in anything but manual work. I told my father that I wasn't sure what I wanted to be in life, but I had no intention of being a mechanic as I believed my life could hold other opportunities and I would be pursuing an academic route.

I was determined that I would pass the subjects I had elected to study at school and give me an opportunity of a great life. So determined was I that I decided to register for additional courses, including A levels at a local college. Not only did I go on to pass enough subjects to get to study at university but the subject matter I studied was mathematics! A few years later I obtained a PhD in mathematical computer science and have gone on to publish papers in top academic journals as well as having written several books across several subjects.

So how did a young boy with learning difficulties transform himself into a person that would eventually earn a PhD? It started with a vision. In my vision I saw my future self as someone being regarded as an expert in mathematics and being able to solve all types of problems. In order to achieve this, I undertook the following steps:

1. I accepted that I had a difficulty with mathematics and other aspects of learning.

2. I was resolved to not make my difficulties limit my potential for the rest of my life.

3. I set myself a target of obtaining a PhD, sometime in the future.

4. I shared my vision with those that could provide me with moral support.

5. I sought out positive role models in the field of mathematics.

6. I studied books that were at least one level higher than my current studies.

7. I blocked out those activities and relationships that could hinder my progress.

8. I broke down my learning into smaller bite-sized pieces.

9. I rewarded myself when I was successful and encouraged myself otherwise.

10. I chose not to dwell on negative thoughts save for knowing how to handle their eventuality.

Let me take the opportunity to go a little further into each of the steps I mention above.

Accepting my current status

Accepting that I had learning difficulties was a crucial part of my journey towards improving my abilities and building self-confidence. It took me a little while, but I came to the realisation that I could not move on until I embraced my issues, acknowledged its presence, and no longer felt uneasy thinking about it. It helped that my school had identified the issues, although late, but late is better than never. I could now put a proper label on my "problems" and stop treating myself as being less than others.

Resolved to make a change

Although I now knew why I was not able to make better progress academically I also knew that I had to make changes in my life to accept the fact that my current limitations were not a prison sentence. I had to condition myself into thinking that a label of "learning difficulties" today did not mean learning difficulties forever.

Set a target for my future state

When I was sixteen, I had no idea what it took to obtain a PhD. I knew, ordinarily, it would be a massive undertaking for someone that was considered academically smart but for me I knew it would be much harder. In any event, it was so far out of my reach that it would take a miracle for me to achieve. However, like the pop group Hot Chocolate, "I believed in miracles" and chose this as my future state. In the world of business, we would call this a stretch assignment. Others would have called it mission impossible. As an adolescent, it was simply my desire.

Sharing my vision

I realised that I had to be careful with whom I shared my vision. Although I knew my mother would be supportive, I felt that I could not really share my vision with her and certainly not with my father. There were only very few friends I could even discuss my plans with, but my solace came in the form of the church.

I had always gone to church for as long as I could remember and at the time, I was sixteen, I was regularly attending a Baptist church close to where I lived. There were several attendees at the church that had gone to university and some were even teachers. Their belief and encouragement in me motivated me to work harder. Later, in life I have come to learn that having a spirit of discernment is extremely useful in the world of business in simply knowing who you can trust and share your vision.

Seeking out positive role models

Although I knew what I wanted my future state to look like I did not know anyone that had completed a degree in mathematics (outside of my school and college respectively). I began to familiarise myself with the works of some of the greats of mathematics such as Newton, Hardy, Ramanujan as well as more recent mathematicians. I tried to imagine what might have inspired them to become so good at what they did. My desire was to be inspired by what they had achieved. I also used this same approach for other subjects that I was studying.

Studying at a higher level

I realised that by doing extra studies of material that was at a higher level than that for which I was to be assessed would give me great confidence if I could successfully understand the material. As such, I regularly sought to read and answer questions that were harder than what I would otherwise have to do.

Since I was not formally taught the extra material, I had to be somewhat disciplined in terms of both finding the material and then devoting the time to study its contents. Unlike today where we can make use of the internet to source material, I used a rather old fashioned, but useful, facility known as a library.

Blocking out hindrances

I knew that I was very easily distracted and did not want to hinder my chances of achieving more than the expectations that several others had of me. I realised that I could not hope to achieve a different outcome by continuing to do the same thing. Many people would recognise this step as being part of an implementation plan to effect change. For me, and at the time, it was simply a mechanism that I used to reduce any distractions from achieving my objectives. I just cut out activities which prevented me from achieving my goals

Breaking down activities

My nature was such that when I was younger, I used to be very impatient and get bored quite easily. For each of my subjects I would break them down into smaller units. For example, if an area of a subject covered 20 pages, I would break this down into 10 or possibly 5. I would make sure I understood this sub-area prior to moving on to the next. By breaking down the study materials in this way I was able to remember the subjects and perform better at answering questions more effectively.

Rewarding and encouragement

Whenever I would achieve success in some aspect of my studies, I would first thank God. Secondly, I would give myself a treat which could be anything from watching a TV show, listening to my favourite music, or just going out. Whenever I did not do as well as I had planned, I would try and identify the reasons why I had not performed as well and identify a way to solve the issue. After this I would encourage myself to be positive, remembering that I am here for a reason and that I am yet to achieve my best and that there is better to come.

Choosing to be positive

It was important for me to remain positive. I chose to see failure not as a failure in me but a first lesson in being successful. As such, when I stumbled, I did not take it so badly as it would simply reveal an opportunity for me to improve on some aspect of my performance.

I applied the above steps to my CSEs, O and A-levels with the result being that I got into university with the label of learning difficulties well behind me. The approach became second nature when I got to university (focusing now on steps 3 to 10) and resulted in me obtaining the highest grade in my class at the end of my undergraduate course. I was awarded a prize of a graduate membership of the prestigious institute of mathematics and its applications. I subsequently went on to obtain masters level qualifications from Oxford and other top-tier universities as well as to publish numerous academic papers and several books.

Enhancing coherency of strategy

Recall that a strategy is, essentially, a plan for how success will be achieved. No single strategy will be applicable across all situations but there are some key things to bear in mind:

1. Clear vision of your desired future state. Without a vision your strategy fits any outcome. This is not a desirable situation. As a leader, you need to be able to manifest your desired outcomes by visualising what your future state should look like. For example, your vision might be to be viewed as an expert in your field within ten years, to be the best engineer in your company by the end of the next two years, to be world champion in your sport in five years' time etc.

2. Identify the abilities you require to enhance or maintain to achieve your vision. To achieve your vision, you might need to enhance several abilities which are underdeveloped. Implementing a successful strategy is not all about playing to your strengths but it is also about knowing how your strengths interact with your weaknesses. For example, if you are not good at seeing things from other people's perspectives or appreciate the things that drive other's but you are good at improvising and have a strong memory you might become a great method actor if you can work on improving your ability to be empathetic and your emotional sensitivity.

3. Identify how you will use your abilities to achieve your objectives. Knowing that you need to and can run fast is necessary but not sufficient to win a gold medal in an Olympic game. You only need to observe the performance of the 100-metre sprinter Asafa Powell at major championships to realise this. Powell has run more sub-10 second hundred meters than any other athlete but has been unable to put this experience into a strategy to win at the biggest championships.

4. Articulation using a variety of media/styles relatable by others. Unless you are planning to do everything for yourself you are going to have to communicate your strategy to someone at some point. In an organisation this could be the board, your boss, or others in the management hierarchy. In your personal life this could be your significant other or

family. If you are an athlete/sport's person this could be your coach etc.,

What is important is that you use a style of communication that is suitable to your audience and this might mean saying the same thing in a variety of ways e.g. text, diagrams, voice, and video. If people cannot relate to your strategy because they do not understand it, they will find it hard to see how they fit in and can contribute to its success. It is also important that you know how others can contribute towards your strategy and that your views and theirs coincide.

5. Simulate your strategy to assess its strengths and weaknesses in the light of current and potential circumstances. I have analysed more strategic plans than I care to remember. One thing that concerns me more than anything is the lack of thought that goes into simulating the plan.

In many organisations, strategies are developed based on making slight modifications to the previous plan. However, these plans often assume a business as usual approach without enough thought given to accommodating changes (or scenarios) and the viability of the plan in the light of these changes. The act of simulating your strategy should go beyond the analysis you conduct in your head and should include soliciting the views of others. At this point one of two things should have occurred: (i) the strategy is deemed to be coherent or (ii) the strategy requires modification. In the case of the latter, steps 1 through 5 should be repeated.

From personal and the experience of others I have come across, one of the biggest obstacles to being able to form a coherent strategy is a poor ability to visualise. If you are unable to visualise then how will you be able to describe your ideal future state either to yourself or to others?

Visualisation

I would hazard a guess that most people have had a dream at some point during their life. Some people can describe their dream in vivid detail and others can only recall the main gist. Being able to imagine how you would like things to be in the future is a bit like dreaming. However, it is a skill that most people can learn to do well if they practice.

I have found the following steps useful in helping to improve visualisation:

1. I imagine that I am in a quiet place and there is no one else around. Although there might be activities going on around me, I block out noise and other distractions by not focusing on these. Sometimes I just close my eyes to prevent visual distractions.

2. In my quite place I imagine my surroundings to be plain e.g. pitch black. I do this because I do not want my mind to be distracted by anything.

3. I now imagine how it would feel if I were in my future state. I begin to think about the sensations I might feel in my body, I think about my surroundings at that time and its colours (which would no longer be pitch black), the people that will be witness to my success etc.

4. I imagine myself holding that certificate of achievement, sitting in that office of the newly promoted, reading the article in the newspaper about my success and I observe how others are reacting to my achievement etc.

5. I imagine the opportunities that my achievement can now afford me, and I evaluate the possibilities. I also imagine how I can make more of a positive impact on the lives of others based on my achievement.

6. I document my vision.

You might find either the above or some adaptation suitable for your purposes. For example, some people prefer to start at (3) rather than (1). Experience suggests that people sometimes have difficulties with retaining clarity of the vision they have imagined for more than a few seconds. Often, this occurs because they have not sufficiently practiced forming mental images in their mind on demand. In such instances it is useful to perform visualisation on something that you can see with your eyes open.

As an example, hold your mobile phone (or some other object) in your hand and look at it from several angles. Take as long as you think you need to memorise its features. Then close your eyes and try and recall the features of your phone or object and then write it down and compare it to the physical object. If your description is far from reality, then repeat this exercise until you are comfortable with your description.

Visualisation is something that must be practiced frequently. If you really want something you do not just think about it once, you think about it many times and from several perspectives. The more often you think about it the more comfortable you become with describing how you feel when your visualisation is realised.

By practicing visualisation on a frequent basis (I recommend daily) and taking into consideration your current situation, you put yourself in a position to identify what changes you need to make (if any) to accommodate your vision. By treating visualisation as a daily exercise and as part of your routine like having breakfast or lunch, you make the exercise second nature. However, as with all things, your vision of the future must be realistic.

To base your vision on something that is largely dependent on luck (i.e. not within your control) is not a good idea. So, for example, if your vision of the future involves random events such as others being fired from work, others being injured on the day of the championship finals etc., then you need to change your vision. Your vision should be one in which you and others can work in concert to achieve your objectives. If luck happens then take it but do not base your life on luck.

You might be of the view that you already implement some or all the above steps and still have problems with your abilities, belief and having a coherent strategy. I would suggest you continue to try and solicit feedback from others on how you can improve. One realisation you might come to is that your ability to grow in your organisation is limited and you need to move on. In a subsequent chapter called "Firing your boss" I provide guidance on when it might be timely to leave your current organisation.

Exercise

Visualise what success means for you.
- Does your current state match your vision?

    If yes, is there anything else you could do to improve your situation? If the answer is no you appear to be in a good place. If the answer is yes, think about what else you could be doing to improve.

    If no, try to determine the reasons why you have not achieved your desired state. Figure out what you can and cannot directly control and where you need help. Then write down (or do some research first to figure out) a strategy for achieving your goals.

Further reading

1. Gawain, S, (2002). *Creative Visualization*, New World Library Pub

Chapter 13

We are all leaders

Introduction
Family
Sports - key steps
Own business
Further reading

Introduction

Having a title, people working for you or having academic qualifications or years of experience does not necessarily make you a leader.

True leaders are those that exhibit additional qualities that we can call soft skills and exhibit the attributes as discussed in earlier chapters. We all have leadership qualities and whether we choose to exercise these qualities for the better or worse is up to us. As also previously discussed, the principles of leadership can be distilled into a simple ABC providing us a conceptually appealing framework to enhance our leadership abilities.

In the following sections, I give some further examples to illustrate how ABC applies to different aspects of our lives.

Most likely, you would have either read and/or heard about the biblical account of the fight between David and Goliath. What image do you have in mind when you think about this account? Is it one where a boy, ill-equipped and inexperienced goes to fight against a formidable mighty warrior? My guess is that most people would reconcile this thought with the account of the fight between David and Goliath. However, they would be wrong!

The Bible does not explicitly state how old David was when he defeated Goliath but various assumptions can be made which puts David in an age range between 16 and 20. In any event, he certainly was not as old and neither was he a seasoned fighter like Goliath so how did he win? From a biblical perspective, we know that David was chosen by God to defeat Goliath but nonetheless it was David that achieved the feat. In other words, David chose to fight Goliath.

Recall the point I have made earlier in this book regarding reasons why some people are not leaders. One of those reasons is due to persons not choosing to take on the responsibility. If a person with leadership capabilities chooses not to be a leader then they will not be leaders, so the first step in becoming a leader is to make the choice to say yes.

What many people may not know was the sling referenced in the Bible was not a toy but a weapon that had been used for thousands of years prior to David and commonly used by the Hebrews in warfare. Typically, high proficiency in the use of a sling required several years of experience and it was customary for children to use slings from a young age. Hence, by the time David fought Goliath he was an expert with the sling and moreover, his age would have been of no consequence.

Moving beyond the story of David, society is witnessing that age is becoming less of an issue for many newly established businesses. There is evidence that more young persons are not only wanting to be entrepreneurs but are setting up their own businesses. Generation Z and Millennials are making up an increasing amount of the workforce across many countries globally and even in established organisations are moving into leadership positions, although perhaps not at the rate at which they ought.

In the biblical account of David versus Goliath you might recall that King Saul was initially incredulous to David's suggestion that he be allowed to fight Goliath. In fact, in 1 Samuel 17:34-36 David finds it necessary to give account to Saul of his fighting credentials in recalling his fights against both a lion and a bear. It was as if David was being interviewed for a job and relaying the relevancy of his prior experience to that of the job at hand. It is unlikely that David had anything more than a slingshot and a shepherd's stick at the time when he killed the lion and the bear.

So, what does the above tell us about David?

* **Ability.** There is an abundance of evidence in the Bible and other historical accounts that suggest that David had the ability to defeat Goliath. Recall that David had previously defeated wild animals. Even if Saul and others had doubts about the veracity of David's claim about killing wild animals it was more difficult for them to doubt his proficiency in the use of the sling. At the very least, David had the potential to hurt Goliath due to his ability to use his sling to great effect.

* **Belief.** David had an unwavering belief that God would guide and protect him throughout all situations. However, this was not just based on his spiritual convictions. If David had, in fact, defeated wild animals then this alone would provide evidence that he could do the same thing to Goliath. In David's plea to Saul to allow him to fight he showed no signs of disbelief in his abilities. Hence David was also able to convince Saul into believing that he had the ability to get the job done and he did this by use of his effective communication skills.

- **Coherent strategy**. David had conceptualised a coherent strategy to defeat Goliath and had clearly rehearsed it in his mind. In 1 Samuel 17: 45-46 David even tells Goliath what he intended to do with him saying that he will strike him down and cut off his head. So said, so done.

Whether you are a believer in the accounts of the Bible or not it is easy to see how the ABC principles apply. In whatever situation you might find yourself, the ABC principles can be applied. For example, consider the origins of the ubiquitous PlayStation games. Did you know that this was invented by Ken Kutaragi who, at the time, was a relatively junior Sony employee?

Mr Kutaragi undertook to develop a sound chip for Nintendo (a project which, initially, he had no approval for) and when his superiors found out they were not pleased. However, Mr Kutaragi was able to convince his CEO that he should continue with the work and this eventually led to a joint venture between Sony and Nintendo, two rival companies.

Even though Sony were initially opposed to the idea of developing video games Mr Kutaragi had the support of the company's CEO and went on to guide the development of the Play Station and later versions.

There are some parallels that can be drawn between the experience of Mr Kutaragi and the biblical account of David versus Goliath:

- **Ability**. Although relatively junior Mr Kutaragi had gained the reputation of being considered a problem solver by colleagues. This would not have been the case had he not demonstrated his technical abilities.

- **Belief**. Notwithstanding his technical abilities, Mr Kutaragi faced opposition from senior members of his organisation and was, potentially, in danger of losing his job for working on an activity not approved by management for a rival company. However, Mr Kutaragi maintained a strong belief in his abilities to undertake the activity and was also able to make a believer out of the organisation's CEO.

- **Coherent strategy**. Mr Kutaragi was able to articulate his strategy to senior management and demonstrate how he would be able to successfully undertake the engagement with Nintendo and how this would be of benefit to Sony.

I doubt very much whether Mr Kutaragi was thinking along the lines of the ABC principle as I have detailed it in this book as most people that are proficient in the application of some skill/ability do so without thinking about it. However, all acts of leadership can be synthesised by the principle and it provides a useful basis for leadership development.

You might be asking; how can I apply the ABC principle to situations in my family or personal life. Here are some examples.

Family

As a parent of three children I know how wonderful and rewarding it can be to see your children grow and develop but it can also be extremely challenging. Being a parent is more than just saying do this or do that or else. Whereas children look for guidance, they also tend to react negatively to hypocrisy. In other words, do as I say not as I do does not work too well.

As a husband I am also aware of the need to consult my wife on most matters in relation to the home as well as my/her professional life. Note that I said most and not all matters. Even though you might be married this does not mean that you have the right to think, speak and act for your other half. It also does not mean that you cannot think, speak, and act for yourself even if such actions are at odds with your other half. You should, however, be cognisant of the implications of any decisions you make by yourself and how this can affect your family and act in the best interest of your family.

Whether you are a single or co-parent, divorced, young or old it makes no difference to your ability to be a leader in your home. Your ability to be a good partner and/or parent has nothing to do with your gender, religious, political, or other beliefs if these are within the laws of the land. However, these attributes will have an influence on the type of leader you are, and the "culture" adopted in your home.

As someone born in the UK, to Jamaican immigrants, I know what it is like to grow up in a home with one culture and to experience a completely different one outside of the home. My parents came to the UK during what is now commonly called the Windrush period. Their hopes and aspirations of building a better life was quickly threatened, due to racism, when they tried to obtain employment and then buy their first house. In both cases their resilience won through and my parents were not only able to obtain employment but were able to buy a house and provide shelter for others that had also made the decision to emigrate from Jamaica to the UK.

Throughout my childhood, there were numerous other similar events, which affected my parents, but it was not until later in life that I learnt of these matters. It subsequently became clear to me that my parents were trying to shield me from harm by not revealing to me the extent to which they had been ill-treated. As a parent I have realised that there is a fine balance to be struck between protecting your children from the knowledge of hate, prejudice/discrimination or other unwarranted acts and educating your children as to how to deal with such situations.

My parents placed a high value on being employed and income security. However, this had an impact on the amount of time we spent together as my parents spent much time at work. Often, they were too tired to sit down with me and help me with my schoolwork. This said, my parents would buy me whatever resources I required to help me to achieve my goals. I guess that this was probably how they were brought up and saw no issue with continuing the same for their children. However, I was adamant that I would want to do more for my children and give them the quality of life and time that they deserved.

By the time I got married in my late twenties I had already started a business but had to close it down, largely to focus on my PhD, and had done enough travelling and reading to have a wide perspective on life. I also became a parent within the first year of marriage. I was sure that I would be a great parent. However, I made a lot of mistakes as a relatively young parent, trying to get too much done in too short a time frame.

I fell into the same trap as my parents becoming too preoccupied with ensuring income security and was continually working up to 12 hours a day and beyond. Yes, my family were living in a relatively nice part of Surrey (a county in the south of England) and we could afford to go on holiday a few times a year and the kids could go to private school. However, even when I was home, I was invariably doing some type of work-related activity. Superficially family life was great, but the reality was quite different. I did not spend the quality time with my kids that I had sworn I would, and I was not the best man I could be and certainly not the best husband.

The main lesson that I learnt from my earlier failures, as a father and husband, can be summarized as follows: I didn't insist on establishing and following a core set of values that I and my family could use to guide our relationship. Establishing a core set of values might seem rather over the top and too formal when it comes to family relationships but, I believe, they work.

As a young Christian I had religious views about ethics and the way in which my family and I should live. However, my life was becoming increasingly imbalanced and work and related activities were dominating my life. Decisions that should have been thought through more thoroughly were either simply not undertaken or acted on without enough consideration. My work and its lifestyle had become my focus and it forced my family into having a bit part in what should have been a leading role in my life.

If I had maintained the focus on my religious views, then I would have prioritised love and family time over the pursuit of money and position. I doubt that this would have negatively impacted on my performance at work and I would have had a much better work-life balance.

My point here is not to suggest that you need to be a fervently practicing Christian to know how to balance work and private life activities but I do believe having an agreed set of core values will help to keep the perspective that the focus should be on the latter. In 1964 the Beatles recorded a song called "Can't Buy Me Love" with the sentiment being that it is not about the money, but the things money cannot buy. Try and keep this sentiment in mind for your own life.

Today we often hear people say nothing is out of bounds when it comes to discussions and behaviour in their home (if it is within the law). Whereas I agree that there should be open communication and freedom of expression I also believe that parents have primary responsibility for setting boundaries of what they perceive to be acceptable norms of behaviour.

Just like school, work, social club or most other institutions, a home should have rules which result in maintaining a set of core values. These values are not, necessarily, set by one individual but is a collective responsibility for the whole family but with the parents as co-CEO's ensuring standards are maintained by all. It is essential, however, that a circle of trust be established in which all family members feel comfortable and capable of raising all kinds of matters in an appropriate way with those subject to the core values.

This is not to say that one cannot seek the opinion of others outside the circle but not where it compromises the integrity of those part of the inner circle.

There will always be a place for those outside of your family inner circle and circumstances might arise in which outsiders become part of the circle for a period, but this should be based on agreement. This said, it is important to realise that there are occasions when outside counsel might be warranted prior to having discussions with those part of your inner circle. Most likely this would occur when someone is seeking support about how they may raise an issue with a family member or where they perceive that such a person has breached the family trust.

The lessons I have learnt, over the years, have made me a better husband and father and can be distilled into the ABC principles as follows:

* **Ability**
    - Knowing and acting on the difference between being a father/mother and being a dad/mum. In general, any man/woman can be a father/mother, but being a dad/mum requires making conscious decisions about: (i) seeing things from the children's point of view but knowing how to say no with love if required, (ii) acting as a good role model to the children e.g. do not adopt a do as I say approach. Point (iii) taking special time out to be with the children (or using technology when you can't be physically there), (iv) praising them publicly (as well as in private) when they do well and being stern but not embarrassing them when they falter and (v) protecting them from harm. Doing these five things well will differentiate you from someone who is merely a father/mother and not a real dad/mum.

    - Knowing and acting on the difference between being a partner (e.g. husband/wife, significant other) or someone in a relationship of convenience. Not every formal/informal relationship will last and there are no hard and fast rules which are generally applicable to all relationships, however, there are some similarities with being a parent: (i) seeing things from the other person's perspective and knowing how to disagree in a loving way, (ii) acting as a good role model to your partner in terms of ethics and conduct, (iii) taking time out to be with your partner other than just at Valentines, Mother's/Father's day or their birthday, (iv) encouraging, supporting and complementing your partner to do well and on their achievements but also being understanding and considerate when they falter and (v) protecting your partner from harm. Doing these five things well will differentiate you from someone merely in a relationship of convenience.

- **Belief**
  - If you doubt your ability to be able to act as a dad/mum and/or partner, do not be surprised if your significant others also share the same doubt about you. It is generally the case that one's actions follows one's beliefs and so thinking positively and making steps to be a good parent/partner is more likely to be successful than if you only went through the motions. You should, therefore, communicate your beliefs to those in your circle of trust with a view to gaining consensus. Relationships are about compromise and it might be that you need to modify your views if your circle is to remain intact.

- **Coherent strategy**
  - If your strategy does not reflect the opinions of your partner and/or children as per the items (i) through (v) above then, most likely, it is not coherent and quite likely to fail.

Sports - key steps

In a previous chapter I gave an example showing how the ABC principles could be used to explain the success of Muhammad Ali. In the current section I will move in the opposite direction and highlight how the principles could be applied to someone that wishes to be a good (or possibly great) sports competitor. It is not my intention to provide a detailed description of the process of being a competitor but how the principles fit in.

Core fitness characteristics

There are several characteristics that any person should possess in order to be able to undertake sports. A commonly chosen subset of these characteristics are speed, agility, strength, endurance, and flexibility. Each different type of sport has its own norms for the right level of each characteristic required to be considered proficient.

One of the first things any budding sports person should do, in relation to the above core characteristics, is to assess their level of fitness as compared to the norms of the sport for someone of their gender, age, weight and possibly disabilities.

The ABC principles apply as follows:

* **Ability**
  - Assess where you are in relation to the norm for your gender, age, weight, and any disabilities for the sport you wish to pursue for each of the five characteristics. You can do this by asking those that are more expert in your chosen sport such as coaches or instructors. Alternatively, you could do some research on the internet. In any event, the five characteristics are the core set of abilities that you would need to develop, beyond the technical skills required to do your chosen sport.

  - Be aware of interactions between your core abilities and how they relate to your technical skills for the sport. For example, although you need a certain amount of strength to be a good 100 metre runner, you do not need to have the strength of a power lifter. In fact, being too good a power lifter could impair your ability to run very quickly.

- Be aware of how your core and technical abilities need to interact with your soft skills. For example, an insufficient degree of humility and patience might result in you being classed as not being coachable irrespective of how well you perform at your sport. The key here is to see how your soft skills can be used to enhance your likelihood of being a better performer.

* **Belief**
    - You can enhance your belief of self by obtaining some wins. The more training and competitive targets you achieve, the more your confidence should improve. Similarly, achieving these targets should also result in enhanced belief of others in you. A key objective is to remain positive even if you have not achieved your targets and to manage self-doubt and thoughts of failure.

* **Coherent strategy**
    - A coherent strategy would involve the identification of targets to assess your performance. These targets might be set by your coach/instructor or by yourself. This strategy should eventually result in you being able to test your sporting skills against others. Key to your strategy is:

        · Being able to visualise what successfully achieving your targets will look and feel like.

        · Monitoring what is working well for you and why.

        · Monitoring what does not work so well and why and assess its potential to impact what you do well.

        · Implement activities that will address what does not work so well and identify timeliness in which this should be done.

        · Understand where your strengths and weaknesses lie with respect to your peers and identify an individual(s) you wish to benchmark your skills against and identify how you will achieve that result.

- Prepare for the next competition/game.

A leader at my level?

It is certainly the case that everyone is not a good leader, but most people can be made into better leaders. For example, you do not have to be the CEO of an organisation or a senior manager to be a leader as even the most junior staff member can be a leader at what they do.

Organisations which respect all their staff members will facilitate for their development and value their contribution in aiding in the direction of the firm. If properly nurtured, these individuals could eventually become future leaders of the firm. However, what if your bosses do not recognise your leadership skills, what should you do?

The first thing you should do is to determine whether you have enough information to verify that your boss is undervaluing your skills. You should do this by making a note of the dates for which you believe you were overlooked. Compare your skills to those of others to assess whether other persons have been treated the same. If you feel confident that your feelings have a basis then you should try and schedule a meeting with your boss to discuss the matter. If you do not feel confident then, initially, try and discuss the matter with a human resource representative and/or a trusted colleague.

The result of the above might be to highlight a deficiency in your abilities or reveal how others perceive your abilities. If this is the case, then highlighting issues with your boss (or others) provides an opportunity to identify areas for your capacity building. However, it might be that your discussions reveal that you are being undervalued and your abilities insufficiently recognised.

If you are being undervalued but you want to remain in your organisation then you need to assess whether there is any realistic possibility of you getting the recognition that you think you deserve. In making this assessment you should take into consideration how long you think it might take and what changes you/organisation need to make to achieve your desired results.

In seeking to remain in your organisation you should:

* **Ability.** Seek opportunities to refine your existing skills and develop new ones. You should also consider augmenting internal capacity building with online and/or face to face certified training. For almost all kinds of employment types there are numerous avenues available to undertake formal training. Certification is important since it shows an independent acknowledgement of achievement at a specified level. You should try and incorporate the suggestions of your boss, HR, and others in your choice of training courses undertaken.

* **Belief.** Once you have achieved a certain level of competence (not necessarily after you have fully completed your capacity building) consider volunteering to shadow those considered expert in your field or just ask to be part of a team working in the same area. This shows that you are confident (or have belief) in your abilities but also provides the opportunity for others to assess your skills.

* **Coherent strategy.** Obtain agreement from your boss and HR that the capacity building undertaken, or skills discussed will be recognised as a competence on your appraisal or equivalent performance review. Further, you should also obtain agreement that the competence/skills will form part of your work duties/tasks or that you be allowed access to job opportunities elsewhere in the organisation.

You should not lose sight of the possibility that it might be that you will never be able to get to where you want in your firm. If you have come to this conclusion then, rather than to remain and be underutilised you should be actively seeking to move to an organisation that values your abilities.

Business owner

According to the UK's Office for National Statistics, as of 2019, around 15% of the labour force were classed as self-employed. This category includes those with and without employees. The figure shows an increase on the 2001 numbers where the rate was around 12%.

The general trend appears to be that more people are becoming self-employed not only in the UK but in other areas of the world. Anecdotal data suggests that there is an increasing number of those classed as non-self-employed (for our purposes, an individual employed to an organisation for which they are not a significant owner) also have other ventures through which they are generating income.

The concept of the ABC leader is as much applicable (if not more) to those that are self-employed as it is to those that have "regular" employment. As a self-employed person you will, largely, be responsible for most (if not all) of your marketing/advertising, administrative activities, technical work, strategy and in some instances, employee relations. Your work hours will often be greater than eight hours per day and you will be responsible for your own personal development. So, how can the ABC principles be applied?

- **Ability**. Before anyone decides to set up a new business for self-employment, they should:

    ○ Determine whether they have the requisite skills for the area of the market they wish to compete. One way of doing this is to compare your skills to those that are currently engaged in the area e.g. viewing profiles on LinkedIn or similar sites. Another way is to send your Curriculum Vitae (CV) to an agency that either recruits or facilitates for employment in your area of interest and use this as a means of getting feedback on your skills. I also suggest that these two things should be done not just at the beginning of self-employment but during the life of a business.

    ○ If having completed your benchmarking exercise you find that there are gaps, then you should identify suitable training that you can undertake to improve your skills. Training which results in some type of certification or recognised qualification should be the preference. As with all types of development, training should not be a one-time thing and self-employed individuals should be continuously seeking to maintain up to date skills.

    ○ You should be able to demonstrate:
        - To potential investors that you have a viable business plan to achieve stated goals/objectives and that the business will be financially sustainable.

- To potential clients that you have the capacity to be able to deliver the type of products/service they require and within specified quality and price levels. Capacity here includes not just your skills but also your ability to attract the necessary talent/systems to aid you in the running of your business.

- To all potential stakeholders that you can effectively communicate your value proposition and potential benefits to you and them.

- That you can balance work and private life without any detriment to the latter.

- That you can realistically earn a living to support the lifestyle you either have or seek to have going forwards.

* **Belief.** Confidence in your ability to succeed in your business is enhanced if you can:

    - Obtain testimonials from others that have first-hand knowledge of your skills and are willing to say good things about you and/or your business. This can be done through several means including LinkedIn, and other social media as well as your company website.

    - Ensure your skills are up to date and in line with best or better practice.

* **Coherent strategy.** You should have a strategy which articulates the growth plans for the business in such a manner that it references your business plans and demonstrates how the business will be sustainable. The strategy should, among other items, identify the means by which success and failure of the business will be measured and the timescales for various initiatives.

Further reading

1. ONS. (2020), *Labour Market Overview, August 2020*, ONS, viewed September 4, 2020, <https://www.ons.gov.U.K./employmentandlabourmarket/peopleinwork/employmentandemployeetypes/articles/coronavirusandselfemploymentintheU.K./2020-04-24>
2. Law, S. (2018), *David Battles Goliath: Is There Evidence?*, Patterns of Evidence, viewed on September 4, 2020, < https://patternsofevidence.com/2018/10/26/david-battles-goliath/>.
3. Leone, M. (2018), *The legacy of PlayStation creator Ken Kutaragi, in 24 stories*,Wikipedia, viewed September 4, 2020, < https://www.polygon.com/2018/11/26/18080492/playstation-history-ken-kutaragi-sony>
4. Wikipedia (2020), *Ken Kutaragi,* Wikipedia Foundation, viewed on September 4, 2020, <https://en.wikipedia.org/wiki/Ken_Kutaragi>

Chapter 14
Good & bad

Introduction
The bottom line
NGO
My way or the highway
It's a man's world
Exercise
Further reading

Introduction

Recall my earlier description of a bad leader as simply being a person in a position of leadership whilst a good leader is simply called a leader. Hence, for me, the term leader only applies to those that are considered good leaders. However, in this chapter I will provide examples of good and bad leadership. The descriptions are not meant to be exhaustive but simply to illustrate common examples of poor behaviour.

The bottom line

One thing I think I need to make clear from the very start is that good leadership is not just about making profit. Consider company X that has generated a year-on-year increase in profits of over 16% (for the last 5 years). You might be tempted to say that this is not bad at all. What if I tell you that this company (over the same period) had an annual staff turnover rate of 13.4% and most of those that left were classified as being either good or outstanding performers. Further, suppose it emerged that turnover at the senior level (i.e. within one or two levels of the CEO but not including the CEO) was even higher at 23%, what would you make of this?

Even in the absence of further information, it is quite clear that company X has a problem. Whilst profit growth appears good it also seems clear that staff retention is not so good and could be indicative of poor leadership. The company is losing good people across the organisation and, most likely, key senior individuals. This is a recipe for disaster which, in this case, is masked by the growth in profits. It is unlikely that this trend will be sustainable but if leadership is all about profits then nothing will be done to rectify the situation anytime soon.

There are many companies like company X. They largely move to the tune of the CEO but are dependent on skilled individuals to get the job done. In such organisations, there is often tension between skilled staff and more senior management largely due to micromanagement. Even when staff require close supervision and guidance micromanagement is not advisable since it can severely restrict the freedom/creativity of individuals.

More worrying, micromanagement can lose perspective of the big picture (i.e. overall objectives) as to why someone was hired in the first place and how they fit into the organisation. Micromanagement can lead to accusations of bullying but is often tolerated by organisations since they claim it gets results or fits into their corporate culture. Naturally, most organisations are unlikely to overtly state that they tolerate micromanagement but will likely rationalise their approach based on culture.

Corporate culture is set at the top of an organisation and a good leader will ensure that policies and procedures are in place to ensure that micromanagement will not be tolerated. A bad leader will be satisfied with ambiguity and with policies that do not clearly rule out the possibility. This latter type of leader will be the first to throw someone under the bus if it means that they are able to save face but will defend their own practices if they are directly accused.

A while back, on a LinkedIn post, I coined the phrase LINO – Leader in Name Only to characterise someone that is in a position of leadership but does not live up to the title of leader. In the UK, Linoleum (Lino for short) has often been used in homes to provide a relatively cheap and easy to maintain floor covering. It can be made to look like wood, but it just is not wood. It is not as trustworthy/durable and presentable. I used this analogy to make a point, leadership is not about a title but about conduct/behaviour as well as abilities and there is no substitute for the real thing.

NGO

Consider a non-governmental organisation (NGO) Y whose main key performance indicator is the number of meetings/events organised with various countries and/or the number of policy papers written. In this respect, the head of the organisation is particularly pleased that they have exceeded the number of outputs for the last year. This type of organisation is, clearly, not driven by profitability. The driving force for this type of organisation is the publicity they generate because of meeting their indicators.

Suppose that Y has met all its KPI's, but that employee turnover is currently at around the 15% level and that over 67% of staff members (based on a survey) feel demotivated? Also, just like Company X, good performing staff members are leaving the organisation.

There are strong similarities between X and Y irrespective of their raison d'etre. Many NGO's operate based on extolling the virtues of the CEO (often called Secretary General- SG). These organisations have communication/press departments whose main role is to promote the photo opportunities and/or column inches for the SG rather than to focus on outcomes. This might seem to be an oversimplification, but my experience is echoed across many individuals that I have met that have worked for a varied number of NGO's.

Why is outcome rather than output important? It is easy for an organisation to produce a piece of work and say that they have achieved some objective. However, it is harder for an NGO to impact governments to the extent to which they achieve changes in government direction as indicated by implementation of new laws, regulations etc. The fact that outcomes are harder to achieve than output should not be a deterrent to using the former as the basis for defining KPI's.

With the above in mind, the mere fact that Y has met its KPI's in terms of events organised and/or papers written does not imply that it has achieved a positive impact in terms of influencing outcomes. Also, with relatively high levels of staff turnover, low morale and good performers leaving the organisation, does not bode well for the leadership of Y. There is clearly a problem with Y on different levels which is highly likely a reflection of poor leadership.

My way or the highway

John Jenkings (not his real name) is the CEO of a technology company he started fifteen years ago. He built the company from a start-up and led its listing on the stock exchange where it now has a valuation in excess of USD $9 Billion. Combined with John's other business interests his personal wealth exceeds $5 Billion.

John is known to be a hard worker and believes his staff should also work hard. He continually works 100 hours per week and believes his dedication to work helps to inspire his employees.

John describes himself as a go-getter and gets easily frustrated when tasks he has assigned are not done in the manner he would expect. He leads by example says some of his employees and provides a clear sense of direction for the organisation. This said, others view him as being autocratic and inflexible and cite this as an example as to why senior management do not hang around for too long.

John likes publicity but does not like it when his employees are also exposed to the media as he believes that he is best suited to manage the image of the company. Whereas John encourages creative and innovative thinking he strongly believes in and values loyalty and expects staff to be 100% focused on their employment at his company.

In the absence of further details, it is difficult to say whether John is a good or bad leader. There are some obvious positives brought about by John's management style including his proven ability to create value (via way of his company being listed), his dedication and his ability to influence others and provide clear direction. However, there are also some potential negatives such as the long hours he works and expects of others; his apparent autocratic style, frustration when things do not go as he planned and loyalty issues. Some people may not see these aspects as being negative, but I include them since they have the potential to erode stakeholder value of a company in the ways I will detail below.

Long working hours

It never fails to amaze me how many people still hold the view that working long hours at work shows dedication and productivity. If performance is rewarded based on the number of hours spent at work, then we all might as well bring a bed to work and stay full-time. However, if performance is based on outcomes achieved then it should be irrelevant how many hours it took so long as it is within expectations.

Focusing on time at work misses the objective of why people are hired in the first place. Of course, there might be instances when employees are required to work longer than their contractual hours, but this should be the exception and not the norm. Moreover, having the expectation that staff will continually work long hours is indicative of poor project management and ignores the balance between work and home life that staff need to maintain a healthy lifestyle both physical and mental.

My advice is that you should be working hard to work smart. In other words, the goal is to work smarter, not harder. As an employee, you know that you are working smart when you can complete your activities without working overtime (unless on rare occasions), go home and detach yourself from work and go to bed without any thoughts (or nightmares) of work. As an entrepreneur, you know you are working smart when you can do your work in normal working hours and go to bed knowing that you are earning whilst you are sleeping.

Autocratic management style

There is nothing wrong with being firm and direct if it is done in a manner which is fair to all concerned. However, when the opinions of others are ignored and/or not solicited, and management become inflexible then this is highly likely to constrain the freedom with which staff can perform their duties. This is likely to create tensions between staff and management with the result being less motivated and productive staff and increased turnover and absenteeism.

Showing frustration to employees

Letting your staff know that you are frustrated with their performance is something that should be carefully undertaken. Not everyone thinks or acts in the same way and expecting people to do things exactly as you would do them is quite unrealistic in most instances.

What is important is that a leader should provide unambiguous guidance as to what they are requesting of others. Moreover, providing staff do not breach any organisational rules then they should be given latitude within which to execute their duties in a manner consistent with their role and abilities.

To show disdain when staff deviate from your ideals might undermine their confidence and erode the duty of care implied in the contractual agreement between employee and the organisation. Criticisms, when valid and constructive, are a welcomed part of feedback required for professional development of staff. However, these should not spillover into personal characterisations or attacks against staff or singling them out for poor performance appraisals.

Loyalty

In my experience, there is a thin line between the desire for loyalty and being insecure. In its simplest terms, loyalty requires an employee to act in a manner which is faithful and not to compete with the interests of their organisation. Consequently, acting for self-interest/benefit or for the benefit of a third party might be construed as being disloyal.

Depending on the formality of the relationship that you have with your employer, you might have a contract of employment which specifies the organisations requirements of what they expect of your conduct. This contract might also be supplemented by organisational policies/procedures which are also meant to form part of your contractual obligations. The details of these documents are meant to convey the "rules of engagement" between employer and employee and deviations from these rules can be interpreted as acts of disloyalty. However, as in most contracts, there will be several areas for which there is no explicit contractual arrangement, and this is where many issues often arise.

Loyalty, like respect is something that must be earned. Just because you work for and have signed a contract of employment for an organisation does not mean that the onus is only on you to be loyal. The fact is loyalty is a two-way street. Gone are the days when most individuals would work for a firm for life. Increasingly millennials (or younger folk) are working less longer for organisations than previous generations. Moreover, with the increased use of zero-hours, fixed-term, and other style of contracts some employers are actively seeking to manage employment lawsuits by reducing the rights of employees.

Adopting a do as I say and not as I do attitude, is unlikely to result in loyalty but could easily bring about resentment, a lack of trust and a reduction in productivity. In the case of John Jenkings, his love for the limelight and his reaction to others exposure to the media might be justified by policy but is unlikely to be for the reasons he mentions.

If John were a true leader then he would realise that leadership is not only about the views of the CEO, but he would consciously work to promote the development and ideas of others in his organisation. However, John not only wants to limit staff exposure but wants to curb the extent to which creativity and innovation are exposed externally. This has the tell-tale signs of insecurity and could be a main reason as to why senior management do not last long at the firm.

It's a man's world

In February 1966, James Brown recorded the song "it's a Man's Man's Man's World". The opening lyrics of the song states: "This is a man's world, this is a man's world But it wouldn't be nothing, nothing without a woman or a girl". This song made the point that many of the everyday items we have become used to were invented by men but that, in many instances, these items would be meaningless without the existence of a women.

Ursula Burns would have been eight at the time of the release of the James Brown song. What might she have made of the lyrics? Ursula grew up in the Baruch housing project in New York. She and her two siblings were raised by a single mother and both her parents were immigrants from Panama. The lessons given to Ursula by her mother resonated as she obtained a Bachelor of Science degree in mechanical engineering from New York University in 1980 and a Master of Science in the same subject matter the year after.

The first job Ursula obtained, after graduating, was at Xerox where she remained until 2017. Ursula had a variety of roles in product development and planning during the eighties and decided to take up an offer as an assistant to a senior executive in 1990. Within a year she was the assistant to the CEO and Chairman. By 2001 Ursula was a senior vice president and became the CEO of Xerox in 2009.

Ursula Burns became the first black woman to head up a fortune 500 company. Shortly after taking over as CEO Ursula also became the Chairwoman of Xerox. However, if this is a man's world, how did she get to the top of one of the most revered organisations in the world? In some respects, the answer is remarkably simple, even men need to rely on the best, and this will not always be found in another man. Ursula did not let the colour of her skin or her gender be a reason for her to be held back.

At the time Ursula took on the CEO role at Xerox, the organisation was in desperate need of change. Its image had become synonymous with the photocopier and it was losing global market share to companies such as Canon and Ricoh. The company had to make a radical decision to move with the times and embrace software technology rather than just to focus on manufacturing.

Ursula led the acquisition of the Affiliated Computer Services company and revamped research and development efforts at the Palo Alto Research Centre. These efforts resulted in a transformation of the organisation from its manufacturing roots towards that of a software technology-based company with increased product and service offerings.

In an interview with the American business magazine publisher, Fast Company, Ursula states that she had to become a better listener to enhance her engagement skills. Although she had a clear idea as to what she wanted to do (i.e. to transform Xerox) it became clear that she needed to listen to and rely on the expertise of others to determine how transformation could be successfully implemented. Since the transformation involved downsizing parts and outsourcing some other aspects it was important that Ursula had the support of key personnel and was seen to be leading from the front but in a consultative manner. In this way Ursula was also transforming herself into a strategist and reinforcing her people-person skills.

Perhaps one way of summarising Ursula's leadership qualities is that she is an inclusive, flexible/reflexive, visionary, problem solver and an effective communicator. She also proved that even though the c-suite of the corporate world might be predominantly viewed as being white and male oriented that women and people of colour are just as effective. As a result, Ursula also showed that its more than just a man's world.

Exercise

Do you consider yourself to be a good leader?

If you answered yes, write down some of the regular things that you do that make you a good leader. If you answered no, write down how you plan to change and by when.

Further reading

1. Vermeulen, F. (2018), *Breaking Bad Habits: Why Best Practices Are Killing Your Business*, Harvard Business Review Press Pub
2. Wikipedia (2020), *Ursula Burns*, Wikipedia Foundation, viewed September 4, 2020, <https://en.wikipedia.org/wiki/Ursula_Burns>

Chapter 15

Your aura

Introduction
Communication
Exercise

Introduction

There are some people that believe a big part of being a leader is looking like a leader, particularly when it comes to dress and grooming. However, wearing a Hugo Boss suit and being a frequent visitor to Harrods Hair & Beauty Salon does not endow you with the qualities of a leader. I often say, it is not what you wear but how you wear it that matters.

Some people will judge you based on how you speak, the university you went to, your culture, religion, race, or gender. None of these are of any importance when it comes to being a leader in the workplace and might form the basis of a lawsuit if used in determining promotion, hiring or other work benefits.

By use of the term aura, I do not assign any type of scientific meaning but instead I take it to mean *the impression you leave on people and how this affects their perception of you.* How people perceive you might not necessarily reflect what you are since we all have preconceived ideas and prejudices which can affect our ability to be completely rationale and objective. However, by continuously seeking to improve our abilities, our decisions should become more objective and defensible.

Perceptions are generally based on two main facets: (1) how you do what you do and interact with others and (2) how you present yourself. The first facet can be broken down into verbal (e.g. written or spoken communications) and non-verbal (e.g. actions or deeds directly or indirectly attributable to you). Indirect actions refer to instructions from you and executed by others.

If you work for an organisation which requires you to wear an outfit and you turn up wearing something different, to other people, then do not be surprised if someone remarks on your appearance. Outside of this and if someone does not dress inappropriately, I do not believe (and have seen no evidence to the contrary) that appearance should be a major determinant in whether a person is viewed as being a leader. Disturbingly, however, there are an increasing number of studies which reveal that black women are not viewed positively (by white workers) unless their hair is straightened. There is only one word for this, **racism.** To treat someone differently on the grounds of their natural hair preferring straight over curly is to denigrate that person's race and culture.

So, notwithstanding prejudice, how you do what you do and interact with others largely determines whether people will view you as a leader or not. The following focuses on the main areas you should work on to improve your leadership aura.

Communication

At any level in an organisation, if you are not able to effectively communicate with staff members at all levels as well as external stakeholders then it will be difficult for people to understand you and buy into you as a leader. Effective communications lie at the heart of every good organisation and is often a differentiating factor between growth and declining organisations.

Based on my experience and research, I have found that effective communicators, often, exhibit the following behaviours:

- Avoid responding to e-mails or other messages when you are either: (1) tired, (2) short of time or (3) do not have enough information to give a proper response. The case of (1) should be obvious, you can easily make mistakes and might not be fully aware of the implications of what you are saying. In case of (2) you should not immediately respond but instead inform individuals of the date or period by which you will be able to respond more fully. In case of (3) you should ask for clarification and/or further and better particulars prior to responding. As a rule of thumb, I would apply these suggestions for all types of communication including verbal.

- Seek verification that you understand requests that have been made of you. A simple way of doing this is to respond to individuals by first summarising the issue at hand and asking them to clarify any misunderstandings that you might have. In this way, you provide an opportunity for people to confirm that you understand what they are talking about and it also confirms that you care enough to ask them their opinion.

- Seek assistance from others. It is always useful to seek the input of others and/or to ask others to comment on proposed communication prior to it being communicated. In this way you can possibly get good feedback/input on your communication whilst building trust and inclusivity.

- Learn to listen more often and pause before communicating. Most of us have been guilty, at some time or another, of cutting someone off in mid-sentence. This might be OK if you are a convener for a debate but not so appropriate during a conversation. My experience is that people just do not listen enough to each other and if they did, they would be in a better position to understand and respond to issues raised by others.

- Have a better understanding of the audience to whom they will be communicating with. I have encountered many instances where positional leaders have not been able to effectively communicate with specific staff members simply because they were presumptuous or just unaware of the background/motivations of such people. In such instances it really is a matter of failing to prepare resulting in preparing to fail. Understanding your audience provides you with an opportunity to tailor your communication so that you can better address their needs.

- Study the body language of your audience to ensure that you are engaging them in conversation. If during a discussion or other engagement at which you are speaking, you find people just not paying attention the issue might not be with them. You should make people feel as if you are approachable and they can ask questions if they desire.

- Be aware of your body language, tone, and speed of delivery. Having made numerous presentations, given lots of team talks and radio and television interviews, I am painfully aware of the need to ensure congruence between the spoken word and body language. You will notice that dynamic speakers do not sit or stand in one place when they are presenting as they have the tendency to more around. Even when they are forced to be in one place, they will gesticulate to emphasise their point. They want to grab and maintain the interest of their audience and use their body language as a visual aid. Clarity of speech is important for any communication, especially if it is to persons where English might not be a first language. In such instances the tone, and speed of delivery should be such that it is easier for those persons to understand. In written communication, you should also use simple language to express your points but in such a manner that it is not viewed as condescending or offensive.

- Be factual, polite and ensure that your communication is fair to all concerned. This is particularly important when dealing with matters of conflict.

To enhance the effectiveness of your actions in being a leader you should:

- **Show respect for all**. As a leader you cannot afford to alienate yourself from one set of people by showing favouritism to another set. Being a good leader requires you to "leave no one behind" and to accommodate the views and opinions of all stakeholders. Although you might not be able to get all on board, if you persist in showing unconditional respect for people then this should eventually enhance their respect for you. Without respect, you are unlikely to get the support you need at the times at which you need it. This goes for external as well as internal stakeholders.

- **Be truthful and direct**. There are likely to be very few people that would say they admire individuals that lie and deliberately try to deceive them yet lies and deceit are common in the workplace. You would quickly lose confidence in your partner if they were often caught in a lie. As a leader, confidence in your abilities and credibility quickly erodes if people cannot trust the words coming out of your mouth. You should always be truthful and direct and rather than distort the truth, it is better to say nothing at all.

- **Encourage teamwork**. I have worked for organisations where rivalry and one-upmanship were encouraged by positional leaders simply to undermine the integrity of others. Whereas this might appear harmless and a "bit of fun", underlying this is the insecurity of these positional leaders. Such individuals have little to contribute so they fear those that are performing well and actively seek to undermine them. They are the first to accuse others of not being team players when what they mean is that you are not willing to play their game. A true leader should encourage the contributions of all and seek ways of breaking down barriers between units/divisions or departments.

- **Be decisive but fair**. As a leader you need to be able to make decisions which will affect the direction of your department, division, or organisation. Some of these decisions will, potentially, have an impact on the job security of individuals under your management. Before making any decision, a leader should ask themselves a couple of questions: (1) how would I like it if I was subject to the decision and (2) is it fair to all concerned and in the best interest of the organisation. Indecisive leadership is not good for an organisation since it can cause unnecessary anxiety for staff and result in potential lost opportunities. On the flip side, fast and poorly considered decisions can also have a significantly detrimental effect on an organisation. A leader must, therefore, demonstrate that they have good judgement, timing and that their decisions are fair.

- **Have a vision and coherent plan.** A leader without a vision for their organisation lacks a clear understanding of what the future state of the firm should look like. As a result, any road will take them there. A leader without a coherent plan for achieving their vision lacks an understanding of how they will realise the goals/objectives needed to achieve the vision. Without a vision and a coherent plan, a leader is not a leader, they will find it hard to inspire and guide individuals as well as to retain the best staff.

- **Show humility and empathy**. Showing people that you are not perfect, not expert in all things and approachable breaks down the barriers between you and them. Asking people for their input and showing gratitude in public strengthens the connection between you and others. Similarly, trying to understand the needs of others puts you in the position of being more empathetic. Both attributes enhance trust between you and others.

- **Belief.** I have already discussed in this book that words and action need to go hand in hand. So, it does not matter what a leader says, if they do not act as if they have belief in what they are saying then others will soon doubt their intentions. Having belief should not be confused with being over-confident or just generally optimistic. Belief, as I have used it in this book, is based on some amount of credible evidence in the abilities of a leader. This belief engenders both trust and enhances the capabilities of a leader to influence others.

Exercise

Take some time to think about and write down the aura you give off. Are you happy with how you are perceived?

Is there anything you could change to improve your aura?

Chapter 16

The wellness leader

Introduction
Feels familiar?
Circwell leadership
Embedding wellness
Further reading

Introduction

I have not taken a survey, but I suspect that if you were to ask most workers why they work they would, likely, say to make ends meet, to be able to afford the things they want or words to that effect. Whether they know it or not, most people are working to fulfil aspects of their well-being.

The well-being of workers has always been important but has not received as much prominence as in the last decade or so. People are becoming more aware of the ill-health impacts of long work hours, poor ergonomically designed offices, and bad bosses. The emergence of the LA3 leader bears testament to the growing importance of being able to effectively manage for the welfare of staff and self.

The UK's Chartered Institute of Personnel and Development -CIPD, through their 2018 Absence Management Survey (now called Health and well-being at work) identify the most common reasons for absence from work as: minor injuries, musculoskeletal injuries, back pain, stress, and mental ill-health. The survey found that a little over 30% of organisations provide training to management to support those with mental health concerns. These statistics are a little concerning as reported instances of work-related mental health is on the rise yet the demands from employers continue to increase.

As a further complication to the above, the UK's National Health Service – NHS are predicting that by 2030, 48% of men and 43% of women will be obese.

Organisations have a responsibility to ensure the well-being of its employees, including mental and physical health. This is not to say that employers are the sole cause of well-being problems, but they are a significant contributor.

Feels familiar?

Jennifer has been complaining that she feels overworked and that she has too much responsibility as compared to others of her grade in her team. Having raised the issue with her boss, she has yet to receive what she believes is a satisfactory response to her concerns. She does not think her boss gives her enough direction or time to undertake assigned tasks, many of which are the responsibility of her boss. Nevertheless, her boss holds Jennifer accountable for all tasks given to her.

Jennifer has been trying to accommodate her workload by staying longer at work as well as taking work home. She believes this is taking a toll on her domestic life and is feeling, somewhat, disillusioned with her job. She is a little reluctant to either raise the issue with her boss again or contact human resources since it appears that her situation is not uncommon in the organisation. Moreover, she is aware that others that have chosen to escalate similar matters have subsequently been sidelined.

Mark has been feeling that his skills are undervalued at work. He does not feel as if he has enough work to do and often ends up creating things to do. However, for scheduled activities (even though it is his responsibility for which he is held accountable), his boss demands to see all his reports prior to these being sent to clients. He often has disagreements with his boss about his reports since he feels his boss never contributes to its substance (as his boss lacks the technical background) but comments on the i's and the t's (i.e. changes in grammar). Moreover, Mark feels that his boss has taken credit for his work and has stymied his growth potential in the organisation. Mark does not feel that he can discuss the matter with his boss as this person does not take well to criticism.

Although the above two examples appear different, they share the same potential outcome – stress. The following issues are likely to result in stress if not effectively managed:

- *Workload.* In the case of Jennifer, it was a case of too much and for Mark too little.

- *Responsibility.* In the case of Jennifer, she was assuming too much responsibility and for Mark too little. Related to this is the matter of accountability. Even though Jennifer was not responsible for her boss's activities she was being held accountable for their completion. In the case of Mark, he was to be held accountable for reports which could, potentially, differ from his true opinions.

- *Poor supervision.* In the case of Jennifer, insufficient direction is given and for Mark there appears to be an overconcern on minute details. A lack of direction is not necessarily indicative of poor management but in an environment when staff have excessive workloads and assume work activities of others then this is a problem. On the flip side, a boss that wants to get involved in the details (beyond their level of competence) and insists on managing micro details could easily lead to conflict situations.

- *Low sense of job fulfilment.* In both cases Jennifer and Mark do not feel satisfied with their job and their morale is likely to be low which could impact on the quality of their work.

- *Poor time management.* Both Jennifer and Mark are not managing their time optimally and this is largely due to the ineffectiveness of project management by their boss and others in the supervision hierarchy.

- *Low sense of job security.* Neither Jennifer nor Mark have confidence that if they escalate matters that a resolution satisfactory to them will be achieved. Their view appears to be predicated on concerns of reprisals (affecting the security of their job) if such matters were to be raised.

If not effectively managed, stress can lead to the following mental health problems:

- Depression.
- Anxiety.
- Bipolar disorder.
- Post-traumatic stress disorder (PTSD).
- Eating disorders.
- Obsessive-compulsive disorder (OCD).
- Phobias.

If your circumstances are like those highlighted for Jennifer and Mark what can you do to take control of the leadership of your professional development? The key steps are as follows:

1. Document the events that are causing you concern e.g. increased workload over the last few weeks, poor supervision on a regular basis. It would be useful if you could also identify when these events occurred e.g. the dates.

2. For each concern raised you should attempt to detail how it makes you feel e.g., I am unable to perform my duties within working hours; I am unable to switch off from work when I get home.

3. For each of the concerns raised detail how the corresponding event occurred and who was responsible. The primary objective is to identify those responsible for initiating the events. It also provides an opportunity to identify whether you are contributory to the issues you have raised. For example, you might not have raised any issues at the time the event occurred for several reasons: shame; fear of reprisals; you thought you could handle it; you were unaware that any issues would arise etc.

4. For each of the concerns raised detail the steps you have taken to mitigate or reduce its impact. The objective here is to identify what initiatives you have explored which do not involve elevating matters to your boss and others and whether these have been successful or otherwise.

5. For any or all the concerns raised have you sought the opinion of a professional to assess whether there are medical consequences (mental or physical)? It is advisable that you seek such an opinion if you are not coping with matters.

    Organisations such as the Mental Health Foundation (a UK charity) provide useful information for individuals and organisations on how to cope and support mental health at work. It is advisable, however, that you contact your doctor to discuss the possibility of stress if you are subject to any of the concerns discussed earlier and are not coping. You should ask your doctor for a written opinion on your situation if you think it would help, especially if it suggests that you are suffering from any form of mental/physical illness.

6. Detail the type of change you desire to have so that you no longer have the concerns raised. Ensure that your desires are realistic and fair even if they are not currently supported by the organisation. Examples could be being allowed to work flexible times; being allowed to work from home on particular days; being subject to objectively verifiable KPI's in respect of work outcomes/output and less supervision; splitting/sharing or removal of certain work activities etc.

7. Remember that your organisation has a duty of care in relation to your

well-being and should provide a facilitative environment to support you. Evidence of this would take the form of policy and procedures explicitly detailing the organisations approach to supporting the well-being of its employees. Moreover, that they treat discrimination on the grounds of mental health in the same manner as other characteristics protected under law such as race and gender.

8. Considering step 7 you should elevate matters to your boss and/or others as per the organisational policies but after you have gone through steps 1 through 6.

9. If having undertaken step 8, you are not able to obtain a satisfactory resolution to the matters raised, you should seriously consider your strategy for exiting your organisation.

Circwell leadership

Circular wellness leadership (Circwell) is a model for leadership that I have developed whose main aim is to support leadership that promotes well-being but in a circular manner.

The benefits of circular wellness leadership are:

1. Improved workplace harmony and collaboration.
2. Improved employee/organisation productivity.
3. More predictable revenue/profitability.
4. Improved organisation sustainability.

Improvements in workplace harmony and collaboration lead to improvements in productivity since staff are more motivated and work with a common purpose rather than at odds with each other. This leads to more predictable revenue and profits since there is less volatility in productivity and outcomes which in turn improves overall sustainability of an organisation. The diagram below illustrates these relationships.

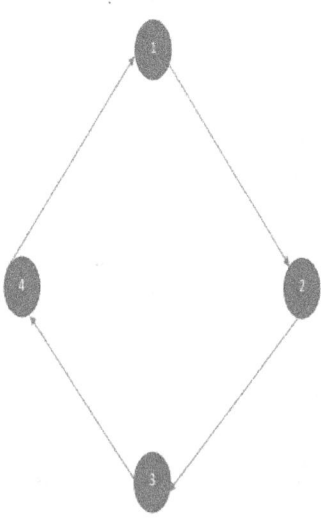

The Circwell model can be thought of as a layered approach as depicted below:

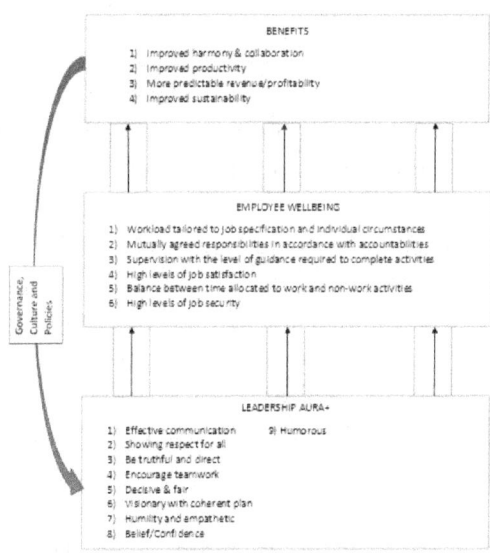

Leadership aura combined with humour provides the foundation for circular wellness. The reader will recall, from the chapter on what is leadership that an LA3 leader has four dominant characteristics: leading by example, communicator, humorous and empathetic. All these characteristics are implied by the skills listed in the above box.

As can be seen from the structure, the qualities that affect leadership aura also affect employee well-being which, in turn, gives rise to the four key benefits highlighted earlier. The circular arrow shows that these benefits should also influence leadership aura through corporate governance and other policies such as the employee handbook as well as the culture of an organisation.

Governance in well-being

One can be forgiven for thinking that leadership is something that is primarily focused on the operational level of an organisation since it is at this level that line management structures exist. However, even though the board of an organisation does not ordinarily get involved in its day-to-day operations the policies approved by the board should be such that they significantly influence the culture and type of individuals employed at the firm.

The board should outline the broad terms of what behaviour and standards they consider acceptable and these requirements should then be embodied in formally approved board policies. Most likely senior management will be given the task of fleshing out and developing such policies, but it must be the board that approves and signs off on these documents.

An important consideration of such governance policies is the importance an organisation places on its stakeholders. Beyond shareholders (or those providing funding), these stakeholders include service providers, clients, regulators and most importantly its employees. As it relates to its employees, a firm's governance policies should address the ways in which it caters for the well-being of its staff either within the governance documents or another document referenced within the policy.

What is tolerated by the board will become common practice at lower levels in the organisation, so it is up to the board to set the tone as to the type of organisation they want. Having set the tone, the board should have procedures in place to ensure they are able to receive reliable performance measures on factors pertaining to the well-being of staff members.

Embedding wellness

Board-level and senior leaders in an organisation can do much to create a wellness culture and make work an enjoyable place to be. These executive and board level personal can institute well-being policies which address a host of physical and mental health issues. The following services lists the better practices I have come across that some organisations offer their staff:

- The provision of educational material on smoking cessation and weight management. This includes free material as well as links to websites of professional organisations that can provide relevant support.

- The provision of free screening sessions for employees and family members for a host of potential physical health issues.

- The provision of free personal and family counselling and stress management.

- The provision of free fitness related activities at work e.g. stretching exercises and dancing.

- Free use of a gym at work or free membership at a gym close to the place of work.

- If the organisation provides lunches, then facilitating for a healthy option.

- Provision of free meditation and mindfulness classes.

- Facilitation of flexible working hours for all staff that have a need.

- Facilitation of time off to undertake volunteering activities. Such time off not counting against holiday entitlement.

- Facilitating the provision of professional development courses aimed at helping staff either in their current or prospective roles at the organisation.

- The provision of catnapping rooms to help staff distress.

➤ The provision of creche facilities for parents with young children.

Many of the above services are offered by the most enlightened institutions. Unsurprisingly most of these are technology or financial institutions whose practices are such that staff can work unusually long hours. Nevertheless, most type of institutions would benefit from incorporating many of the services listed above.

Further reading

1. CIPD (2018), *Health and Well-being at work*, CIPD, viewed September 4, 2020, <https://www.cipd.co.U.K./Images/health-and-well-being-at-work_tcm18-40863.pdf>

Chapter 17
Manager versus Leader

Introduction
Changing mindset
Further reading

Introduction

You might have come across people that are in a managerial position and wondered how on earth they managed to reach so high given their level of incompetence. Like me, you might have thought "surely they will be found out and fired". At least this is what I used to think around thirty or so years ago.

According to a researcher by the name of Laurence J Peter, people will rise to their "level of incompetence". Peter argues that there is a level at which people are "super competent" and once they get promoted (i.e. move up the hierarchy) they become less competent since the skills in the lower-level role might not translate into what is required at the higher level. Eventually a person will reach a plateau (a level at which they are not able to go beyond) and become incompetent at that level.

My experience is that the "Peter Principle" is alive and kicking today and driven by many organisations' insatiable desire for immediate or near-term results. Let me explain. People only truly reach their level of incompetence if they are not allowed the time and opportunity to develop their skills to required levels. However, the emphasis is on individuals to want to learn/develop their skills and to have the capacity to reach to the required levels within a reasonable time. If time and other constraints are imposed on an individual's ability to grow, then this might adversely affect their level of performance and perceived competence.

Different organisations are likely to be affected in different ways by the Peter Principle. For example, a fast-moving environment such as investment banking is likely to give people less time to adjust to a higher-level position than let us say an NGO. With the former, since the business model is, largely and increasingly, sensitive to market timing, e.g. announcement of an initial public offering (IPO); Merger or bond offering, incompetent staff will be found out very quickly and the impact of their decisions might immediately result in financial and reputational loss.

In the case of an NGO more time is, generally, allowed for transitioning into a higher position and the business model is much less time dependent. Consequently, mediocrity and/or incompetence might either go unnoticed or tolerated over a relatively long time-period.

Organisations will "tolerate" incompetence for several reasons including feeling that they do not have much choice, being oblivious or by design e.g. "it's their turn to be promoted". This latter reason occurs quite often in public service roles. However, if organisations want to reduce the risk of the curse of the Peter Principle leaders would be well advised to take on board the following approach:

- For new hires at a technical level, ensure that they also possess relevant soft skills e.g. such as those described in the chapter on the aura of a leader. In this way, both the individual and the organisation is better prepared for when that person is promoted.

- Consider having performance related compensation schemes to reward good and outstanding performance. Such a scheme might be used as an alternative to promoting an individual that is either not ready for a more senior or leadership role (based on them not having the relevant skills) or simply does not want the role.

- Consider having management and leadership training available to those that wish to develop the relevant skills. You could consider having competency-based training in which those wishing to be promoted should be able to demonstrate that they have attained required levels of competency. Such training should be mandatory for those already in managerial and leadership positions.

- If you are in a managerial or leadership role but feel that it is becoming all too much for you, consider asking for feedback from staff and others (including your boss) on areas where they think you could improve as well as what they think you do well and ask for examples. Do not be afraid, showing humility and openness are traits expected of a good leader so it should not come as a surprise if you come across in this way. Your goal should be to try and work on the areas where you are deficient and learn how to combine these with your strengths.

- Organisations could consider having flatter hierarchies. In such an organisation, emphasis is placed on empowering individuals to collaborate and take control of their assigned areas of responsibility. More emphasis is placed on ensuring that the right process for delivery is followed such that it is inclusive and delivers to mutually agreed outcomes.

Other than helping to reduce the risk of the Peter Principle, the aim of the above approach is to encourage organisations to promote individuals based on their abilities to undertake a new role and not just on what they have achieved in the past.

Changing mindset

Society and the workplace have become, increasingly, aware that because someone is a manager this does not imply that they are a leader. Typically, management, amongst other things, is concerned with planning, command, and control.

Managers are concerned with *planning* from a budgetary perspective. They see it as their responsibility to fight for and defend *their* budgets. Although they may ask for input from their direct reports, they often have a firm view as to how the resources should be allocated and act accordingly. Better managers will ask for input and be guided but your typical manager will make decisions on what they think can be achieved with the resources over the budget period.

Managers are concerned with issuing *commands* and ordering individuals to perform various tasks. They see departmental resources as *theirs* to be used how they see fit. Typically, their concern is ensuring that persons are engaged in activities assigned to them and that these persons only report to the manager for feedback. Better managers will ask for input from their employees and make decisions considering a wider array of opinions.

Managers are concerned with exerting *control* over their employees either directly or indirectly. When managers make decisions, which result in changes in budgets they can end up exerting or releasing pressure on individuals. This would be an example of an indirect method of control. Unscrupulous managers have often used this as a tool to either reward or punish employees.

When managers make decisions dictating how an employee's work will be performed and ensuring that such work is only undertaken according to rigid instructions this amounts to micromanagement. Micromanagement is an often-used method of directly controlling an employee's work. Better managers would be aware of the skills/weaknesses of their staff and allow them to control how they do their job, if they are capable.

Underlying the above traits, of a manager, one will often find two additional characteristics. Managers are often in their positions because of the perception that they possess certain *technical* skills. We know, from the Peter principle, that this might not be a valid assumption but, nonetheless it is quite common. Managers are also *tactically* minded in that their actions are guided by short or near-term considerations. Most immediately, managers are concerned with ensuring that tasks/activities are completed within time frames specified by project plans and fall within budgets.

The following table can be used as a guide to differentiate manager and leader mindset:

Manager	**Leader**
Planning	Creative thinking
Commanding	Empowering
Controlling	Well-being
Technical	Inspiring
Tactical	Strategic

The right-hand side of the above table details the characteristics that are exemplified by good leaders. These characteristics have already been discussed in this book, including how persons can enhance their skills.

Whereas leaders often need to manage, their overall focus is on leading the future direction of an organisation. When in manager mode they employ the methods on the left side of the table. Note that these methods are, primarily, performed by the manager and not staff.

When in leader mode the methods on the right-hand side are facilitated by the leader. That is, they are either jointly performed by the leader and staff or exclusively by staff.

The following steps can be used to guide the process of your transition from manager to leader:

1. *Understand the role, your expectations, and the expectations of others for you.* It is perhaps, no exaggeration to say that many people that move from

a management to leadership position do not have a full understanding of what is required of them. Many assume that the biggest difference is that they will have a bigger portfolio with more people reporting beneath them. Whilst this might be true, it still accentuates the control aspect of management and not the focus on development of people and broad strategic objectives. In assessing expectations, some things to consider include:

    a. Understanding of what more senior leaders require of you and the dates by which you are to achieve these requirements.

    b. Understanding of how existing leaders behave and what is considered good leadership in your organisation.

    c. Understanding of what your new direct reports like and dislike and their views on how to improve working relations and business development.

    d. Understanding of what you expect from the role and whether these are consistent with (a), (b) and (c).

2. *Determine which leadership style is an immediate requirement for your organisation.* It might be that you have a particular style of management that you favour but based on (1) you find that it is not exactly what is required at this point in your organisation. Your objective should be to determine whether you are able to take on this style of management in the timescales required for you.

3. *Work on developing/improving the leader characteristics in the transition table.* Start your leadership development by working on improving your skills for each of the characteristics listed in the transition table.

The process of transitioning from a manager to a leader mindset will not result in immediate beneficial results for some people. In fact, some people may never be able to effectively transition from manager to leader. Experience suggests that what you put in is what you get out of leadership and depending on the maturity of your mindset and your willingness to change this will impact on the timing of your growth to leadership.

A manager that is used to producing strategic plans is likely to find it less difficult to think strategically than someone that has no experience. This said, being a leader that is strategic goes beyond creating a strategic plan and requires leaders to be visionary and to be able to assess the impact of decisions today on business practices tomorrow.

A manager should not expect that they would be able to transition to leadership mindset at the same time for all the characteristics detailed on the left side of the table. Again, the timing of the transition is very much likely to depend on your existing mindset maturity and willingness to change.

One way to gage your maturity is to seek feedback from others as to how they think you perform in relation to each of the leadership characteristics. As always, you should also seek out those that you believe exhibit good leadership qualities and, whilst remaining true to yourself, emulate what you believe makes them successful.

Further reading

1. Kelly, D and Kelly, T. (2015), *Creative Confidence: Unleashing the Creative Potential within Us All*, Harper Collins Pub
2. Peter, L and Hull, R. (1969), *The Peter Principle*, William Morrow & Co Inc

Chapter 18

Firing your boss

Introduction
Underutilised
The monies not right
Weaknesses
Limited growth
Poor well-being
Toxic environment

Introduction

Have you ever wondered when the right time would be to leave your organisation? If you have not given this much thought I would suggest you pay close attention to what follows. Gone are the days when people commit to only work for one organisation for the rest of their lives. This is not just my opinion, this is fact. It is highly likely that someone within the age group 24-36 would have an average work tenure less than that of someone with an age between 53-65.

Organisations expect loyalty but their strive for market share often means that they do not always reciprocate the loyalty shown to them by employees. Consider the contraction of investment banks when profits drop below a level that they believe to be acceptable. Even though the banks might still be earning several UK £ billions per quarter they are not averse to shedding thousands of jobs to protect shareholder dividends and market share.

Employers are not the only reason for the reduced tenure of employees. Perhaps more than at any other time we live in an era where many people seem to want instant gratification. People are demanding more from their employers and if they do not get it within a short period they are not hanging around for much longer. This said, some employers and recruitment consultants do not place much value in persons that have had too many short-term permanent roles. So, there could be a potential conflict between the desire to find that dream job and how frequent a person moves from job to job.

Underutilised

Believe it or not, you are the one that should be in control of your destiny as it relates to professional development. Your happiness also depends on you. Understanding your role in your life is fundamental to you being able to say what you like and do not like and what you can and cannot do well.

A common issue I come across when discussing work-related matters with people is, they feel that they are not being fully utilised. They say things like I am bored, I am not learning anything, my talents are going to waste, I feel like I am vegetating. In only a few instances have these same people raised their concerns to management and/or HR. Whether for fear of repercussions or just not knowing what to do, these people are in danger of becoming slaves to their fear. One thing is for sure, you cannot expect anything to change unless you make that change happen.

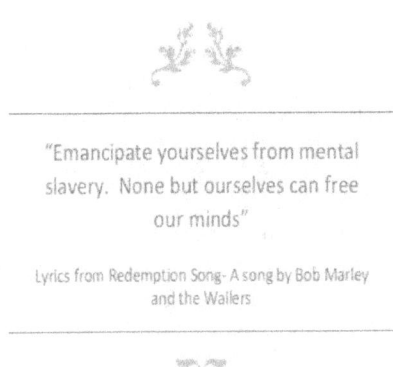

"Emancipate yourselves from mental slavery. None but ourselves can free our minds"

Lyrics from Redemption Song- A song by Bob Marley and the Wailers

The above quote from Bob Marley exemplifies the fact that we need to be prepared to reject apathy, adopt new ways of thinking, and take control of our destiny. So, if you are being underutilised at work say so. Remind your managers of your strengths and the additional value that you could bring to the organisation if they only made better use of your skills. My point is, before you decide to leave see if there is anything you can do to make your life better at work.

If after having made your case, you still feel you are likely to remain underutilised you should create your exit strategy. In determining when to move, you should bear in mind whether you would need to demonstrate to a future employer that you have kept abreast of the latest developments in your area of expertise. This might be a little difficult if you are working for an organisation where you were not utilising much of your skills. In this respect, you might want to think whether undertaking external professional development/academic courses could help prior to applying for new roles.

The monies not right

There might be individuals where underutilisation is not the issue. However, they might feel that they are not receiving the level of compensation consistent with their work activities. Whereas you might not be able to control how much you earn you should be able to make an argument for a pay rise based on your contribution and results obtained.

In some instances, getting a pay rise might be not possible given the pay structure of an organisation e.g. pay bands based on experience. If this is the case and your organisation follows industry practice, then you might not get much joy elsewhere unless you switch to a new role. However, if your organisation does have the flexibility to award you with a pay rise but refuse then it is an easier decision to make about leaving.

I think a word of warning is warranted. You should never adopt a habit of leaving an organisation just because you want to earn more money. Money will be one of several physical benefits of working for an organisation, but my experience suggests that psychological benefits (e.g. stimulating environment, recognition of your abilities) have an equal role to play.

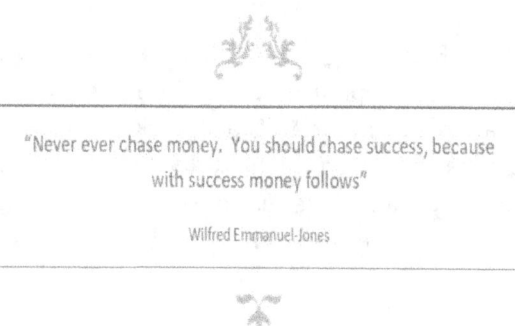

"Never ever chase money. You should chase success, because with success money follows"

Wilfred Emmanuel-Jones

Weaknesses

Another area where people could focus more attention on is their weaknesses. I have found that many people are not aware of the impact their weaknesses have on their fortunes at work. In fact, there are many I have come across that are unaware that they have weaknesses.

Such persons become critical of others instead of reflecting on their own performance. This lack of reflective thinking makes them feel that others are the problem, increases their anxiety and desire to move on. By carefully following the guidance of the previous chapters, those persons would be in a better position to appreciate their strengths and weaknesses and what they need to do to improve. However, to do this a person has to realise that they are the ones that need to make a change.

In a good organisation, it is likely that management would have identified areas for improvement for their staff and agreed a plan whereby development objectives would be measurable and time-bound. However, I have come across instances where organisations refuse to provide adequate support for staff leaving them with few internal remedies to aid their development. In such instances, individuals should either seek external development or take the organisations approach as a cue for them to find alternative employment.

> "I'm hungry for knowledge. The whole thing is to learn every day, to get brighter and brighter. That's what this world is about. You look at someone like Gandhi, and he glowed. Martin Luther King glowed. Muhammad Ali glows. I think that's from being bright all the time and trying to be brighter."
>
> Jay Z

Limited growth

It sometimes happens that persons reach the 'limit' of their growth in an organisation. They might be happy with how they are being paid, utilised in their role and could even be 'star' performers. However, they require more from the organisation. This tends to happen more with individuals that have skills which go beyond the job for which they are currently employed and wish to move to a different role in the organisation.

Given the volatility of the global job market, it is likely that this will become more common especially for those that have had varied careers. In some instances, it might not be possible for persons to transition into a new role given financial/organisational constraints. Under these circumstances, it makes perfect sense to seek opportunities elsewhere since persons will not be able to realise their growth objective in their organisation.

It also makes sense to move on if your organisation simply refuses to facilitate for your growth even though you are qualified to work elsewhere in the organisation. Be careful not to be caught in the endless you will get what you want soon saga where every year your organisation promises you the earth but asks you to wait a little longer. When the year comes around, there is another excuse/reason for why you cannot get what you want.

> "Change will not come if we wait for some other person or some other time. We are the ones we've been waiting for. We are the change that we seek"
>
> Barack Obama

Poor well-being

If you feel that your well-being is being threatened and that you have done everything you can to manage yourself and help others to address your concerns, without success, then it might be time to move on.

Some pointers that your well-being might be at risk include *increased anxiety at the prospect of going to work, bad working relations with colleagues, inability to complete work on time/constantly taking work home, always thinking about work, abnormal weight loss/gain and lack of interests outside of work.*

As previously discussed in this book, it is important for people to work in an environment which is conducive to their well-being whilst achieving the technical/functional objectives of the job. It is however, up to you to constantly monitor your well-being and seek guidance where necessary. Asking for help should not be viewed as a sign of weakness and organisations that see things this way are not worth working for. You should also not see yourself as weak for asking for support. Issues, however, do arise when organisations unreasonably refuse to provide needed support, and this should be taken as a signal for you to make plans to move on.

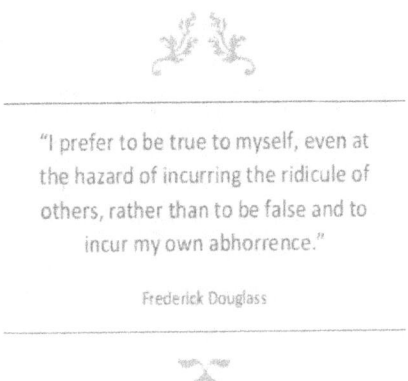

"I prefer to be true to myself, even at the hazard of incurring the ridicule of others, rather than to be false and to incur my own abhorrence."

Frederick Douglass

Toxic environment

Discrimination, harassment, bullying or any other form of unwarranted conduct should not be tolerated by individuals. This said, in the UK, the number of employment tribunal claims are rising year-on-year. This suggests an increasing disconnect between employers and employee.

Despite this, there are many issues occurring at work which do not end up in the tribunal, not because there is no merit but because of other reasons. For example, many people I have spoken to simply do not want the hassle of a tribunal or even to raise a grievance as they feel it would lead to victimisation and/or cause them to be viewed as being difficult to work with.

One thing is clear, you should not have to put up with unwarranted behaviour or be victimised for having made a complaint. If, however, having made an internal complaint you feel side-lined or unable to continue to effectively work for the organisation, you should move on.

Continuing to work in a toxic environment will do nothing to improve your morale and, if you let it, will have an impact on the quality of your work and health. However, we all have different circumstances and what might be tolerable for one might be unbearable for another person.

It might be that you feel unable to leave as you do not have a job lined up, do not have savings to rely on, feel that your age will work against you in finding another job etc. Under these circumstances, it might be better to 'manage' the toxicity rather than to resign immediately.

Managing toxicity effectively requires you to *not engage in unprofessional behaviour, document your interaction with others and retain for future use if needed, find a quiet place to eat/have coffee or some time to yourself to get away from others, find a confidant external to the firm to discuss matters, do not be a slave to work for fear of being victimised and find an external activity to do after work to avoid bringing the toxicity home.*

Most importantly, start planning for your exit by looking for a new job.

"No one is born hating another person because of the colour of his skin, or his background or his religion. People learn to hate, and if they can learn to hate, they can be taught to love, for love comes more naturally to the human heart than its opposite"

Nelson Mandela

Chapter 19

Dear black people

The sacrifices of others
Uncle Tom
Board positions
Unconscious racism?
Further reading

The sacrifices of others

> "You are where you are today because you stand on somebody's shoulders. And wherever you are heading, you cannot get there yourself. If you stand on the shoulders of others, you have a reciprocal responsibility to live your life so that others may stand on your shoulders. It's the quid pro quo of life. We exist temporarily through what we take, but we live forever through what we give."
>
> Vernon Jordan

The above quote from Vernon Jordan should be a constant reminder to all people of colour that others have gone before them paving the way for their acceptance in the workplace and wider society. Unfortunately, there are those that appear to have forgotten the sacrifices of others and that what they do will have an impact on the fortunes of those to come. They act as if they have a God given right to be where they are and try their hardest to prevent other persons of colour from being elevated to higher heights.

Uncle Tom

You have probably heard the phrase 'Uncle Tom' being used to describe persons that curry favour from white folks often by putting down other people of colour. This might be more common than what you think, and I have seen and experienced this throughout my working life both in the UK and elsewhere in the world.

What some black folks seem to ignore is the fact that what they do is highly likely to impact how white people view other black people in the future. Putting down another black person, largely, because you want to be the black person of choice is akin to being an Uncle Tom. You might get that 'pat on the head' from the boss but you should be aware she is probably treating you like a pet.

As a black person, showing true leadership does not mean denying your cultural identity to fit into a white person's view as to how you should look, walk, and talk. It should not mean that black women need to straighten their hair or lighten their skin. It should not mean that you give the next black person a hard time because you had one. To quote a line from Bob Marley and the Wailers: "Who feels it knows it, Lord".

As a black person in a leadership position you would probably have come across racism in its many forms. Armed with this, you should be aware of the 'dynamics' of the office and how these might affect others from your culture/race or other persons of colour. You should see it as one aspect of your job to ensure the well-being of your staff members by ensuring that they are not treated in a manner that could be construed as being culturally inappropriate.

If I had to choose, I would rather have an overt racist white manager than one that is an Uncle Tom. I have discussed this subject with many people, and I have yet to come across any black person that disagrees with this view. You know what you are going to get with the racist they say, but the Uncle Tom will smile in your face and later stab you in the back. Their insecurities will consume them to the point where they can think of nothing more than how to undermine the up-and-coming black brother/sister.

Other than overt racism, the biggest issue that has held black people back from achieving more corporate success has been the Uncle Tom. These people need to realise that the black race could get much further if they treated other black folks with the respect that they give to white people. The legacy of slavery runs deep.

These people come in all forms and guises. They are heralded as the voice of black Britain when they justify the discriminatory profiling and targeting of black persons going about their business. They are promoted to higher highs when they do the master's/mistresses' bidding and put that brother/sister 'in their place'. They are lauded as great Thespians when they willingly smile and act the buffoon by playing the 'coon'. Still, none of these persons are likely to be Prime Minister in the UK, to be CEO/Chair of the largest of UK organisations and none are likely to win a Bafta or Oscar any time soon.

In case you were wondering, the probability of the average black person becoming the UK Prime Minister is around 1 in 17 million compared to 1 in 1.4 million for the average white person. These figures where revealed in 2016 in a BBC documentary (BBC, 2016).

Segregation was a favoured approach of churches, schools, restaurants, and many other establishments in America. In the UK, the term segregation was not used as much but colour bar existed across many organisations including lettings of private landlords, workplaces, pubs, and other establishments. The technique of divide and conquer was often used by slave masters (in the Caribbean and America) whereby they would choose a few women and men and treat them differently from the others.

Manifestation of segregation could take the form of appointing a male slave to be an 'overseer' (supervisor of other slaves). It might also have taken the form of making some slaves servants/maids in the master's house. In some instances, the impact of the differential treatment was devastating and led to animosity between the house and the field slave. Although the book by Harriet Beecher Stowe – "Uncle Tom's Cabin or Life Among the Lowly" (Stowe, 1852) was meant to show how Christian love could overcome the brutality of slavery, in the years that have followed, the term Uncle Tom has very much taken on a negative connotation.

The legacy of slavery has resulted in some black people adopting a divide and conquer approach to work, play etc. They appear not to be happy unless they are the only ones speaking on behalf of all black people. These black people are not woke, they do not understand what it means to be a true leader and only engage in social activities which furthers their own interests.

Whether consciously or subconsciously the actions of these people amount to mental slavery. It is as if they have forgotten that slavery officially ended (in the UK) on March 25, 1807 with the passing of the Slave Trade Act and December 1865 (in the US), with the passage of the 13th Amendment to the Constitution.

Given the above, it is easy to see how the actions of a few (Uncle Toms) could influence the views of many white people especially if those few are influential. As previously discussed, the actions of black leaders are likely to impact on the prospects of others. This is an unfair situation since the actions of one white person does not, generally, impact the fortunes of other white people.

I cannot imagine a situation where if the white CEO of a large white-run corporation were fired the organisation would have a problem with hiring another one. However, if that CEO were black the chances are it would take a while before they hired another one. Similarly, I do not know of an example where a white person has been fired for being too white. Yet there are numerous examples where black people have been fired for being themselves. According to the American actress, Gabrielle Union, this happened to her, most recently, when her contract on America's Got Talent was not renewed.

Another situation where the acts of a few black people have an impact on the majority is when it comes to crime. The violent/criminal acts of a few black people do not imply that most black people are criminals. Yet policing policies (under various political leaders) would suggest otherwise. There have been several special initiatives established by the Metropolitan Police, for example operation Trident, to investigate black-on-black gun crime and homicide. However, there does not appear to be similar initiatives for investigating white-on-white crime despite the homicide rate for this category being higher than black-on-black. Patently this is discriminatory.

If one buys into the concept of unconscious bias, then it is likely that white people are more willing to accept negative than positive stereotypes of black people. Therefore, it is important for black people not to feed into or conform to harmful stereotypes even if it makes their lives easier. One such stereotype is the view that light-skinned are more attractive than darker-skinned women and another is that black men cannot be trusted.

If white people see that black folks, generally, prefer lighter-skinned black people then guess what, many will interpret this as confirmation that lighter is preferential to dark. Again, this is a legacy of colonialism and slavery.

Whether you believe in the Bible or not, its many words of wisdom are as relevant today as it was when they were written down. In Mark 3:25 (of the New International Version) it states that "If a house is divided against itself, that house cannot stand". So, if you are a black person in a position of leadership and want to be woke, ask yourself this question, when was the last time you went out of your way to support other black people trying to move up the corporate ladder?

The callous treatment of George Floyd by the Minneapolis police has reignited the issue of race not just in the United States of America but in many other countries around the world. In the UK, several organisations have apologised for historic links to the slave trade. These include Green King, Lloyd's of London insurers and the Bank of England. However, much more is needed.

Many so-called leading black figures in the UK, US and other countries were uncharacteristically quiet during the height of public uproar following the circumstances leading to the death of George Floyd. This should not be a surprise since many high-profile white folks were also silent on the subject. However, being a woke leader requires you to speak out and take a position on matters of social importance. Saying nothing because it might affect your street credibility, affect the share price of your company, or affect the likelihood of your organisation receiving funding is not an excuse, it is, however, a reason for preserving your own self-interests.

As the above discussion illustrates, being black is not sufficient to be woke. Being woke requires knowing what and not what to do or say.

Board positions

When it comes to black persons holding the most senior positions in the UK the statistics are not good reading. Based on research, published last year (Haughton, 2019), the following table provides a breakdown of membership of Financial Times Stock Exchange group (FTSE) 100 companies (in 2019) based on race:

Category	Percentage of total FTSE 100 directors
People of colour (BME)	10.13%
Female black	0.86%
Male black	0.67%
UK black	0.76%
UK people of colour	2.96%
White persons	89.87%
Others	0%

A white woman is around thirty times as likely to be on the board of a FTSE 100 company than either a black man or black woman. For a white man, the multiples are twice as large as that for a white woman. The picture is not that much different at the senior/executive level in many of the FTSE 100 companies.

One can put the lack of black representation down to several issues including: lack of relevant experience/qualifications, few applications from black people, overt racism, unconscious bias. What is worrying is that the general trend has persisted for many years and does not appear to be getting better quickly.

Unconscious racism?

Black people, how often have you heard the phrase unconscious bias of late in relation to the 'unwitting' actions of white people concerning the under-representation of BME's in the corporate workforce? Probably quite a lot. However, all persons have some amount of unconscious bias, not just while people. The question is how do you manage this bias and recognise when it is occurring?

A cottage industry has sprung up in which unconscious bias awareness training courses are popping up all over the place. As it relates to the workforce, this training is aimed at, largely, white run organisations since most of their senior management are white. In many of these organisations, black and other persons of colour are vastly under-represented and tend to occupy lower paid roles.

If you are a white person in a position of leadership in your organisation, you should ask yourself whether you believe your organisation's hiring/retention policy induces an implicit bias. For example, does it preserve the gender/race composition as it currently stands, or does it provide a fair basis for increased inclusivity?

It is all too easy to blame unconscious bias for the lack of proportionate black representation at more senior levels in UK organisations. Especially when one considers that little has changed, of significance, for decades. You remember the saying: "Insanity is doing the same thing over and over again and expecting different results". The evidence is overwhelming, diversity increases productivity, profitability, and sustainability (BCG, 2018). Therefore, organisations which are laggards in the race for a more diverse workforce are doing a disservice to their board and organisation.

Based on several Meta-Analysis of research, see for example Forsher et al. (2019), conducted into implicit/unconscious bias, little evidence can be found which supports the conclusion that changes in bias attitudes leads to changes in discriminatory behaviour. In other words, unconscious bias training whilst useful in highlighting bias tendencies does not provide a means of effectively reducing the tendency to act in a biased way.

Tests for unconscious bias were popularised with the Implicit Association Test (IAT) developed by Tony Greenwald (in 1995) who is currently a Professor of Psychology at the University of Washington. The test is the most widely used measure of unconscious bias. In undertaking the test (for race bias) a user is presented with images of black and white people as well as words implying good and evil things.

Users are then asked to identify black and white faces and words which imply good/evil by clicking a certain key for good and another for evil etc. The test applies a score based on the number of correct answers as well as the time in which a user responds. This latter aspect appears to be key since even if all questions are answered correctly one can be assessed as being prejudiced against black people if the response time for identifying a black person is longer than that for a white person. Although the IAT does not provide a definitive means to predict whether a person will act in a discriminatory manner, it does provide an indication of tendency of thinking.

Since unconscious bias derives from several inter-related sources including culture, religion, schooling, and experiences to which one might have been exposed to for years, changing your "whole existence" overnight will not be easy and practically impossible. It is, perhaps, better to focus on:

1. Identifying those areas for which you have unconscious bias. One way of doing this is to take an Implicit Association Test (IAT) to test for bias in race, gender, or other legally protected characteristics. There are several websites which can facilitate for this.

2. For each of the areas identified in (1) determine whether any bias identi-

fied has resulted in you taking discriminatory actions or acting in a discriminatory way. One way to do this is to educate yourself about discrimination and assess whether any of your actions falls into this category.

To increase objectivity, it is useful if step (2) is undertaken with other people (e.g. select colleagues, external diversity, and inclusion specialists or friends). This step works better if you have adopted and practice reflective leadership and work in this manner with others.

Reflective leadership naturally lends itself to an individual assessing the potential implications of their thoughts and decisions. The reflective thinker does not rush to make decisions or take actions. This reduces the likelihood of bias having an impact on behaviour.

When a reflective leader embeds visioning as part of their daily activities, she makes it easier to reduce the propensity to dwell on unconscious biases. She achieves this by visioning a future state in which she can be empathetic to others. Daily practice increases her ability to be more quickly aware as to when her thoughts amount to biases which could lead to unfairness and discrimination. Being empathetic then allows her to understand what it might feel like if she was subject to actions resulting from such thoughts. The quest for continuous process improvement would then inspire the leader to change her ways (e.g. dwelling and acting on implicit bias).

The above discussion is predicated on the assumption that learnt behaviours can be superseded by employing other behaviours. For example, if you are right-handed, the chances are your right arm is stronger than your left. However, it is perfectly possible for you to train your left to be just as strong as your right arm. To do this requires practice, a willingness to change and visioning what life would be like if you were ambidextrous coupled with a strategy for making this happen.

You see, there is no real excuse for white people to use unconscious bias as the reason why they have very low numbers of black people in senior roles since such bias can be controlled by appropriate behaviour. The question to ask, therefore, is why such behaviour is not consistently and persistently applied across many white controlled organisations?

One answer to the above question arises from knowing that discrimination is much more subtle than it was fifty, forty or even ten years ago. Rather than to say we only want white people; companies might advertise that they want to fill a board position but that the applicant must have relevant and extensive board-level experience in a similar environment. This requirement is likely to exclude a disproportionate number of females and people of colour since they are less likely to be on boards in the first place.

It is also the case that, in many organisations, actions which fall short of overt racism (but are racially motivated) often do not get treated as discriminatory despite the lack of a plausible explanation otherwise. Often, if such organisations need to draw an inference to conclude that discrimination has occurred and that such inference is consistent with the facts, many are unlikely to 'do the right thing'. So here is an opportunity for white leaders to do the right thing. They can ensure that the HR policies in relation to discrimination and victimisation treat allegations of unfair treatment arising from unconscious bias the same as overt discrimination.

Of late I have noticed various public and private sector organisations include questions (as part of their application process) on whether an applicant attended private or state school. Whether the applicant received free school meals and whether their parents went to university. I have no doubt that many of these organisations believe that this will provide them with a better means of improving the diversity of its workforce.

What such an approach cannot guarantee, however, is that a higher proportion of black people will apply and/or be recruited for a job. For some unscrupulous employers they might even use the disclosed information to exclude certain applicants. Since positive discrimination is illegal in the UK under the Equality Act, 2010, employers could not use the fact that they want to recruit a 'poor black applicant' just because they fit this description.

An employer could, however, choose to hire a black person over a white person if they were just as qualified/experienced as other applicants. This is termed positive action (which is legal) and, unfortunately, is where many organisations fall short. This often occurs at the point at which an employer is assessing whether a candidate is 'the right fit' for their organisation. In forming their conclusions, some individuals are not able to get beyond seeing the word 'fit' as a euphemism 'for looks like me' or 'acts like me'.

Until and unless some form of positive discrimination is allowed in the UK all woken individuals should strive to make their and other organisations accountable for more inclusive workplaces.

Further reading

1. Haughton, H. (2019), *The Privileged Few Benefit From Racial Inequality*, Centre for Labour and Social Studies, viewed September 3, 2020, < http://classonline.org.U.K./blog/item/the-privileged-few-benefit-from-racial-inequality>
2. Stowe, H. (1852), *Uncle Tom's Cabin; or, Life Among the Lowly,* Jewett and Company, Boston
3. Greenwald, A. G. & Banaji, M. R. (1995), *Implicit social cognition: Attitudes, self-esteem, and stereotypes.* Psychological Review, 102, 4-27.
4. Forscher, P. S., Lai, C. K., Axt, J. R., Ebersole, C. R., Herman, M., Devine, P. G., & Nosek, B. A. (2019), *A meta-analysis of procedures to change implicit measures.* Journal of Personality and Social Psychology, 117(3), 522–559
5. Project Implicit (2019), *Project Implicit,* viewed October 3, 2020, <https://implicit.harvard.edu/implicit/takeatest.html>
6. Rothstein, Richard, (2017), *The Color of Law: A Forgotten History of How Our Government Segregated America,* Liveright Pub
7. Akala (2019), *Natives: Race and Class in the Ruins of Empire,* Two Roads, Pub
8. BBC (2016), *David Harewood: Will Britain ever have a black prime minister?,* BBC Magazine, viewed October 11, 2020 < https://www.bbc.co.uk/news/magazine-37799305>
9. BCG (2018), *BCG Henderson Institute, How Diverse Leadership Teams Boost Innovation,* viewed October 11, 2020, available at < https://www.bcg.com/en-us/publications/2018/how-diverse-leadership-teams-boost-innovation>
10. Ogunnaike, L (2020), *The State of Gabrielle Union,* Marie Claire, viewed on October, 11, 2020, available at < https://www.marieclaire.com/celebrity/a34206870/gabrielle-union-interview-october-2020/>

Chapter 20
Afterword

Having read this book you should be in no doubt that you have the attributes to be a leader, but it requires you to adopt a leader's mindset and be willing to change. As simple as it might seem, change is the hardest thing to do for many people and their failure to do so results in them not being regarded as good leaders.

This book has taken a pragmatic approach to leadership. It has identified emerging leadership styles and detailed a set of key characteristics exhibited by good leaders. For each such characteristic the book describes how persons can enhance their ability to be more proficient. This said, realising that we live in a digital era, the book expands on the type of skills required to be an effective leader in this age of technology.

The book introduces and develops the ABC principles as a means of providing a framework for the enhancement of leadership skills. It demonstrated the interplay between abilities and belief and the necessity of having a coherent strategy for achieving leadership success.

Real world examples have been used throughout the book to reinforce the ideas and thoughts discussed. This is important because you need to be able to see how to apply this in your day-to-day life. Do you recall that the ABC framework can be applied to personal as well as professional development? It is not a concept that is to be used only in the workplace.

Increasingly well-being has become a topic of great importance both outside and within the working environment. The book has introduced a theory which supports well-being leadership known as Circwell. This type of leadership will have important ramifications for enhancing well-being at work.

You may need, and it is advised that you read this book several times through. Although this book is meant to inspire you to achieve greater success as a leader it is not a feel-good book. It is intended that the reader study its contents and determine how they can adapt their behaviour to achieve the desired objectives. Remember, as with most things in life, you tend to get out what you put in. So, wake up to the possibilities in you as a leader and work smart, not hard!

Index

A

ABC of leadership 214
  Ability 214
  Belief 217
  Coherent strategy 219
  Muhammad Ali 214
Apple 76
Aura 221, 280, 281, 285, 293, 294, 301
Autocratic 17, 18, 19, 129, 271

B

Black people 164, 315, 316, 317, 318, 319, 321, 322, 323
Building systems knowledge 64

C

Circular leadership 11
Cirwell 292
Communications 165, 281
Conflict 60

D

David and Goliath 252

E

Eight perceptions of leadership 58
Empowering leader 23, 24, 27, 29, 30, 33, 36, 40, 41
Enhancing your ABC's 225
  Enhancing abilities 226
  Enhancing beliefs 235
  Enhancing coherency of strategy 245
    Visualisation 246

F

Facebook 17
Family 255
Rotary Four-Way test 10

H

Healthy conflict 62

I

Influencers 135
  Ann McKee 165
    Tenacity 167
    Truth seeking/Integrity 169
  Chloe Kim
    Excellence 171
  Issa Rae 158
    Creativity 161
    Humour 160
    Mentoring 162
  Jesmyn Ward 163
    Communications 165
  Kenneth Frazier 151
    Strategic leadership 154
  Satya Nadella
    Encouraging challenges 151
    Inspiring others 150
  Tarana Burke 140
    Demonstrating your passion 144
    Persistency 142
Intrinsic motivation 18

L

LA1 20, 21, 24, 37, 40, 47, 77, 97, 130, 131, 186
LA1-Workplace Example 37
LA2 19, 20, 21, 46, 47, 67, 70, 130, 131
LA2- Workplace Example 67
LA3 19, 20, 21, 76, 77, 86, 89, 130, 131, 288, 294
LA3-Workplace Example 86
LA4 19, 20, 21, 96, 97, 106, 109, 130, 131
LA4-Workplace example 106
Laissez-faire 17, 18, 19
Leaders and staff needs 116
LOTS 25, 27
Loyalty 273

M

Managers 299, 302, 303
Micromanagement 205, 268, 269, 302
Morally 11, 167

P

Peter Principle 300, 301, 302, 306

R

Reflective leader 45, 131
Resolve 60

S

Selection bias 4
Server-leader 2
Shared leadership 17, 18, 21
Social media 2, 189, 190, 198, 202, 203, 233, 265
Sports 259
Stakeholder leader 95
Stewardship 2, 11
Synchronicity 60

T

Technology 180
  Automation 183
  Being nimble 197
    Kodak 199
    Nokia 199
    Toys R Us 200
  Connected working 209
  CSR
    United Airlines 203
  Global value chains
    Greta Thunberg 190
  Knowledge assets 207
  Talent management 205
  Technology risks
    Equifax 193
    Twitter 193
Tesla 186, 187, 211

U

Unconscious bias 321, 322, 323, 324
Ursula Burns 274, 277

V

Verify 60

W

Warren Buffet 17
Well-being leader 75
Wellness 89, 90, 287, 292, 293, 295

Woke leadership 113
  Switching leadership styles 128
  Woke leadership behaviour 120
    Assess quality of outcomes/outputs and process 127
    Create a shared vision and strategy 125
    Demonstrate dependability 124
    Demonstrate well-being 123
    Demonstrating self-awareness 122
    Demonstrating strategic thinking 122
    Empower 128
    Facilitate conflict resolution 125
    Facilitate for creativity 125
    Facilitate for development 128
    Facilitate shared approach to teamwork 126
    Facilitate well-being 128
    Inspire 127
    Motivate 123
  Woke leadership, needs matter 115
    Leaders and staff needs 116
    Organisational needs 119
    Team needs 117
      How 119
      Strategy 119
      What 118
      Why 118
Woken leaders 4

Z

Zappos 17